Signatures of Time

(A collection of 232 Letters written by Swami Dayanand Sarasvati in 19th Century India)

Compiled Edited and Translated into English
By
Prof. Ravi Prakash Arya
Ved Prakash Bhatia
Vinita Arya

AMAZON BOOKS, USA
In association with
INDIAN FOUNDATION FOR VEDIC SCIENCE
1051, Sector-1, Rohtak-124001, Haryana, India
Ph.No.: 09313033917; 09650183260
email:vedicscience@gmail.com;vedicscience@rediffmail.com
website: https://vedic-sciences.com

First Edition

Kali era: 5117 (c. 2016)
Kalpa era: 1,97,29,49,117
Brahma era: 15,55,21,97,29,49,117

ISBN: 9788187710950

Contents

To Gangadatta Sharma of Mathura 15
To Gangadatta Sharma 17
To an office-bearer of the Eta Pāṭhaśālā 18
To Babu Shiv Sahay Gaur 19
To Gopal Rao Hari Deshmukh 21
To Gopal Rao Hari Deshmukh 24
To Gopal Rao Hari Deshmukh 27
To Gopal Rao Hari Deshmukh 29
To Gopal Rao Hari Deshmukh 31
To Gopal Rao Hari Deshmukh 33
To Shri Chhabil Das, Devi Dass and others 35
To Max Mýller 36
To Lal Ji, Laxman Sastri, Purnananda, Nathu Ram and others.. 37
To Pundit Bhim Sen Sharma 39
To Pundit Sundar Lal 40
To Ramadhar Vajpai 41
To Shri Banmali Singh 42
To Shri Sundar Lal Har Narain Sharma 43
To Pundit Kalu Ram Sharma 44
To Pundit Kalu Ram Sharma 45
To Pundit Sundar Lal Ram Narain 46
To Pundit Ramadhar Vajpai, Allahabad 47
To Pundit Ramadhar Vajpai 49
To Pundit Ramadhar Vajpai 50
To Pundit Ramadhar Vajpai 51

To Shri Ram Narain 52
To Babu Harish Chander Chintamani 54
To Pundit Ramadhar Vajpai 55
To Pundit Gopal Rao Hari Deshmukh 57
To Shri Ram Narain 59
To Pundit Ramadhar Vajpai 60
To Shri Babu Dina Nath Ganguly 61
To Various Critiques of Vedabhāṣya 63
To Members of Arya Samaj at Lahore 70
To Members of Arya Samaj at Lahore 71
To Pundit Gopal Rao Deshmukh, Lucknow 72
To Lala Mansukh Rai, Amritsar 74
To Pundit R.R. Gopal Rao Hari Deshmukh 75
To Pundit R. R. Gopal Rao Hari Deshmukh, Mumbai 77
To Shri Ram Narain 79
To Pundit R. R. Gopal Rao Hari Deshmukh, Mumbai 80
To Pundit R.R. Gopal Rao Hari Deshmukh, Mumbai 82
To Pundit Ramadhar Vajpai 83
To Pundit Ramadhar Vajpai 84
To Pundit Ramadhar Vajpai 85
To Pundit Ramadhar Vajpai 86
To Pundit Sukh Swroop Kalu Ram, Lucknow 87
To Pundit Ramadhar Vajpai 89
To Babu B.H.Chintamani 91
To Shri Madho Lal 93
To Lala Jiwan Das 94
To Lala Jiwan Das 95

To Shri Mool Raj, Jiwan Dass, Sain Das, and Bal Das........... 96

To Babu Madho Lal 98

To Babu Madho Lal 100

To Pundit Ram Narain ji...102

To Henry S. Olcott, Madame H.P. Blavatsky and other Members of the Theosophical Society 103

To Kaviraj Shri Shyamal Das 106

To Pundit Sundar Lal Ram Narain 108

To Pundit Sundar Lal Ram Narain ji...............................109

To Pundit Sundar Lal Ram Narain 110

To the Secretary and Members of Arya Samaj....................113

To Pundit Sundar Lal Ram Narain 115

To Pundit Sundar Lal Ram Narain 116

To Pundit Sundar Lal Ram Narain 117

To Pundit Sundar Lal Ram Narain 118

To Lala Mohan Lal, the President and Lala Sain Dass, the General Secretary 119

Unknown Addressee..121

Unknown Addressee..122

To Pundit Sundar Lal Ram Narain ji...............................123

To Pundit Sundar Lal Ram Narain 124

To Shri Shyam Lal Ji Krishan Verma.............................125

To Pundit Sundar Lal Ram Narain 127

To Babu Madhava Lal ji 128

To Henry Steel Olcott...129

To Pundit Sundar Lal Ram Narain ji...............................141

To Babu Daya Ram Ji 142

To Lala Mool Raj Ji, M.A. 143
To Lala Mool Raj ji, M.A. 144
To Thakur Bhoopal Singh Ji 145
To Lala Mool Raj Ji, M.A. 146
To Babu Madho Lal Ji 147
To Pundit Sundar Lal Ram Narain Ji 148
To Maulvi Mohd. Kasim Ali 149
To Maulvi Mohammed. Kasim Ali 150
To Maulvi Mohd. Kasim Ali Saheb 155
To Maulvi Mohd. Kasim 158
To Babu Madho Lal ji 171
To Lala Mool Raj ji, M.A. 172
To Secretary(Mantri) Arya Samaj Multan 173
To Maulvi Mohd. Kasim 174
To Maulvi Mohd. Kasim 175
To Captain W. Stuart 176
To Maulvi Mohd. Kasim 177
To Lala Mool Raj, M.A. 178
To Lala Mool Raj ji, M.A. 179
To Lala Mool Raj ji, M.A. 180
To Pundit Ram Narain ji 181
To Pundit Ramadhar Bajpai ji 182
To Maulvi Abdullah 183
To Lala Mool Raj, M.A. 184
To Pundit Ram Narain 185
To Babu Madho Lal ji 186
To Lala Kishan Sahai ji Saheb 187

To Pundit Ram Narain ji 188
To Lala Kishan Sahai 189
To Babu Madho Lal ji 190
To Pundit Sunder Lal ji 191
To Pundit Shyam ji Krishan Varma 192
To Pundit Shyam ji Krishan Varma 193
To Babu Madho Lal ji 194
To Babu Ramadhar Bajpai 195
To Munshi Samarth Dan 196
To Pundit Ram Narain 197
To Pundit Sunder Lal Ram Narain 199
To Babu Ramadhar Vajpai 200
To Babu Samarth Dan Charan 201
To Pundit Shyam ji Krishan Varma 202
To Babu Ramadhar Vajpai 204
To Babu Ramadhar Vajpai 205
To Babu Madho Lal 206
To Pundit Shyam Ji Krishna Varma 207
To Col. H.S. Olcott 209
To Munshi Samarth Dan 210
To Pundit Ram Narain 211
To Pundit Shyam ji Krishna Varma 212
To Sardar Ganda Singh, Granthi Ropar, District Ambala 213
To Pundit Gopal Hari Deshmukh 214
To Pundit Shyam ji Krishna Varma 215
To Pundit Sunder Lal Ram Narain ji 217
To Pundit Sunder Lal Ram Narain ji 219

To Pundit Shyam ji Krishna Varma 220
To Pundit Sunder Lal Ram Narain ji 221
To Pundit Sunder Lal Ram Narain 222
To Pundit Sunder Lal Ram Narain 223
To Pundit Shyam ji Krishna Varma 225
To Pundit Sunder Lal Ram Narain ji 226
To Babu Pyare Lal, Member, Arya Samaj, Lahore 227
To Pundit Shyam ji Krishna Varma 228
To Pundit Shyam ji Krishna Varma 229
To Lala Ram Shran Dass Jiva 231
To Kripa Ram Swami 232
To Pundit Shyam ji Krishna Varma 233
To Pundit Shyam ji Krishna Varma 235
To Pundit Shyam ji Krishna Varma 237
To Munshi Samartha Dan 238
To Col. Olcott 239
To Lala Madho Lal 240
To Munshi Samartha Dan 241
To Munshi Samartha Dan 242
To Munshi Samartha Dan 243
To Swami Vishuddhananda 244
To Pandits for Debate 245
To Pandits desirous of a debate 246
To Munshi Samaratha Dan 247
To Lala Madho Lal 248
To Munshi Samaratha Dan 249
To Babu Madho Lal 250

To Munshi Samaratha Dan 252
To Munshi Samarathadaan....................253
To Secretary, Arya Samaj, Shahjhanpur....................254
To Babu Madho Prasad and others 258
To Munshi Samaratha Dan 262
To Munshi Samaratha Dan 263
To Pranji Das....................264
To Munshi Samaratha Dan 265
To Munshi Samarath Dan....................266
To Pt. Shyam ji Krishna Varma 267
To Sahu Shyam Sunder Das 270
To Colonel H.S. Olcott 271
To M. Blavatsky 273
To Munshi Samaratha Dan 278
To Munshi Samaratha Dan 279
To Munshi Samaratha Dan 280
To Pundit Ramadhar Vajpai....................281
To Pundit Ramadhar Vajpai....................282
To Pt. Angad Shastry and others 283
To Pt. Angad Shastry 288
To Munshi Samartha Dan....................289
To Munshi Samaratha Dan 290
To Babu Madho Lal of Danapur 291
To Pundit Sundar Lal Ram Narain 292
To Munshi Samaratha Dan 293
To Babu Madho Lal 294
To Pt. Sundar Lal Ram Narain....................296

To Babu Madho Lal 297
To Munshi Samaratha Dan 298
To the Press Manager 299
To Babu Madho Lal 300
To Babu Ramadhar Vajpai 301
To Babu Madho Lal 302
To Babu Madho Lal 303
To Munshi Samartha Dan 304
To Mr. Bal, the Magistrate, Kashi 305
To Shri Jaisraj Goti Ram 306
To Pt. Sundar Lal Ram Narain 307
To Munshi Inderman Jiva 308
To Col. Olcott and Blavatsky 310
To Chaudhary Laxman Das 311
To Munshi Manohar Lal 312
To the Editor, Theosophist 313
To Lala Mool Raj 314
To Mukand Singh 315
To Col. H.S. Olcott 316
To Raja Shiva Prasad 317
To Raja Shiva Prasad 320
To Munshi Bhaktawar Singh 321
To Munshi Bhaktawar Singh 323
To Munshi Bhaktawar Singh 324
To Munshi Bhaktawar Singh 327
To Rama Bai 329
To Pundit Gopal Rao Hari 332

To Shyam ji Krishna Varma....................333
To Ramabai....................335
To Pundit Bhim Sen....................337
To Col. H.S. Olcott and H.P. Blavatsky....................339
To Babu Mulraj....................342
To Babu Mulraj....................345
To Prof. G. Wise....................347
To Shyam ji Krishna Varma....................348
To Atma Ram....................351
To Pundit Bhim Sen....................357
To H.P. Blavatsky....................360
To Pundit Jwala Dutt....................369
To Pundit Jwala Dutt....................370
To Atma Ram....................372
To Mahadev Govind Ranade....................379
To Col. H.S. Olcott and H.P. Blavatsky....................380

Signatures of Time
(इतिहास के हस्ताक्षर)
Introduction

The present work is a compilation of 231 letters written by Swami Dayanand Sarasvati in the 19th Century to his followers, opponents, and other scholars contemporary to him. These letters from Swami Dayanand Sarasvati will give you an idea of Dayanand's lifestyle, his way of working, dealing with his subordinates, and the treatment meted out by him to his rivals and to other people who came into his contact. He was very disciplined and ordered when performing different tasks. He used to reply to letters regularly on a day to day basis. It was astonishing for the authors to find out that he always travelled with two and often three carts. One horse-driven cart which was called a "Baggi" was for himself, and another cart was used to carry his library and other books published by him. He was always on the move, forever observing whilst travelling the entire length and breadth of the country. This peripatetic lifestyle of Swami ji points to the hectic schedule he was undergoing daily.

From reading his letters, it is evident that Swamiji used to pay a very handsome amount to his clerks. During the 1870s he used to pay from Rs. 20 to Rs 35 to his clerks and even to teachers deputed by him in his Pāṭhaśālas.

Here, we would like to inform readers that we have made strenuous efforts to retain the terminology and style of the English letters dictated by Swami Ji to his clerks. We have however made amendments wherever necessary and where it was deemed unavoidable. For many letters, some spellings of nouns have been changed to make them more up to date, e.g. Swami Ji's clerks' spellings 'Dehllee' and 'Lallah' are now 'Delhi' and 'Lala' respectively. The 'u' sound which was spelt 'oo' and 'pur' which was spelt 'pore' in a Bengali style, have also been modified by the present authors according to the current usage. In letter No. 111, the scribe writes 'I have *appointed* the Arya Samaj in Meerut' instead of 'I have *founded* the Arya Samaj in Meerut'. At such places, the authors were obliged to make the necessary amendments.

Here it may also be known that most of the letters were preserved by Pt. Bhagvaddatta, Prof. Dhirendra Verma, Arya Samaj Danapur of Bihar, Arya Samaj Lucknow and the Paropkarini Sabha. Pt. Lekhram and Devendra Nath Mukhopādhyāya also cited many letters in their biographies on Swami Dayanand. In the present compilation the authors have dwelt heavily on the book titled 'Rishi Dayanand Sarasvati kā Patra Vyavahāra Aur Vijñāpana, compiled and edited by Pt. Bhagavaddatt, BA, enlarged and amended by Pt. Yudhisthir Mimansaka, published by the Ramlal Kapoor Trust Bahalgarh, Sonepat, Haryana. It is earnestly hoped that both readers and researchers will find this compilation a very significant addition to the general historical studies of 19th century India and the Arya Samaj movement in particular.

Prof. Dr. Ravi Prakash Arya
Maharshi Dayanand Saraswati Chair (UGC)
Maharshi Dayanand University, Rohtak, Haryana

Letter No. 1

To Gangadatta Sharma of Mathura

(Bhadra Śukla 6, Saṁvat 1927 or Sept. 1, 1870)

Gangadatta Chaube was a classmate of Swami Dayanand in Mathura. In this letter, Swami Ji wanted to assign to Gangadatta Chaube the teaching work of the Pannalal Pathshala, Farrukhabad. This letter, originally written in Sanskrit, was sent from Farrukhabad to Mathura on Sept. 1, 1870.

May God bless you!

Blessings from Dayanand Sarasvati Swami to Gangadatta Sharma, who can be compared to the noblest of men. Everything is in good form here. Hope all is well there. I received your letter and got the details. A wise person like you keeps me posted, but don't show up in person. It is indeed amazing. I would like you to come immediately after receiving this letter. The day you join the Pathshala, you will be paid one month's salary in advance which you can send to your family back home without any problems. You need not harbour any doubts about your job here. In the beginning, one rupee per day will be paid to you, but the same will be enhanced as and when your talent will be revealed in the Pathshala. For now you should stay here and you should consider your job as being permanent regardless of whether it is here or elsewhere. I don't want you to have any doubts about your job being terminated in my absence. Here, everything will run smoothly. This letter is being written on the 6th day of the bright half of the

Bhādrapada month, Thursday, Saṁvat 1927.

Do bring along with you the following books on the Vedas:

Mahābhāṣya (a commentary on Pāṇini's grammar), Aṣṭādhyayī (Pāṇini's grammar), Dhātupāṭha (a book dealing with verbal roots in Sanskrit), Uṇādipāṭha (a book dealing with the formation of Sanskrit words with the help of suffixes prescribed by succinct aphorisms called Uṇādi Sūtras), Vārttikapāṭha (supplementary formulas to Pāṇini's grammar), Paribhāṣāpāṭha (collections of definitions given by Pāṇini in his Sanskrit grammar) and Gaṇapāṭha (a group of certain Sanskrit words that undergo a similar treatment in Pāṇini's grammar).

Swami Dayanand Saraswati

Letter No. 2

To Gangadatta Sharma

(Date not known)

This letter, originally written in Sanskrit, was sent to Mathura from Hathras through a messenger named Baldev Singh before Swami Ji reached Mathura. It has been referred to by Pt. Lekhram in his book on the Biography of Swami Dayanand.

Please try to find out in Vrindavan, such a house which is free from the menace of monkeys and devoid of stones.

Swami Dayanand Saraswati

Letter No. 3

To an office-bearer of the Eta Pāṭhaśālā

(Caitra Śukla 6, Saṁvat 1930, Saturday)

It is not exactly known to whom this letter was addressed. But, from the contents of the letter, it appears that this letter was written to some office bearer of the Eta Pāṭhaśālā. The letter depicts the disappointment of Swami Ji at the mismanagement of the school. This letter was written in Hindi.

Vishuddhananda (the name of a student) has left. Inform me about the facts behind this episode. Also, write the address of Mulakdass's bungalow which is located close to Vrindavan Seth's bungalow. I can very well imagine that Yugal Kishore was not able to teach or there may be some other reason. If the students continue to desert the Pāṭhaśālā in a row, then the teachers will be considered at fault. Let me know the whole episode. Also, let me know who is teaching what. Whatever may be the condition, do write.

Swami Dayanand Saraswati

Letter No. 4

To Babu Shiv Sahay Gaur

(Jyeṣṭha Śukla 13, Friday, Saṁvat 1931, i.e May 29, 1874)

This letter in Hindi was written to Babu Shiv Sahay Gaur of Kanpur from Kashi. This person was involved in raising funds from different quarters at the behest of Swami Dayanand for the foundation of a Pāṭhaśālā in Banaras. This letter was written to him when he was in Farrukhabad (See Biography of Swami Dayanand in Hindi by Pt. Lekhram, p.814). Here it may also be pointed out that Shiv Sahaya Mishra was the secretary of Arya Samaj Kanpur (See the newspaper Bhārata Sudaśā Pravartaka, March 1880, p.8).

Blessings from Dayanand Sarasvati Swami!

Your letter of the 7th day of the waxing of the moon was received and I was able to get all the details from it. I have a plan to stay here for one month. Here the management of Pāṭhśālā is very good. One teacher, excelling in all of the six Śāstras, has been appointed. Similarly, a grammarian has been engaged. On the Daśāśvamedha Ghāṭa, a very good place is procured. Here the Pāṭhśālā will commence after the full moon day. The Kedāra Ghāṭa place was not appropriate. Now we have a Pāṭhaśālā (school) in Bagh (This bagh belonged to Sarju Prasad Bania, see Pt. Lekhram: 814. Now it is known as Benia Bagh). We have a good batch of students. Send money and books immediately as soon as you receive this letter. Do not delay even for a moment. Give one copy of Mahābhāṣya to Dinesh Ram and send the rest of the books here. If Dinesh Ram refuses to hand over the books to you, then we will need to decide what to do. You send the money and books that are in your possession immediately by post. If Gopal or somebody else wants to study, he is welcome. Neither Brahmachari Lakshmi Narayana has reached here, nor your letter. Everybody is fine here. Convey our greetings to Yugal Kishore Mehta, Gopal Dutt, and Dinesh Ram.

Swami Dayanand Saraswati

Letter No. 5

To Gopal Rao Hari Deshmukh

(Phālguna Kṛṣṇa 2, Saṁvat 1931 or February 22, 1875)

Gopal Rao Hari Deshmukh was a learned Judge at Allahabad. In this letter (from Mumbai) Swami Ji discusses developments around the founding of the 'Arya Samaj' at Bombay (Mumbai) and exhorts Gopal Rao Deshmukh to set up an Arya Samaj at Allahabad. Swami Ji also touches upon the subject of the nomenclature of the society preferably being the 'Arya Samaj' and not the 'Prārathanā Samaj'. Here one may get an idea that the Arya Samaj was founded by Rishi Dayanand along the lines of the 'Prārthanā Samaj' just to fulfil the current need. From this letter the reader gets an indication of the progress of the publication of the Satyārtha Prakaśa and that of the publication of the Sanskāra Vidhi and Pañca-mahā-yajñavidhi books which were all on the anvil. This letter was originally written in Sanskrit.

Blessings from Dayanand Saraswati Swami to Sh. Gopal Rao Deshmukh.

This is to acknowledge the receipt of medicines and an umbrella sent by you, but the song ("Bhajan") book from the Prāthanā Samaj is still awaited. A lecture is organized here for which a place is being constructed. The efforts of the Arya Samaj are appreciable. Please continue to work hard towards setting up an Arya Samaj in Allahabad. Have you received the four copies of the Satyāratha Prakāśa (with up to 120 printed pages) sent through your son - one for you, one for Bholanath Ji, one for Mahipatiram Ji, and one for Vechar Bhai? If not received, please inform me by letter.

Have you started the Arya Samaj by now or not? If not please do it quickly, as there should not be any delay in executing good deeds. Please (also) see that it is named the 'Arya Samaj'. This name will not invite any blame or criticism. Any other name, and (people) will not join it for God's Prayer. Hence, (the nomenclature) should be the 'Arya Samaj', which means a Samaj of Aryas or Śreṣṭhas (noble and spiritual) persons. If we name it the 'Prārthanā Samaj', it will be against our ethos. Actions like stuti (recollecting or chanting God's name), prārthanā (prayer), upāsanā (meditation) and sadupadeśa (sermons) stand contrary to our intended sense. So, the nomenclature should be in coherence with the intended sense, so that it may not appear misleading. Hence, the 'Arya Samaj' is the only right name and not the 'Prārathanā Samaj'. The setting up of the 'Arya Samaj' should not be delayed. It is in the interest of all.

Please don't worry. The preparation for bringing out the book "Sanskāra Vidhi" has begun, as has also that of 'Āryābhinaya', a book containing Veda mantras on stuti (the chanting of God's name and attributes), prāthanā (prayer), and upāsanā (Meditation). And printing of the book Sabhāṣya Sandhyopāsanādi Pañcha Mahāyajña Vidhi (Five great Yajñas with a commentary) has also begun. It will be ready within two to four days and (then) it will be shipped to you. Please convey my due regards to Baldeva Datt and to Mandan Rao. You can place a demand for as many copies of 'Veda Virudha Mata Khaṇḍana' (A Reply to anti-Veda propaganda) as you want, as they may go out of stock after some time. Moreover, you may ask for as many copies of the Satyārth Prakāśa as you want, which is presently available at the price of one rupee per copy.

Please do write about the new developments at your place. Also, send the song (bhajan) book to me. A prompt reply is expected.

Swami Dayanand Saraswati

Letter No. 6

To Gopal Rao Hari Deshmukh

(Phālguna Śukla 9, Saṁvat 1931 or March 16, 1875)

This letter was written in Sanskrit from Mumbai to Gopal Rao Hari Deshmukh, a learned judge at Allahabad. In this letter, Swami Ji discusses developments at Mumbai, where the misconceptions of a local Pundit about Swami Ji's knowledge of Sanskrit grammar were dispelled and the shallow knowledge, in particular that of Pundit Vishnu Shastri, Editor of Indu Prakash, and other Pundits in general, about Sanskrit grammar and Vedic interpretation, was exposed. The recipient has been exhorted to arrange the foundation of an Arya Samaj at Allahabad.

Blessings from Dayanand Saraswati Swami to Sh. Gopal Rao Hari Deshmukh.

Your letter was received and I was able to find out all the details from it. Four books of songs, one umbrella, one inkpot have been received. In Kot Maidan of Mumbai, devoted householders have built up a Maṇḍap (Platform), where lectures followed by a question and answer session are being held. The Pundits of Mumbai were claiming that Swami Ji did not have a good grasp of (Sanskrit) grammar. When we came across this false propaganda, a workshop on grammar was organised, which was attended by these Pundits. When queries on Sanskrit grammar were raised, the Pundits failed to reply and kept silent. Then, all people assembled there convinced them to accept the reality that Swami Ji possesses a very good knowledge of Sanskrit grammar. Then the Pundits were asked to write two questions and bring logical answers to them. From this time onwards everyone has become convinced about Swamiji. Preparations are in full swing for setting up the Arya Samaj at Mumbai.

It seems that someone among you might have sent a letter to Vishnu Shastri, the editor of the 'Indu Prakash' requesting the meaning of the mantra 'ākarṣṇeneti.' Whatever he wrote about it is false. And there is no doubt that this Vishnu Shastri is ignorant, a crook, a stubborn, prejudiced person and a liar. Here is a example of foolishness on his part, which even a student would not have committed: he writes that from root √ṛ, meaning 'to go', 'to receive' the word 'ratha' or wheel is derived, but not from the root √ 'ramu meaning 'to play'. Such a meaning is both illogical and baseless. He is ignorant both on the inside and on the outside. I give here evidence from Uṇādipāṭha as written by Pāṇini. Accordingly, the word ratha is derived from the root ramu with the suffix kthana. Also according to Yāska, the author of Nirukta: the word ratha is derived from the root Öraṅha 'to move' and the root ramu 'to play'. Thus, the interpretation by Vishnu Shastri becomes baseless. He was invited to a meeting, but he didn't turn up. He is in the habit of telling lies while sitting comfortably at home. The letter written to him was merely a waste of time and writing material. There is no end to the misleading statements of such foolish people. In the meeting, criticism of his wrong interpretation was done and he was also informed about the same, but the crooked man would not write it in his journal. And do write to him to publish our clarification along with his criticism. If he does not publish the same, then it will be published elsewhere. Why do you people ask those who possess destructive and prejudiced minds to pronounce judgement on such serious matters (while even Sāyaṇācārya, etc. couldn't interpret the meanings of the Vedas rightly)? How can their followers possess right knowledge? Therefore, we don't accept such crooked people as competent to make statements on such matters (like Sanskrit grammar and the interpretation of the Vedas). This is because their intellect has been ruined due to a lack of correct knowledge and greed. The behaviour of almost all of the Pundits coming from Ahmadabad and other places is almost similar to that of Vishnu Pundit. They start walking upside down after hearing our name. Whichever Pundit is asked to clarify matters, he invariably comes up with misleading statements. They don't even possess an iota of knowledge about Vedic interpretation. The books sent by you have been received. It will be appreciated if you could expedite the matter of setting up an Arya Samaj (at Allahabad).

Swami Dayanand Saraswati

Letter No.7

To Gopal Rao Hari Deshmukh

(Caitra Śukla 6, Saṁvat 1932, (1931 according to Gujarati Pañcāṅga) or April 11, 1875)

This letter from Mumbai was written in Sanskrit to Gopal Rao Hari Deshmukh, a learned judge at Allahabad. Here Swami Ji discussed developments at Mumbai culminating in the setting up of the Arya Samaj at Mumbai on April 10, 1875. Through this letter, it becomes crystal clear that the Arya Samaj was founded in Mumbai on Saturday, April 10, 1875. Accordingly, it was the 5th day of the bright half of the Caitra month of Vikrama Saṁvat 1932, instead of the 1st day of Caitra month, as it is often held. This letter mentions the Vikrama year 1931 which is according to the Gujarati Pañchāṅga. The Gujarati Pañchāṅga is six month behind, because it starts from Kārtika Śukla Pratipadā. As such it appears that the stone installed in the premises of the Arya Samaj Mumbai, that mentions the foundation day of the Arya Samaj as Caitra Śukla Pratipadā (1st day of the bright half of Caitra month) is false and fictitious. This building was constructed seven years after the foundation of Arya Samaj. Maybe somebody has written this so that Arya Samaj Foundation day may be celebrated along with Bharat's New Year's day.

Blessings from Dayanand Saraswati Swami to Sh. Gopal Rao Hari Deshmukh.

The Arya Samaj was started blissfully in Mumbai on Caitra Śukla 5, Saṁvat 1931 (1932, according to the North Indian Pañchāṅga or April 10, 1875, Saturday) at 5:30 P.M. With God's grace, everything went very well. You should also not delay and set up an Arya

Samaj at Allahabad as early as possible. It is also being done at Nasik. Now the Rules for the Arya Samaj and the book on 'Sanskāra Vidhi' will be published shortly.

It seems that Pundit Vishnu Shastri, Editor of Indu Prakash has not corrected himself, instead he is proving rather incorrigible. A rebuttal of his statements was sent to him but he didn't publish it. He appears to be a person with a prejudiced mind. We will get it printed elsewhere now. The books on 'Sandhyopāsanādi' and 'Pañcamahāyajña Vidhān bhāṣya' have since been printed. Ten copies are being sent to you for distribution amongst good (Arya) people. Two of the ten rules, are of particular significance; that pertaining to marriage ceremonies and the other concerning death or some joyful event. On these occasions, donations (as per one's conscience) to the Arya Samaj must be done. The second rule is that until employees and employers are available in the Arya Samaj, no-one else should be engaged; and both (employer and employees) should treat each other equitably (yathā yogya vyavahāra) and both should work in harmony. The place provided by Dr. Manik Ji for the Arya Samaj is inadequate. With the (likely) increase in members, some new place would be acquired for the Arya Samaj. It is a matter of great pleasure that all of you have declared your commitment in the interest of the country. With God's grace, may it progress day by day. Ten books on 'Sandhyādi bhāṣya' are being sent through your son.

Swami Dayanand Saraswati

Letter No.8

To Gopal Rao Hari Deshmukh

(Caitra Kṛṣṇa 9, Saṁvat 1932 or May 29, 1875)

This letter was written in Mumbai. It was written partially in Sanskrit and partially in Hindi. The part containing the address was written in Sanskrit and the rest of the contents were in Hindi. It was addressed to Gopal Rao Hari Deshmukh and others. Swami Ji informs them about the progress regarding the composition of different books.

Blessings from Dayanand Saraswati Swami to Sh. Gopal Rao Hari Deshmukh, Bhola Nath Mahipati, Ram Sharma, Baichara, and others. Here everybody is fine and I hope the same for you.

The two chapters of Aryābhivinaya have been composed. The remaining four chapters have yet to be written. The Sanskāra Vidhi book will also be composed as soon as I find the time. The Principles of Arya Samaj and their explanations will also be published soon. The fourteen sheets of the Satyarth Prakash have come out of the printing press, and they will also be sent to you through your son. I am planning to visit Poona before or after the 15th day of the dark half of Jyeṣṭha month. You can inform the appropriate people there. I shall come to Baroda at your invitation. You must also start an Arya Samaj there. It will be very beneficial. On reflection, only this name seems correct but you are free to do as you wish. The people of our country, in any case will benefit from the Arya Samaj. Here everyone is fine, and hope you are too. There is no need for any further elaboration. You are intelligent enough to make out what I mean to say.

Saṁvat 1932, Caitra Kṛṣṇa 9. Saturday. The book on the rebuttal of Śikṣāpatri with commentary in Gujarati has also been done. Its printing may cost fifty to sixty rupees. Would you like to get it printed there instead of Mumbai? It will however be better if it is printed at Mumbai. Please send a prompt reply to this matter.

Swami Dayanand Saraswati

Letter No.9

To Gopal Rao Hari Deshmukh

(Śrāvaṇa Śukla 8, Saṁvat 1932 or August 10, 1875)

In this letter (from Pune) to Gopal Rao Hari Deshmukh a learned Judge at Allahabad, Swami Ji discussed developments at Pune about setting up the Arya Samaj there and shared his itinerary with him.

Blessings from Dayanand Saraswati Swami to Sh. Gopal Rao Hari Deshmukh, Bhola Nath Mahipati, Ram Sharma, Baichara, and others.

We are in good health here and hope you are having a wonderful time there. In Pune, Mahadev Govind Ranade, Madhava Rao Maheshwar Kunte and Cantt. Gangaram Bhau and other people, have arranged lectures. They have also published these lectures. They have also collected some funds for engaging a Pundit to teach the Vedabhāṣya. You must make efforts to set up an Arya Samaj at Allahabad. An organising committee has been set up for holding a meeting (Sabha) twice (daily). We are going to organise a meeting shortly in which the President, General Secretary (Mantri) and Treasurer, etc. shall be nominated for setting up an Arya Samaj (at Pune). It is very likely to be done shortly. You might have already got to know this through the current 'Gyan Prakash' news. We are likely to go either to Satara or Baroda shortly. When we leave here to go to Mumbai via Satara, we would like to stay at Dadar Railway Station for a day or so. You will be informed by telegram from Dadara. After being informed by you by whatever means we will decide whether to come directly to Baroda or to Baroda via Surat and Baruch. Mahadev Govind and other people have decided to engage a Pundit for a salary of fifty Rupees (per month). Mathuradass Lauji, Chhabildass Lallubhai and other Arya Samaj members have invited shares of Rs. one hundred to Rs. ten thousand in order to collect Rs twenty thousand for the Vedabhashya; and it seems that they will get to the twenty thousand rupees mark soon. Raja Jai Krishan has agreed to engage one Pundit. Mahadev Govind and I would like you to employ a Pundit for fifty rupees. You may do this as you deem fit. It may be known that none of the Pandits at this place dared to challenge us, but criticism continued from distant quarters.

It's by God's grace that I am very happy and I wish you great joy also. Convey my blessings to everybody at your end.

Swami Dayanand Saraswati

Letter No.10

To Gopal Rao Hari Deshmukh

(Āśvina Kṛṣṇa 2, Saṁvat 1932 or September 17, 1875)

In this letter, written in Hindi from Pune or Satara, addressed to Gopal Rao Hari Deshmukh at Allahabad, Swami Ji discussed developments at Pune and Satara and the collection of funds for the Vedabhāṣya.

Blessings from Dayanand Saraswati Swami to Sh. Gopal Rao Hari Deshmukh.

You might have become aware of developments at Pune and Satara through recent letters. The latest news is that an Arya Samaj has been set up at Pune. You might have come to know from newspapers that two meetings were held (earlier) at Pune for that purpose. However, when I reached Pune from Satara then it was decided that Mahadev Govind Ranade would be President and Keshav Rao Godbole General Secretary (of the Arya Samaj). All the members including those of the Prārathanā Sabhā, Baba Gokul, Kashi Nath Gadgil, Ganga Ram, and others from Pune Cantt. totalling around sixty or seventy and much more, are likely to join. From Satara Kalyan Rao Treasurer, Headmaster, and others are going to enrol themselves as members, but I have told them not to rush. However, they are likely to do so shortly.

Further, I plan to stay in Bombay until the Queen's son's (Edward VII) arrival and departure for Calcutta. Afterwards, I would like to proceed towards Surat, Baruch, and Baroda. The Mumbai Arya Samaj has been progressing in leaps and bounds. For the Vedabhāśya, five thousand rupees have already been collected and a further collection is ongoing. We are likely to collect twenty to twenty-five thousand rupees. Search for a Pundit, as the Sanskar Vidhi book has already commenced. Unfortunately we have not achieved any success so far. So, if you can find one (Pundit) there, please pay him a monthly remuneration of thirty to fifty rupees. May God keep all of you healthy and strong. We are also keeping well by His grace. Please convey my blessings to Bholanath Sarabhai, Vechar Dass, Ambai Dass, Mahipat Ram, and others.

Swami Dayanand Saraswati

Letter No.11

To Shri Chhabil Das, Devi Dass and others

(Āśvina Śukla 3, Saṁvat 1932 or October 2, 1875)

This letter was written in Sanskrit to Chhabil Dass, Devi Dass, Dwarika Dass, Shyam Ji Ram Dass Verma and others. This letter depicts Swami Ji's arrangements for future trips to Mumbai and Pune.

Blessings from Swami Dayanand Saraswati to Sarvashri Chhabil Dass, Devi Dass, Dwarika Dass, Shyam Ji, Ram Dass Verma, Girdhari Lal, Shri Navin Chandra, Jhala, and others.

All is well here. I do hope you are having a good time there. I'd like to inform you that your letter was received today (on Āśvina Śukla 3, Saṁvat 1932, Saturday) and a reply was also written on the same day. Furthermore, I have accepted your request to visit Mumbai. Although I would like to visit Gujarat, I have however decided to cancel my plans so that you can visit Mumbai. I would really appreciate it if the Balkeshwar residence used before could be arranged for my stay there. If it is not available, please choose some other place. After finalizing the accommodation, please a send a message to Justice Mahadev Govind Ranade at Pune. It is confirmed that during the ensuing Aṣṭami (on Thursday), I will be reaching your place after visiting Pune. I may at the most, stay at Pune for eight days and then come to Mumbai. But it all depends upon a quick response at your end about my staying arrangements.

Swami Dayanand Saraswati

Letter No. 12

To Max Müller

(Date not known)

A summary of this letter written to Max Mñller was published by Pt. Lekhram in the Biography of Dayanand. In the same book the reader is informed that when Swami Ji received this letter, Bhatis present there promised Swami Ji to get him to the ship.

Although I do really wish to come, as people consider me an atheist here, I may not be able to come until I convince them about the type of atheist I am.

Swami Dayanand Saraswati

Letter No.13

To Lal Ji, Laxman Sastri, Purnananda, Nathu Ram and others

(Āśāḍha Vadi (Kṛṣṇa) 9, Saṁvat 1933 or June 16, 1876, Friday)

This letter was handed over by Pt. Ram Sahaya, Mahopadeshaka of Rajasthan Pratinidhi Sabha to Yudhisthir Mimansak. It was written in Hindi to Lal Ji, Laxman Sastri, Purnananda, Nathu Ram, and others in Kashi. It shows how Swami Ji used to arrange the publication and distribution of literature.

Blessings from Dayanand Saraswati Swami to Sarvashri Lal Ji, Laxman Sastri, Purnananda, Nathu Ram, and others.

Letters have already been posted first to Lalchand, secondly to Keshav Lal Nirbhay Ram, thirdly to Harish Chandra Chintamani and this is the fourth letter in this series. The accounts of all books should be handled by one person. The sums of seventy-five rupees and one hundred fifty rupees from Seth Hanumant Ram Pitti Ji might have been paid to Laxman Sastri Ji for the printing, etc of 'Āryābhivinaya' and one thousand books might have been kept with Keshav Lal Nirbhay Ram Ji. If no action has been taken in this regard, it should be done quickly on a priority basis. Furthermore, five hundred copies of Āryābhivinaya should be sent as soon as possible by Keshav Lal Ji to Pundit Sunder Lal Ji in Prayaga (Allahabad) c/o the residence of Postmaster General at Kacheri. If Laxman Sastriji has up till now not been able to keep the books there, please kindly send one thousand books to Keshav Lal and one hundred and fifty rupees. Make him send copies of the Āryābhivinaya to Hanumant

Ram Pitti and Keshav Lal at the above address at Allahabad. Please do it quickly, as there are many people (customers) in this country who want to buy this book. Delay may harm the cause. Please convey my warm blessings to all the members of Arya Samaj there. Here, we are in a blissful state.

Swami Dayanand Saraswati

Letter No. 14

(Summary of the letter)

To Pundit Bhim Sen Sharma

(Date not known)

This letter was written to Bhim Sen Sharma originally in Sanskrit. The summary of this letter was published in the biography of Bhim Sen Sharma written by Purna Singh Verma in 1918. It appeared on page 93. This letter shows that Bhim Sen Sharma was engaged by Swamiji as a scribe. Bhim Sen himself requested Swami Dayanand to teach him Darśana Śāstra and offered his writing services in return. Here it may be pointed out that it was Bhim Sen Sharma who inserted a lot of interpolations in the writings of Swami Dayanand. So whatever appears to be wrong in Swamiji's writings, Bhim Sen and others should be held responsible for such errors. Swamiji, it must be noted, was not able to proofread and check manuscripts, etc. due to the lack of time.

Please see me immediately. I will teach you one of Darśana Śāstras daily for an hour and during the remaining four to five hours I will give you dictation. You will be paid eight rupees per month for this job. You will also be paid for your meals and clothing.

Swami Dayanand Saraswati

Letter No. 15

To Pundit Sundar Lal

(November 14, 1876)

This letter was written in English from Bareily. It was sent from Lucknow or Shajahanpur to Mumbai. This letter is preserved in the collections of Propakarini Sabha.

Today I have sent an application to the Post Master General, N.W.P for registering our monthly Tract Vedabhāṣya, which is going to be issued from December 1876. Please do the needful. I shall send two tracts, as soon as they are printed, to the Post Master General, N.W.P. I am all right here and hope the same for you.

P.S. Please try to get as many subscribers as you can for the Vedabhāṣya and send a list to my representative at Banaras. He will send you the pamphlets monthly. You can distribute it among your friends. For the time being, you can collect Rs 3/10/6 (Rs. 3 annas 10 and paise 6) from each subscriber for a whole year. 500 Shlokas will be issued monthly @ 4/- four annas including postage. But in the first issue, there will be 1000 Shlokas in two pamphlets. Therefore, I have kept annas 4/6 in excess.

For further information write to my representative Banamali Singh at Banaras.

I will proceed for Moradabad in a week and after a weeklong stay, I will move to Chalasar and Delhi.

Swami Dayanand Saraswati

Letter No. 16

To Ramadhar Vajpai

(November 18, 1876)

This letter was written in English by some scribe of Swamiji to Ramadhar Vajpai, the Head Clerk Govt. Telephone Office, Lucknow. Ramadhar Vajpai was one of the fans of Swami Ji who dedicated himself in propagating the publication of Swamiji.

The first copy of the Vedabhāṣya will be issued shortly. So, you should make concerted efforts wholeheartedly to secure as many subscribers as possible in your town. For getting the tract published and for distribution among subscribers, my clerk will proceed to Banaras on Monday. On his downward journey, he will take a break at your town for a day. I have told him to stay at the Pathshala if Ganesh Swami happens to be there. Please inform him about it.

About my activities at Shahjahanpur and here, I think, you might have already heard from Ganesh Goswami and the rest that you can learn from my clerk (Babu). I don't think there is any need for giving further details here.

Hope you are enjoying perfect health. My blessings to all of you.

Swami Dayanand Saraswati

Letter No.17

To Shri Banmali Singh

(Pauṣa Śukla 4, Saṁvat 1933, December 19, 1876)

Banmali Singh was a clerk (Babu) engaged in writing English letters. This letter, written in Hindi, was sent from Delhi to Kashi.

Blessings from Dayanand Saraswati Swami to Shri Banmali Singh.

We have reached Delhi on Pauṣa Shuddi 2, 1933 (Sunday). Kindly send 1000 advertisement folios and 1000 Vedabhāṣya books immediately; the balance should remain with the Lajras Press. Having received my letter, 2000 books along with letters should be dispatched in my name. Please bring along with you the index which was prepared for the Vedabhāṣya, as now you will have to stay with me. Your railway fare will be reimbursed to you. The books under binding may also be carried along with you. There is nothing else to write.

Swami Dayanand Saraswati

Letter No.18

To Shri Sundar Lal Har Narain Sharma

(Pauṣa Śukla 5, Saṁvat 1933, December 20, 1876)

This letter, written in Hindi, was also sent from Delhi. In Delhi, Swami Ji stayed at Ramdhan's garden on Gurgaon Road. This letter has been quoted on page 26 in the biography of Kaluram Sharma written by Sh. Jai Narain Poddar.

Blessings from Dayanand Saraswati Swami to Shri Sundar Lal Har Narain Sharma.

We are staying in Delhi at Ramdhan's garden, which is located at Gurgaon Road. Letters and parcels coming in my name at the address of Ajmeri Gate near Paharganj may kindly be sent to this address. If three Sanskar Vidhi books are sent by Keshavlal Nirbhay Ram from Mumbai, please receive them and acknowledge your receipt to him. I may stay here for fifteen days. Please convey my blessings to all.

Swami Dayanand Saraswati

Letter No. 19

To Pundit Kalu Ram Sharma

(Date not known. Probable year that it was written 1876. It was sent from Delhi)

Kalu Ram Sharma was a resident of Ramgarh (Sikar) in the Riyasat of Jaipur. He was well versed in Yoga. Once he happened to meet Swami Ji in his dream. Since then he accepted Swami Ji as his Guru. After a long period, he got a chance to meet Swami Ji in person. Due to his unflinching influence, the people around Ramgarh came into the fold of the Arya Samaj. It was due to him that Swami Ji got a devoted person like Munshi Samarthdan as his caretaker. He left his mortal body of his own will on Jyeṣṭha Śukla 10, Saṁvat 1957.

Blessings from Dayanand Saraswati Swami to Pundit Kalu Ram Sharma.

Regarding the clarification you sought on Dharma, whatever views have been expressed in the Satyarth Prakash and other books written by me concerning Sva-dharma, may be followed.

Swami Dayanand Saraswati

Letter No. 20

To Pundit Kalu Ram Sharma

(Māgha Kṛṣṇa 4, Saṁvat 1933, or January 3, 1877)

This letter was written in Delhi. The original letter was sent to Pt. Bhagavaddatta by Pt. Ram Sahay who received it from Swami Swarupananda, a disciple of Pt. Kalu Ram Sharma. This letter was written on pink coloured paper.

Blessings from Dayanand Saraswati Swami to Pundit Kalu Ram Sharma.

Preta means departed soul and the term 'adyatana' (today) denotes time till ensuing midnight. Thus, the day commences from midnight. Moreover, we cannot count the number of followers of the Vedic path. Out of countless people, very few write about it e.g. Maharajas of Indore and Baroda; Vikram Singh, Maharaj of Kapurthala, Raja Jai Krishan Dass, Thakur Mukand Singh, and Lala Laxmi Narain of Bareilly. These may be considered among the followers of Vedic Dharma.

In addition, it must be said that it is difficult to reach your place at present. Maybe at some other opportune time. Meerut will probably be my next destination.

Swami Dayanand Saraswati

Letter No. 21

To Pundit Sundar Lal Ram Narain

(January 20, 1877)

This letter, written in English, and was sent from Meerut to Allahabad. This letter is preserved in the collection of the Paropkarini Sabha.

Will you please inform me whether you have received five hundred (500) copies of Sanskarvidhi from Bombay. Lala Keshav Lal and Nirbhay Ram were requested long ago by me to send you the above number of copies immediately. I am nowadays in Meerut and will continue to stay here for about a fortnight; so please send me your letter at the following address at Meerut: Swami Dayanand Saraswati, c/o Suraj Kund, Kothi of Dy. Mahatab Singh Ji, Meerut.

Swami Dayanand Saraswati

Letter No. 22

To Pundit Ramadhar Vajpai, Allahabad

(Phālguna Kṛṣṇa 9, Tuesday, Saṁvat 1933, February 6, 1877)

This letter, written in English, was sent from Meerut. The original letter is preserved in the collection of the Arya Samaj Lucknow.

This is to acknowledge the receipt of your letter (undated) and I feel elated to know that you could manage a large number of subscribers for the Vedabhāṣya. Please inform all those subscribers who are ready to buy monthly tracts, to send their subscription money to Banaras to the address of M/s E.J.Lazarus & Co., Medical Hall Press, Banaras. The Vijñāpana Patrikas (advertisements) or notices are not for sale but intended to improve the number of subscribers for Vedabhāṣya. So, please display them and distribute them among all of your friends and neighbours who are expected to be subscribers for the Vedabhāṣya. E.J.Lazarus and Co. will acknowledge receipt of the money despatched to them, but all subscribers are expected to send their respective correct addresses for receiving their copies from them M/S Lazarus and Co.

I hope you will continue to put your utmost efforts into increasing the number of subscribers. Hope you and your family are keeping well. I am to stay here up to the 15th instant and then will depart for Saharanpur. An early reply will oblige. The annual subscription for Vedabhāṣya is 4/8/- (4 Rupees and 8 annas) only.

Swami Dayanand Saraswati

Please let me know the total number of subscribers already managed by you in Lucknow. I have mentioned five copies in my list against your name. Others can get more copies on advance payment of their annual subscription of Rs. 4 and 8 annas (i.e. 4.50 Rupees).

Swami Dayanand Saraswati

Letter No. 23

To Pundit Ramadhar Vajpai

(Phālguna Kṛṣṇa 30, Tuesday, Saṁvat 1933 i.e. February 13, 1877)

This letter, also written in English, was sent from Meerut to Allahabad. This is also preserved in the collection of Arya Samaj Lucknow.

I received your letter dated 9th February and feel much pleased to send you herewith ten more copies of Vijñāpana Patras (advertisement papers) as you wished to distribute (them) there.

Well done, my dear, this is only (to be) expected from you. Let Sanskara-viddhi (books) come from Mumbai soon, as expected, and then not only one, but ten to fifteen copies will be dispatched to you without fail.

I will leave Meerut on the 15th of this month for Saharanpur and so your reply should reach me there instead of here. Hoping you are well with your family.

Swami Dayanand Saraswati

Letter No. 24

To Pundit Ramadhar Vajpai

(Caitra Kṛṣṇa 1, Wednesday, Saṁvat 1933, i.e. February 28, 1877)

This letter, also written in English, was sent from Saharanpur to Allahabad. The original letter is preserved in Arya Samaj Lucknow.

I am very glad to inform you that I will now visit the Chandrapur Religious Fair scheduled to be held in Ruhilkhand, Shahjahanpur District, where the fair-organisers and others have repeatedly invited me. The fair is held for bringing together different religious philosophies of India to discuss and deliberate upon the issue of 'God's true religion to be followed for Salvation'. I will leave Saharanpur by the 11th March and reach the site of the fair on the 15th and so you are expected to join the fair, which will continue for a week, (being extended from three days to a week) with all your friends, who wish to attend it. The fair will be most interesting and worth attending, as a great many Pandits, Maulvis, and Padrees from every nook and cranny of India will attend it and grace the occasion.

Hope you are keeping well along with your family. Have you received the required number of copies from Banaras. An early reply will be appreciated.

Swami Dayanand Saraswati

Letter No. 25

To Pundit Ramadhar Vajpai

(Caitra Kṛṣṇa 10, Friday, Saṁvat 1933 i.e. March 9, 1877)

This letter, also written in English, was sent from Saharanpur to Allahabad. This letter is also preserved in the collection of Arya Samaj Lucknow.

I am in receipt of your letter dated 6.3.1877 and in its reply, I am pleased to inform you that five more copies of Vedabhāṣya have been sent to you with my permission and M/S E.J.Lazarus is not mistaken this time. Please distribute them among the subscribers about whom you had informed me some days ago. I will reach Chandrapur fair on the 15th March which will now continue for the whole week from the 19th March. Please let me know how many Sanskara-viddhis do you require? Address me after the 11th at Chandrapur fair and not Saharanpur, as I will leave Saharanpur for (the fair) on the aforesaid date.

Please accept my best Āśirvāda (blessings) and attend the fair, if possible.

Swami Dayanand Saraswati

P.S. You can send the subscription for the five copies you received twice to the Medical Hall Press, Banaras, with addresses.

Letter No. 26

To Shri Ram Narain

(April 8, 1877)

This letter, written in English, was sent from Ludhiana. A copy of the letter is preserved in the Paropakarini Sabha. This letter shows that Swami Dayanand Saraswati had opened an account with M/S E.J. Lazarus & Co. Banaras for his credits and debits. The money used to be sent to E.J. Lazarus & Co. by various followers of Swami Ji from different parts of India who were in charge of the distribution of literature of Swamiji in their respective areas.

My dear Ram Narain,

In reply to your letter dated the 5th, you are informed not to send any more Sanskara-viddhis to me this time. I don't require them at all. It was written to you by mistake and you may now keep them in your custody. Please send the remaining subscription Rs. 2.28 for five copies to M/S E.J. Lazarus & Co. who have a credit balance of Rs. 350/- against my name for the months of February and March regarding the publication of Vedabhāṣya.

I have delivered many successful lectures at Meerut and Saharanpur and now I have reached Ludhiana. Daily sabhas are held here and the lectures are still going on with the same lustre indeed as were being held in the beginning. I will visit Amritsar next.

My ashirwad (blessings) to Pundit Sunder Lall as well as you. The Vedabhāṣya copies are published twice only i.e. for February and March, and not before as you suppose. The year for the work issue commences from February 1877. You received copies for the 1st and 2nd months, but for the third month (April) you will get them next time.

Your well-wisher,

Swami Dayanand Saraswati

Letter No. 27

To Babu Harish Chander Chintamani

(Vaiśākha Śukla 3, Monday, Saṁvat 1934 i.e.April 16, 1877)

This letter, written in English, was sent from Ludhiana to Mumbai. A copy of this letter was received by Pt. Bhagavaddatta from the collections of Prof. Dhirendra Verma.

I was happy to receive your letter dated 17th March. It was good to know that Mr. Shyam Ji will be staying in England for three years. In my opinion, this is a good opportunity which he must grab without fail. It will prove mutually beneficial indeed for both countrymen and will enhance their success in many ways. Your incentivisation of him in this respect, will undoubtedly, in the future be considered as being first-rate, and I forsee that he will be crowned with high honours by the intelligentsia in both England and India for such a praiseworthy attempt when he makes his successful return. Will he take his wife with him? Why does his father-in-law Seth Chhabil Dass, not agree in general with your views? Please give me more information on this matter. I am very comfortable expressing the view that, Mr. Shyam Ji would not be considered a wise man if he stepped back from this venerable undertaking. Now I will leave Ludhiana for Lahore on 19th April 1877 and will stay in the garden of Rattan Chand Darhiwala. Please send all your letters to the above address until further notice.

My best Āśirvāda (blessings).

Swami Dayanand Saraswati

Letter No. 28

To Pundit Ramadhar Vajpai

(Jyeṣṭha Śukla 2, Tuesday, Saṁvat 1934 i.e. May 15, 1877)

This letter, written in English, was sent from Lahore to Allahabad. It appears from the language of the above-cited English letters that Swami Ji's English translator was somebody from a Bengali Background. The style of spellings and other things prove this fact. The present editors and translators have corrected spellings, but have kept the style and sentences as they are, so that readers may also be acquainted with the style of writing English in 19th century India.

I received both letters and got all the details. The reason I could not reply to you was that the books required by you were not ready in my hand to despatch and so I waited to receive them all the while till this date.

I have now got some of them. However, though in very limited number I can send you a few copies, whatever I have with me, on your informing me of how many books of the Satyārth Prakāśa and Aryābhivinaya, etc, will suffice you, to be sold for ready payment because I also stand in need of money in my visiting places and at least fifty copies are required for Lahore and Amritsar.

Please send me an estimate of books, necessarily required for your Sabha and then I will send you some copies indeed.

May Parmātaman (God) bless your object of establishing Satya-Nirupaṇa-Sabha (Society for

Revealing Truth), which is expected to result in the good for the public. Hoping you are well with your friends. Accept my Āśirvāda (blessings).

Swami Dayanand Saraswati

Letter No. 29

To Pundit Gopal Rao Hari Deshmukh

(Jeṣṭha Kṛṣṇa 10, Wednesday, Saṁvat 1934 i.e. June 6, 1877)

This letter, written in English, was sent from Lahore to Lucknow. From the contents of the letter, it is crystal clear that the printing of Yajurveda was also started along with the printing of Ṛgveda at the advice of Gopal Rao Hari Deshmukh. This letter also shows that Swami Ji funded Shyam Ji Krishna Varma's expenses during his stay at Oxford.

I am glad that I got your letter of 30th May. It made me happy. Your boldness to tread the virtuous path is beyond measure, and your exertions in Indian welfare unparalleled. By the laws of nature, you are deserving a good reward and very soon your opulence will progress in leaps and bounds.

I am willing to follow your advice and I am ready to translate the Śukla Yajurveda as you wish. But in this case, I will require two more Pandits and the printing charges will increase for the double issue of the work every month. Therefore, you can yourself think over the matter properly and inform me then of your final opinion on the matter, so that I may employ two more writers and begin to translate the work with certainty.

I have every reason to believe that the darkness of ignorant India, which has reduced the people to such a low condition in which they seem to be careless, will one day be banished away if the sun of civilization shone over and the true knowledge of the Vedas is diffused over the country.

Noble and high-spirited persons like you and your companion only can be expected to undertake this mighty task for the public good and though such souls are very few, their rarity is better than their abundance.

I wish that Shyam Ji Krishan Varma should come to me for some time before starting for Oxford, (as) I wish to give him some of the most important hints on the Vedas which are necessarily required for him. He must not care for his expenses or anything else and I will indeed furnish him with all necessities. In my opinion, his trip to England is very useful for him, but let me know what is your opinion about the matter. I will also write directly to him. I have got no copy of Mahā Nirvāṇa Tantra with me but it is procurable from Calcutta.

Hoping you are well. Please let me know Shyam Ji K. Varma's reply to my inquiry.

My Āśirvāda (blessings).

Swami Dayanand Saraswati

Letter No. 30

To Shri Ram Narain

(June 7, 1877)

This letter, written in English, was sent from Lahore. A copy of this letter is available in the collection of Paropkarini Sabha.

My dear Ram Narain,

Your letter (of) 3rd May is to hand. You need not worry about anything; let (Mr.) Prasad assign its cost as he deems fit and suitable.

Wait some time more for Shukla Sarju Prasad's reply from whom I have received a letter this morning. He wishes to send me some money for purchasing Punjab's woollen cloth for him and perhaps he will also include the cost of the books in his money order. I have replied to him today.

Hope you are well with your uncle Pundit Sundar Lal.

My Āśirvāda (blessings) to all of you.

Swami Dayanand Saraswati

Letter No. 31

To Pundit Ramadhar Vajpai

(Jeṣṭha Vadi 12, Saṁvat 1934 or June 8, 1877, from Lahore)

This letter, written in English, was sent from Lahore to Lucknow. The original letter is preserved in the collection of Lucknow Arya Samaj.

My dear Pundit,

Please let me know whether you require some more copies of Sanskāra-viddhi or Satyārath Prakāśa for your Sabhā, as you requested once earlier. Have you received the twenty Sanskāra-viddhis and have you sold all of them to the people?

The other books are not ready. As soon as they are received, you will be informed at once. Successful lectures are going on here every day and with good results.

Hope you are well with your children.

My Āśirvāda (blessings).

Swami Dayanand Saraswati

Letter No. 32

To Shri Babu Dina Nath Ganguly

(Āṣāḍha Śukla 11, Saturday, Saṁvat 1934 i.e. July 21, 1877)

This letter, written in English, was sent from Lahore to Darjeeling. It was traced from the collection of Devendra Nath Mukhopadhaya. Mamraj Ji secured it from Adv. Ghasiram and handed it over to Pt. Bhagavaddatta. It stands preserved in the collection of Pt. Bhagavaddatta. From the contents of this letter, it appears that Swami Ji reached Amritsar on 12th July 1877. But the Biographies of Swami Dayanand written by Pt. Lekhram in Urdu (p. 321), Devendra Babu and Pt. Ghasiram Adv. (p. 429) mention that Swami Ji reached Amritsar on July 5. Thus with the help of these letters, the dates in various biographies of Swami Dayanand can be amended.

My dear Babu!

I received your letter of the 17th instant and got to know that by the grace of Almighty (Parameśvara), you are enjoying sound health.

According to your request and wishes, I herewith send a pattern of Veda's monthly commentaries (and) also a copy of the prospectus of the same for your information. The subscription for the current year has been fixed at Rs. 4.50/- only including postage, but for the future years, the amount of subscription will be increased or decreased according to the size of the work. I will be very glad to inform you now and then all about my gradual progress in my undertakings and regular movement from place to place without fail.

Hoping you are well and rejoicing. Please accept

my best Āśirvāda (blessings). I intend to stay at Amritsar up to the end of August, having arrived here on the 12th from Lahore.

Swami Dayanand Saraswati

P.S. Address me at Amritsar in the garden of Mohammad Jan Raees of the station.

Five parts for the five past months have already been published up to the end of June and the year for the work commences from February 1877.

Letter No. 33

To Various Critiques of Vedabhāṣya

[Published in 'Dayanand Digvijyarka, Vol II (Pages 82-88)]

Before reading this letter, the readers should be informed about the history behind this letter. Swami Ji met the Lt. Governor of Punjab on Monday 14th May 1877, at about 10 am. On the same day, after a meeting with the Governor, Swamiji wrote a letter to the Punjab government requesting a grant for financial aid for the publication of the Vedabhāṣya. Along with the letter, a specimen copy of the Ṛgvedādi- Bhāṣyabhūmikā and the Vedabhāṣya was also enclosed. The Punjab government sent the specimen copies to the Registrar at Punjab University College Shimla for review. The Registrar invited the views of some Indian and foreign scholars regarding Swamiji's Vedabhāṣya. Those views were naturally against Swamiji. This letter was written as a reply to the criticism made by the reviewers. The reply of Swamiji, written in Hindi, was sent by Arya Samaj Lahore to Dr. G.W Lightner, M.A. Bar-at-Law, the Registrar, Punjab University College Shimla along with its own letter written in English.

I came to know from the 'Vakil- a-Hind' newspaper and from papers published by University College Punjab that some gentlemen (Sahibs) have given adverse opinions on the Vedabhāṣya written by me. Therefore, I proffer my reply verbatim to clarify their doubts.

First is the reply to the doubts expressed by Mr. R. Griffith, M.A., Principal, Banaras College.

During the last five thousand years Vedic

knowledge (Vidyā) has disappeared, whereas before the Mahābhārata, the entire Vedic knowledge was intact, but after that period, such books of learning and teaching were forgotten and the system changed altogether. Since then the wrong system is in vogue. Although some people in some places were able to learn true Vedic Granthas (books) by heart and thereby guard its knowledge, the true meaning of the terminology used in the Vedas, and other books of Grammar, etc. are no longer known. The latter containing the meaning of Vedic terms, was being taught beforehand and it was used to assist scholars in understanding the meaning of the Vedas. The (so-called) modern Vedabhāṣyas compiled by Mahidhara and others, which are available nowadays, are highly corrupt (mahābhraṣṭa) and add to the ignorance (about the true interpretation of Vedas). The people who rely on such Bhāṣyas are unlikely to comprehend the Vedabhāṣya (Vedic commentary) written by me. My Vedabhāṣya provides the true meanings of the Vedas in consonance with the original old Vedabhāṣyas. This will be understood only when the old (original) books on Bhāṣyas, etc. are referred to for assistance (in this regard).

I have written the true meaning of each Mantra clearly along with full evidence in support of such interpretations from very ancient books of learned grammarians. Had Mr. Griffith studied the ancient original commentaries and my commentaries (Vedabhāṣya), supported with evidence and examples, he would not have proffered the adverse opinions, which he has recently given. The (Veda)Bhāṣyas written by Uvaṭa, Sāyaṇa, Mahidhara, Rāvaṇa, etc. are totally at variance with those by the ancient Vedabhāṣyas. Only the English translation of the former has been done by Professors like Wilson and Max Müller. Therefore, I don't consider such Vedabhāṣyas to be correct and justifiable. Due to such (literally translated) books, Griffith Saheb and others are biased and they malign me by saying that Swami Ji has given a different interpretation to serve his own objectives. But their argument is totally baseless. Everywhere I have cited from Aitreya and Śatapatha Brāhamaṇa and quoted evidence from Granthas like Nirukta and Pāṇini, etc. true grammars, while writing the true meaning for each mantra. Had Mr. Griffith seen my interpretation, he would not have written this. I think that he has published his own biased suggestions without looking into my Vedabhāṣya.

I fail to understand why Griffith Saheb considers my labour as being pointless when there are more than one thousand people of great standing and repute who have purchased my Vedabhāṣya, and every day I receive more and more requests from the new customers of my books. Among my customers, there are many Sanskrit learned scholars and many great scholars of English. The last comment of Griffith Sahab that 'Vedic Ṛcas' containing names of many gods, would have been appreciated by me and by other scholars if he would have cited some particular ṛcā in that context.

In support of the above, the following excerpts (uddharaṇa) are given:

(a) From the book 'The Vedas' by H.T. Colebrook

(b) From 'Mythology of the Vedas' by Charles Coleman.

(c) From the Preface to the book 'Bhagavad Gītā' translated by Padari Garrett

(d) From 'History of Ancient Sanskrit Literature' (page 567 onwards)

In the very first mantra in Ṛgveda there is mention of the word 'Agni', which in his first cited statement, has been translated by Mr. C. H. Tanny, MA, Principal, Presidency College, Calcutta as meaning 'fire'. That fire element is also recognised in the Vedas. But no ancient Ṛṣi or Muni (Seer) has invoked 'fire' for prayer (Pūja). Moreover, the apparent meaning of Agni as 'fire' has been used only for worldly (materialistic) affairs. But in sentences where the context is the glorification of God, prayer, and request, the word 'Agni' denotes 'Parmeśvara' (Supreme God). This meaning is not an untrue meaning imagined by me. Such logical interpretations have been made in the Brāhamaṇas and Nirukta granthas.

Lastly, the view expressed by Mr. Tanny is that the Vedabhāṣya has been written by me in order to condemn as being incorrect, the Vedabhāṣyas of Sāyaṇa and English translators. I cannot be blamed on this subject. If Sāyaṇa committed a mistake and English translators have accepted him as their guide, they may do, but I cannot deliberately commit that mistake. Wrong opinions (interpretations) cannot stand for long, as only truth prevails and untruth fades away quickly as compared to the truth.

Pundit Guru Prasad, Head Pundit of Oriental

College Lahore, by stating that 'the many errors which have crept in the Swami Ji's Vedabhāṣya, are not printing errors' has hurt my good intentions. Still, I am thankful to all the critics. It is not a small thing that they have expressed confidence in the printer of my Vedabhāṣya. But I feel that whatever mistakes are assigned to the printer are in reality my mistakes. They should express themselves boldly (with confidence), and unless further details are known, nothing can be concluded. Secondly, their attempt to defame me by saying that I want to propagate my own faith (pantha), is I feel, quite painful and wounding. I think that they are quite ignorant of Vedic knowledge. Had they studied the ancient commentaries (Vedabhāṣya), they would not have come up with such statements.

They also say that Swami Ji has erroneously coined his own meanings of the words 'Indra', 'Vṛtra' and 'Tvaṣṭā'. To clear their doubts on that score, I present to them evidence of (our) advertisement for the Vedabhāṣya, in which the appropriate meanings of these words have been given. However, while considering all these aspects, I am constrained to say emphatically that they possess very little knowledge of ancient Sanskrit.

The fourth defect alleged by them is that in my Vyākaraṇa (grammar), I I have used ātmnepada instead of parasmaipada. This shows that the Pundit Ji himself does not possess knowledge of grammar. Here, I give several separate examples as proof (evidence) from the books (granthas) of Kaiṭa (Bhāṣya Pradīpa), and Nageśa, Ramashram Acharya, Anubhuti Swarup Acharya, and others. They consider my use of the term 'vidadhīmahi ' as correct. For the authenticity of the term 'vadāmahe', I have cited Pāṇini grammar (1.3.47) as evidence, of which I can send a relevant copy to them to prove to what extent my usage (of the term) is correct. However, without proper knowledge of grammar, they cannot comprehend all this.

The fifth doubt expressed by them is about my use of one Chhanda, (metre) which is quite laughable. If I reply to it briefly it would be more emphatic. To solve their doubt, I cite separately from Paiṅgala Sūtra with clear cut proof from its commentator (Bhāṣyakāra) Halāyuddha Bhaṭṭa. By referring to it, they should (now) feel comfortable.

It seems that Pundit Hrishikesh Bhattacarrya and also Pundit (Guru Prasad) of Oriental College Lahore and all other Pandits are followers of Pundit Guru Prasad. Therefore, the answer (reply) to their doubts may be read as the same as written (indicated) before. In the word 'upacakre', their doubt is separate. To make them understand the same, my use of the term is very much clear, for which I cite evidence from Pāṇinian Grammar(1.3.30), which should satisfy them.

Now remains (the doubts expressed by) Pundit Bhagwan Dass, Assistant Professor, Government Sanskrit College, Lahore. His doubt is not different. So, whatever I have said above will suffice. He should also finally be satisfied.

To conclude (lastly), it appears to me that the intention behind the energy spent by these critics, is so that my Vedabhāṣya may no longer be allowed to exist in all the colleges of India. However, this is a blunder (great mistake) on the part of my critics. My

Vedabhāṣya, is based on evidence from the (ancient) Vedabhāṣyas prior to Mahābhārata and also it is opposed to the views expressed by the European scholars. It will undoubtedly create such a furore, that it will unravel the truth and enhance ethical (moral) values in our colleges. Hence, due to this reason, our Vedabhāṣya needs patronage by the government.

Swami Dayanand Saraswati

Letter No. 34

To Members of Arya Samaj at Lahore

(Bhādrapada Śukla 3, Saṁvat, 1934 i.e. September 10, 1877, Monday)

This letter was written by Swamiji from Amritsar to the members of Arya Samaj at Lahore to share developments at Amritsar and his future itinerary for Jalandhar. It was found quoted in Swami Ji's Biography by Pundit Lekha Ram (Hindi, page No. 365). The original letter is not traceable.

Blessings from Dayanand Saraswati Swami to all the members of Arya Samaj (Lahore).

With the grace of the Almighty, the fame of Amritsar Arya Samaj is increasing every day. Arya Uddeśya Ratna Mālā containing one hundred rules is likely to be printed and bound shortly (in a day or two). We shall (then) send five hundred copies of this book to Lahore and fifty to Gurdaspur. It may be known that I will proceed to Jalandhar by train at 9:30 morning on Bhadra Śudī 6 (Thursday), Saṁvat 1934 (September 13, 1877). Replies to letters containing adverse views about Vedabhāṣya have been sent to Mumbai and other places. It will be very good if these are published in newspapers there. Regarding the rest, you all may do as you wish.

Swami Dayanand Saraswati

Letter No. 35

To Members of Arya Samaj at Lahore

(Bhādrapada Śudī 8, Saṁvat 1934, i.e. September 15, 1877, Saturday)

This letter, written in Hindi, was sent from Jalandhar to the members of Arya Samaj Lahore. This letter has been quoted in Swamiji's Biography written by Pt. Lekh Ram in Urdu (p.341).

Blessings to all the members of the Arya Samaj, Lahore.

I have reached Jalandhar and I am staying in the garden of Sardar Suchet Singh. Sardar Vikram Singh (brother of Sardar Suchet Singh son of Maharaja Nihal Singh of Kapurthala) is a gentleman. Further developments will be shared with you later.

Has the sixth volume of the Vedabhāṣya been received or not? After stamping it, was the stamp sent to Amritsar?

Swami Dayanand Saraswati

Letter No. 36

To Pundit Gopal Rao Deshmukh, Lucknow

(Āśvina Kṛṣṇa 10, Saṁvat 1934 i.e. October 2, 1877)

This letter, written in English, was sent from Jalandhar and was probably addressed to Pundit Gopal Rao Deshmukh of Arya Samaj, Lucknow. The original copy of the letter is available there with Lucknow Arya Samaj. Through this letter, we have come to know that the composition of Ṛgvedādibhāṣya Bhūmikā was completed by Swami Ji by the end of Sept. 1877.

My dear Pundit,

I hope you might have received one hundred copies of Āryoddeṣya Ratna Mālā from Amritsar, which have been sent with my permission to your address by Mansukh Rai of Arya Samaj. Please acknowledge receipt of them, if duly received, and inform me about your sound health.

Daily lectures are being delivered here and hopefully, these will bear good results. I will stay here for about nine to ten days more and then visit the next place or perhaps Lahore once more.

You can address me at Jalandhar city care of Sardar Vikram Singh of Kapurthala.

Please accept my blessings. The (above) said copies are to be sold at (the rate of) one and a half annas (9 Paise) each.

Swami Dayanand Saraswati

The Vedabhāṣya Bhūmikā (An Introduction to the Commentary of Vedas) has nearly been completed and the commentary of (the main) Vedas is to commence soon.

Letter No. 37

To Lala Mansukh Rai, Amritsar

(Āśvina Śukla 5, Saṁ. 1934 i.e. October 11, 1877, Thursday)

This letter, written in Urdu, was sent from Jalandhar. This letter was given by Pt. Rudradatta of Amritsar in Oct. 1926 to Pt. Bhagavaddatta. The letter was in a dilapidated condition. Half of it was missing and the remaining part was in a very bad condition. One side of this letter has an Urdu version and the other side has both Urdu and English versions.

Blessings to Lala Mansukh Rai Ji!

May you be happy. Everything is going well here. Now I will not inform you about matters through telegrams. I will leave for Amritsar on the 15th on the 7:30 morning train and will reach Amritsar Railway Station at 10:30 am and on the next day (16th instant) will proceed to and deliver a lecture, if possible. About (the status of the) books, I will tell you everything in person to you when I am there. On another matter, by mistake the name of Narain Singh has crept in instead of Baba Narain Singh, which please could you kindly correct. Please arrange for a house for my short stay overnight and half a day there. My blessings to all the members of Arya Samaj.

Swami Dayanand Saraswati

Letter No. 38

To Pundit R.R. Gopal Rao Hari Deshmukh

(Mārgaśīrṣa Kṛṣṇa 8, Wednesday Saṁvat 1934 or November 28, 1877)

This letter, written in English, was sent from Rawalpindi, present Pakistan to Torman. This letter points out that the Vedabhāṣya is being done under his guidance. This points out that Swami Ji used to dictate only the Sanskrit portion of the Vedasbhāṣya. The Hindi Bhāṣya was done by Bhimsen, etc. This is perhaps why we do not find coherence in the Sanskrit and Hindi Bhāṣya.

Dear Pundit,

Enclosed herewith is a specimen copy of my Vedabhāṣya (publication of which is to commence soon) exhibiting a style and method of interpretation of the text in a peculiar way for the facility of the readers. I will do my best to address all the most difficult points in plain Sanskrit and Devanāgarī (Hindi) so that even children with insufficient knowledge of Sanskrit can grasp it without any aid. Please go through it yourself first and then circulate it in Ahmedabad, Bombay, and other places to the relevant people for comments and suggestions. I do hope that you will not delay the matter and will communicate your final opinion to me, to either preserve the style or change it to a better one.

The work of (the main) text of the Vedabhāṣya has since commenced and is being written daily under my personal guidance. Thus, any delay in conveying your opinion and of other persons like Moreshwar Kunte is not advisable. Address me at Rawalpindi care of the postmaster only. For the publication of two volumes of the Ṛg and Yajurvedas during the next year 1878, I have sought views of (prospective) subscribers through this month's Volume 9 of the Vedabhāṣya and another notice for raising the subscription of the same will be published next month.

Please reply to my other letter and accept my best Āśirvāda (blessings). I am very glad to hear that you visit Bombay Arya Samaj every fortnight and deliver beautiful lectures there on different topics of public interest. Hope you are keeping well and rejoicing.

Swami Dayanand Saraswati

Letter No. 39

To Pundit R. R. Gopal Rao Hari Deshmukh, Mumbai

(Mārgaśīrṣa Śukla 2, Thursday, Saṁvat 1934 i.e. December 6, 1877)

This letter, written in English, was sent from Rawalpindi to Pundit Hari Deshmukh in connection with the correction of proofs of the Vedabhāṣya and shows Swami Ji's determination to undertake the work of the Vedabhāṣya and of the Yajurveda as well. This letter also sheds ample light on Swami Ji's cost-consciousness concerning the printing of his books.

Dear Pundit,

Yours of the 30th ultimo (last month) is to hand. To correct proof sheets in Hindi must be my constraint, and I will do that twice or thrice on my own every month. Although you will have no difficulty at all in doing such work, yet you are to take care of many other works, which you can only do. I think Babu H. Chintamani is well-qualified and intelligent enough to supervise the work, but tell me first what would you like to do in this case? I have not given any contract of the work to Dr. Lazauras for any fixed length of time, but his charges have been settled as follows:

Monthly expenses for 3100 copies-

Charges for printing and paper @ Rs. 6.70 per 6 page is Rs. 161.90/-

For printing of covers including folding and

stitching @ Rs. 15 per 1000..Rs.46.50/-

For office allowance and agency Rs 30/- per month.

The list of subscriptions paid and unpaid with full particulars will be sent to you at the close of the current year.

If God is willing, I will publish the Yajurveda as well. At what rate per ream the papers like that of Sanskāra-vidhi is procurable at Bombay? Hope you are keeping well and rejoicing. My Āśirvāda (blessings) to you. Send me letters at the Rawalpindi address.

Swami Dayanand Saraswati

P.S.

What will be the printing cost of such size of copies as printed at Dr. Lazauras press in Bombay, if I supply paper at my own cost separately? If you find the printing cheaper there, let the printing be done at Bombay. There is no objection at all at my end.

Letter No. 40

To Shri Ram Narain

(December 10, 1877)

This letter, written in English, was sent from Rawalpindi. A copy of this letter exists in the collection of Propalkarini Sabha.

I received your letter of 5th ultimo and got all the details.

I have accepted Rs. 30/- as a donation for the Vedabhāṣya from Rao Gopa Mangesh Manjeshwarkar with thanks and give much credence to him for his generosity for the cause of truth. I also enclose a separate receipt for the amount given by him, as also a reply to his inquiry.

I am very happy that Pundit Sundar Lal will be at Ambala but unfortunately, I will be too far to see him. Rawalpindi is located far away from the railway line. Please inform your uncle not to take unnecessary trouble in snow-clad weather. I am happy to hear that he is enjoying sound health. He should not undertake such a long journey. Please convey to him my best Āśirvāda (blessings) and the same for yourself.

Your well-wisher

Swami Dayanand Saraswati

P.S. Lala Shiv Dayal, Assistant Engineer, is going to Allahabad on public duty and will see you within a fortnight. I have given him a letter about your address, so please receive him, kindly.

Swami Dayanand Saraswati

Letter No. 41

To Pundit R. R. Gopal Rao Hari Deshmukh, Mumbai

(Mārgaśīrṣa Śukla 7, Wednesday, Saṁvat 1934 i.e. December 12, 1877)

This letter, written in English, was sent from Rawalpindi to Pundit Hari Deshmukh about the price of the Vedabhāṣya and Swami Ji's green signal for its publication from Banaras, if cheaper. This letter reveals Swamiji's cost-consciousness in getting the Vedabhāṣya printed at the lowest possible rates. He conveyed his approval to hire the services of Pundit Shyam Ji Krishna Verma at Rs. 30 to 40 per month if he had no objections to supervising the printing work of the Vedabhāṣya. According to Pt. Bhagwaddatta, the copy of this letter was preserved in the collection of J.N. Rana (Mumbai). This letter is in a dilapidated condition.

Yours... of the 6th ultimo is to hand. To know that the .... of Vedabhāṣya of Rs. 31 ... of 24 pages ....do include the cost of paper... include it..

I have no objection if the work is printed at the lowest market rates in Banaras.

If Shyamji Krishna Verma is not proceeding to England and willing to supervise the printing and distribution of Vedabhāṣya, I'll (be) glad.. and that.. upon desire.....hand allowing.. in the meantime Rs. 30 or even Rs. 40 per month, including house rent for keeping the printed copies in a store, as I pay. Lazarus for the same duty, except the postage expenses. Shyamji Verma is a very good Pundit and can do proofing of both Sanskrit and Hindi------ properly.

You, yourself and Babu H. Chintamani will have to supervise the regular progress of the work either through correspondence or personally, while for myself, the translation of the Vedas and propagation of the true doctrine all around the country is a priority. My Āśirvāda (blessings) to you.

Your Well-wisher

Swami Dayanand Saraswati

Letter No. 42

To Pundit R.R. Gopal Rao Hari Deshmukh, Mumbai

(Mārgaśīrṣa Śukla 8, Thursday, Saṁvat 1934 i.e. December 13, 1877)

This letter, written in English, was sent from Rawalpindi to Pundit Hari Deshmukh regarding the sample paper for the Vedabhāṣya, and what is noteworthy is the particular style of reminding him and others to renew their subscriptions.

Dear Pundit ji!

In continuation of yesterday's letter, I again inform you about something more which I remembered afterwards.

I want to have a sample of the paper which is to be used and selected for the printing of the Vedabhāṣya, and also you should bear in mind that the aforesaid Bhāṣya must be published in three different types according to my Ms. i.e., 'M' large, round and small bands.

Please remind the Baroda subscribers to renew their subscriptions without further delay.

Your well-wisher

Swami Dayanand Saraswati

Letter No. 43

To Pundit Ramadhar Vajpai

(Pauṣa Kṛṣṇa 8, Thursday, Saṁvat 1934, i.e. December 27, 1877)

This letter, written in English, was sent from Jehlum, Pakistan to Pundit Ramadhar Vajpai at Lucknow regarding the purchase of papers for the Vedabhāṣya. What is noteworthy again, is the particular style of reminding him to renew his subscriptions.

Dear Pundit Ji!

I am so glad to receive your letter. I got all the details which made me happy.

I have reached Jhelum today, i.e. 27th of Dec. I intend to stay here for about a fortnight. At least you can remit the money to me freely to my above address care of the Postmaster only. However, don't send me tickets as you did before because I find some difficulty in encashing them. Better, send currency notes or money orders. Both are the safest ways indeed. Hope you are keeping well and rejoicing.

Your well-wisher

Swami Dayanand Saraswati

Letter No. 44

To Pundit Ramadhar Vajpai

(Pauṣa Kṛṣṇa 9, Friday, Saṁvat 1934 i.e. Dec. 28, 1877)

This letter, written in English, was sent from Jehlum to Pundit Ramadhar Bajpai at Lucknow regarding the Sandhyopāsanā book, of which the improved and enlarged edition was underprint. The original letter is preserved in the collection of Arya Samaj Lucknow.

Dear Pundit Ji!

Please tell me how many copies of Sandhyopāsanā you wish to have for sale in Lucknow. These are the best copies with good translations in Hindi paragraph by paragraph. This is an improved and enlarged edition. The average price per copy has not been fixed as yet because the said book is still in the press, but on its coming out of the press, everything will be settled and decided with goodwill.

However, I can give you an idea that the price would be under half a rupee per copy. This would prove to be an excellent work for the Aryans indeed.

Since yesterday evening, it is raining here so heavily that the entire building, except for a few spots, is leaking.

Hope all is well.

Your well-wisher

Swami Dayanand Saraswati

Letter No. 45

To Pundit Ramadhar Vajpai

(Pauṣa Śukla 1, Friday, Saṁvat 1934 i.e. Jan. 4, 1878)

This letter, written in English, was sent from Jehlum to Pundit Ramadhar Vajpai at Lucknow regarding the printing of Sandhyopāsanā and Pañca Mahāyajña Vidhi books, of which 100 copies would be sent to him shortly. This shows how meticulously Swami Dayanand utilised every bit of time in bringing out these books at the earliest. The above-mentioned letters also clearly show that during his visits to various cities and places, Swami Ji used to receive letters addressed to him directly from the postmasters of the concerned cities. This shows his popularity with the public and with government employees.

Dear Pundit Ji!

The Sandhyopāsanā and Pañca-mahāyajña-vidhi with simple and lucid translation in Hindi are now ready for use and you will soon get 100 (one hundred) copies of it from Banaras Press shortly.

The price per copy has been printed on the covers and if you wish to have more of them, you can be furnished with the required numbers on (receipt) of your further request. I believe you would have received my other letters also in the due course of time. I do hope all the family are well.

Your well-wisher **Swami Dayanand Saraswati**

Send me letters at the Jhelum city address care of the Postmaster only.

Letter No. 46

To Pundit Ramadhar Vajpai

(Pauṣa Śukla 3, Sunday, Saṁvat 1934 i.e. Jan. 6, 1878)

This letter, written in English, was sent from Jehlum to Pundit Ramadhar Vajpai at Lucknow regarding the imminent likelihood of setting up an Arya Samaj at Jhelum. It shows how consistently he wished to spread the Vedic message to more people through the Arya Samaj. All letters written to Ramadhar Bajpai are preserved in the collection of the Lucknow Arya Samaj.

Dear Pundit Ji!

I am writing to say thank you for your letter of the 3rd instant and a currency note of ten Rs. only. Nothing is new here worthy of being mentioned, but I hope sincerely that an Arya Samaj will also be set up here shortly.

Hope all is well with you and all the family are also well.

My best Āśirvāda (blessings).

Your well-wisher

Swami Dayanand Saraswati

Letter No. 47

To Pundit Sukh Swroop Kalu Ram, Lucknow

(Pauṣa Śukla 4, Saṁvat 1934 or Jan. 7, 1878)

This letter, written in Hindi, was sent from Jhelum to Pundit Sukh Swroop Kalu Ram at Lucknow informing him about the publication of the Vedabhāṣya of the Ṛg and the Yajurveda in 1878 and developments regarding the starting of Arya Samajs in Panjab. He has also thankfully acknowledged receipt of financial assistance for the Vedabhāṣyas.

Sukh Swarup Kalu Ram Ji,

Greetings!

Your beautiful letter of Pauṣa Kṛṣṇa 7, 1934 (Dec. 16, 1878) made me happy. From next year i.e. Saṁvat, 1935 (1878 AD) two issues of the Ṛg and the Yajurveda Bhāṣya shall be despatched to you and Samarthdana. I congratulate you all for your assistance in the cause of the Vedabhāṣya. May God shower His blessings upon you.

Sandhyopāsanā Bhāṣya in Hindi (Devanāgarī) with comments has been printed very nicely. 25 copies will reach you from the Banaras Printing Press shortly. Please acknowledge the receipt of the same. In the future, any new book published will be sent to you. Part II of Satyaratha Prakash could not be printed despite our best efforts. The Arya Samaj has been set up at Rawalpindi and it is hoped that it will be set up in Jehlum also. In Punjab, Arya Samajs have been set up in many places. It is a sign of the great progress of

Vedic Dharma.

Here it is very cold and raining heavily. Nothing more to write. My blessings to Samarthadana and others. You can address me, care of the Postmaster/Post Office Jehulam.

Swami Dayanand Saraswati

Letter No. 48

To Pundit Ramadhar Vajpai

(Pauṣa Śukla 10, Saṁvat 1934 i.e. Jan. 14, 1878)

This letter, written in English, was sent from Gujrat (now in Pakistan) to Pundit Ramadhar Vajpai at Lucknow giving information about the printing of the Vedabhāṣya. This letter was sent by Pt. Ram Sahay Ji Mahopadeshak from Ajmer to Pt. Bhagawaddatta. The original copy existed in the collection of Pt. Bhagawaddatta.

Dear Pundit Ji,

Your welcome note of the 9th instant is to hand and I was given to understand the whole matter.

Your cherished wish for raising the Vedabhāṣya's subscription for the current year will soon come true. The only delay is the consent of the Bombay people, I am now making some better arrangements for the (Veda) Bhāṣya's publication, both in terms of paper and type (style). All this will soon be finalised with the combined efforts of (all of) us and a notice will be circulated through the 11th or 12th part of the Vedabhāṣya for public information in this matter. The subscription for this year is to be fixed, with definitely some reduction so that people will be able to buy both the Ṛg and Yajur (Veda) at a low cost.

I dare say that all the subscribers for this year (1878) will be fully satisfied to find (everything written on) good paper and (in a) fine order of interpretation, which is essentially required to know the actual and factual meaning of the mantras. On my return from

Punjab, I will tell you whether and what time I will be able to visit Lucknow. My visit will go through certainly eventually. I hope all is well with you. My best Āśirvāda.

Your ever well-wisher,

Swami Dayanand Saraswati

Letter No. 49

To Babu B.H.Chintamani

(Pauṣa Śukla 12, Wednesday, Saṁvat 1934 i.e. Jan. 16, 1878)

This letter, written in English, was sent from Gujrat (now in Pakistan) to Babu B.H. Chintamani at Mumbai, stating not to go for English and Urdu and other vernacular translations of the Vedabhāṣya until and unless the Sanskrit and Hindi version is completed. It shows Swami Ji's will to propagate Sanskrit and Hindi through his Vedabhāṣya instead of English or Urdu. The original letter was preserved by Prof. Dhirendra Verma in his collection.

Dear Babu,

Having consulted with Munshi Inder Mani (a famous scholar of Arabic and Persian) and other experienced persons of the North West Province, I have come to the conclusion that we should not go for a translation of the Vedabhāṣya in English or other vernacular languages until the whole of the Vedabhāṣya has been completed. It is because if we translate it in English or Urdu, people will remain unconcerned about Sanskrit and Devanāgarī (Hindi) when they would achieve their goal by studying it in English or Urdu. Under the circumstances, there is no need to get it translated into English or Urdu, as the same will have a negative impact. First, let us get it completed in pure Sanskrit and Hindi Bhasha, and if the need is felt later to get the Vedabhāṣya translated in other languages, then you people would be free to do so as per your desire in the public interest.

Some time back Shyam Ji Krishna Verma had

selected and accompanied me to a new shop for samples of papers in Bombay. The paper is available there @ Rs. 16 per ream. Please sort out this matter early, and have a mutual agreement with the printers (of the Vedabhāṣya) drafted on stamp paper without further delay.

If Shyam Ji Krishna Verma is ready to work for me, I will be glad to engage him even at an extra cost of Rs. 10 or Rs. 15 on our monthly exchequer. Seek his consent and hold a meeting of your friends for proposing some better scheme about the Vedabhāṣya's publication, if possible.

The first year is to end and the second is to commence from February, so I want to finalise the subscription after you reach a settlement with the printers and advise me of the rate of the subscription for both the Vedas, in view of the printing cost. The buyers will be unwilling to pay high fees if the Hindi translation is added with the Sanskrit one.

Gujrat, Fatehgarh, and Wazirabad (all in Pakistan) have been blessed with Arya Samajs in December last (1877) and January 1878. Address the correspondence at Gujrat city care of the postmaster only.

My Āśirvāda (blessings).

Your well-wisher

Swami Dayanand Saraswati

Letter No. 50

To Shri Madho Lal

(Pauṣa Kṛṣṇa 10, Monday, Saṁvat 1934 i.e. Jan. 28, 1878)

This letter, written in Hindi, was sent from Gujrat (now in Pakistan). The reference to this letter is registered at page 358 in the Urdu Biography of Swami Ji by Pt. Lekhram. The previous part of this letter is not available.

I am excited to meet you on my arrival in the Bengal region (area) from Punjab. I am glad to know that you are anxious to contribute your bit to the cause of the progress of your countrymen. May the Creator bless you with good health and prosperity. I felt intensely rejoiced to know that you are keen to put your efforts into improving the condition of your country. There is no doubt, your selfless efforts will be fruitful. My Āśirvāda (blessings) to all.

Swami Dayanand Saraswati

Letter No. 51

To Lala Jiwan Das

(Māgha Śukla, 7, Saṁvat, 1934 or February 9,1878)

This letter, written in Hindi, was sent from Gujranwala (Now in Pakistan). We also find the reference to this letter in Urdu Biography of Swami Ji by Pt. Lekhram on page 365 (Hindi version, p. 404).

Upon the receipt of the invitation from Dr. Jaswant Rai Saheb from Multan, I will visit that place.

Gujranwala, 9 Feb. 1878

Swami Dayanand Saraswati

Letter No. 52

To Lala Jiwan Das

(Phālguna Kṛṣṇa, 2 Saṁvat 1934 i.e. February 19, 1878)

This was a telegram given in Hindi from Gujranwala. By that time Swami Ji was in Gujranwala. Afterwards, he proceeded to Lahore. He stayed there from March 3 to March 12. The subject of this telegram suggests that Swami Ji had a debate with Christian missionaries in Gujranwala.

Lala Jiwan Dass!

Lectures are being held here daily. Nothing special to mention presently. I will be writing shortly. Today, there will be a debate with (Christian) Priests.

Swami Dayanand Saraswati
Gujranwala

Letter No. 53

To Shri Mool Raj, Jiwan Dass, Sain Das, and Bal Das

(Caitra Kṛṣṇa 11, Saturday, Saṁvat 1934 i.e March 30, 1878)

This letter, written in Hindi, was sent from Multan. It has been quoted by Pt. Lekhram (p.370 of Urdu version and p. 410 of Hindi version).

Dear Moolraj, Jiwan Dass, Sain Dass and Bal Dass,

Greetings to all of you!

Letters from Ram Rakha will be forwarded, as soon as they are received or when new letters will be written and posted. However, like before, all efforts will come to nothing, if the matter is not printed. As with the finalizing of the rules of the Antraṅga Sabhā (Executive Council), which still remain unfinalised, this should not happen here. I am writing this to ask you to complete the work as scheduled. Timely completion of work is a sign of wisdom. We are having a good time here, and I hope you are also having a wonderful time.

As the only clerk I have nowadays, is unable to carry out all his duties, there is an urgent need to appoint someone well versed in English, Persian, Devanāgarī (Hindi), and who is also very skilled in accounting, and map work. If a person with the above qualifications is not available, then one who knows English, Persian, and Urdu at least and who can read and write letters (in these languages) should be appointed. However, he should not be lazy and should have a good temperament. His salary should not exceed Rs. Twenty-five (25.00) per month. All the four of you may select such a person with a salary payable between Rs 25.00 and Rs. 20.00 and inform me.

Here, lectures are being held daily. There is also the likelihood of setting up an Arya Samaj.

Swami Dayanand Saraswati

Letter No. 54

To Babu Madho Lal

(Caitra Kṛṣṇa 14, Monday, Saṁvat 1934 i.e April 1, 1878)

This letter, written in Hindi, was sent from Multan to Danapur, Bihar. The letter is preserved in Danapur Arya Samaj.

Dear Madho Lal Ji,

Greetings!

I got your letter dated 24.3.1878 and I came to know of its contents. As you desired, we have sent two copies of the Ten Principles of the Arya Samaj printed on 31st March 1878. Today we are sending one more copy containing sub-rules and thus I assume that you have both copies containing the rules and the sub-rules. Kindly send us the receipt as soon as possible. One must understand these rules properly and should take up the initiative wholeheartedly and with full dedication for the well-being of all, particularly for the reform of our Āryāvartta country as directed in the Vedas. Working for the well-being of all is the greatest Dharma. Similarly, there are many instructions in the Vedas, following which our great Rishis and Munis imparted the true sciences and advised them about the true path of Dharma creating much prosperity and progress. This country was the source of knowledge and prosperity for the whole globe because the ever-existing Vedas are the treasure trove of all: the true sciences of God. For such things like rules and sub-rules, behaviour, worship, etc. you can refer to our books. You must keep the title 'Arya Samaj' in place of 'Hindu Sat Sabha'. This is because our name is 'Arya' and our country was known as 'Āryāvartta' in the Vedas.

Arya means 'a noble, spiritual and righteous person. The word 'Hindu' is the corrupt name given to us by our enemies, the Muslims. 'Hindu' symbolizes a 'slave', 'kafir', and a 'dark-skinned' person. Keeping in view of all the above-mentioned reasons, you must name your association 'Arya Samaj' as per the Vedas . All members of the association should use the salutary address 'Namaste' and not 'Salam' or 'Bandagi'.

Swami Dayanand Saraswati
Multan

Letter No. 55

To Babu Madho Lal

(Caitra Śukla 10, Friday, Saṁvat 1935, or April 12, 1878)

This letter, written in Hindi, was sent from Multan to Danapur, Bihar. This letter depicts Swami Dayanand's joy over the setting up of more and more branches of the Arya Samaj, which he considered a sign of national reform.

Be rejoiced Babu Madho Lal Ji. Your letter dated 7th April is received and its contents are known. The following books are being sent to you, receipt of which may please be sent early at the Lahore address:

	Rs	Annas	Pai
1 Satyāratha Prakāśa	2	8 (50 paise)	0
1 Sanskāra Vidhi	1	10 (60 paise)	0
1 Āryābhivinaya	0	8 (50 paise)	0
1 Sandhyopāsana	0	6 (40 paise)	0
1 Aryaodeśya Ratanmālā	0	1 (6 paise)	2
1 Chandapur Fair (in Urdu)	0	1 (6 paise)	1
1 Praśanottara (Question Answer) Haldhar	0	1 (6 paise)	0
Total cost of 7 books:	5	12 (75 paise)	3

Postal charges :	0	5	3
Total cost :	5	9 (55paise)	3

The total cost will be five Rs. and 55 Ps.

I am highly pleased to know that you have named your society 'Arya Samaj'. Now, 'national reform' should be your objective and vision. Nothing more to pen down.

Swami Dayanand Saraswati

Letter No. 56

To Pundit Ram Narain ji

(April 13, 1878)

This letter, written in Hindi, was dispatched to Pt. Ram Narian. It is available in the collection of Paropkarini Sabha.

Be rejoiced Pundit Ram Narain Ji. I have sent you a letter dated March 15, (1878) from Multan, requesting that you send 50 copies of Sanskāra Vidhi to Lala Ballabh Dass Ji at Lahore. However, up to now neither have the books reached there, nor have I received any reply to my letter. We have not been informed of the receipt of the letter by you. Anyway, send 50 copies each of Sanskāra Vidhi and Āryābhivinaya to Lala Ballabh Dass, Treasurer, Arya Samaj, Lahore quickly, without any further delay, because the books are in great demand and are not in stock.

I received a letter (from the Treasurer, Mumbai Arya Samaj) on Phālguna Kṛṣṇa 5, Saṁvat 1934, which states that a parcel of books containing 100 copies of Aryābhivinaya and two more books have been shipped to your uncle, Pundit Sundar Lal Ji. Please acknowledge receipt and also inform me about the status of books in your stock. Please pass on 50 copies each of Sanskāra Vidhi and Āryābhivinaya, on my behalf, to Lala Ballabh Dass Ji.

Further, Arya Samaj has also been set up at Multan. I have made it to Lahore on April 11, 1878, and may stay here for some more days.

Please convey my blessings to Pundit Sundar Lal Ji and others at your place.

Swami Dayanand Saraswati

Letter No. 57

To Henry S. Olcott, Madame H.P. Blavatsky and other Members of the Theosophical Society

(Vaisākha Kṛṣṇa 5, Tuesday, Saṁvat 1935 i.e. April 21, 1878)

This letter was written in Sanskrit. The translation has been done from the original Sanskrit.

My choicest blessings upon the one who is well-accomplished and endowed with excellent qualities in head and in heart, who is ready to renounce false beliefs, is the lover of true Sanātana Dharma, inclined to believe in one God, and belongs to the fraternity of Mr. Henry S. Olcott, President, Madam H.P. Blavatsky and other Members of the Theosophical Society.

We are happy here, hope you are as well. I was pleased to receive your letter through Shri Mool Ji Thakkar and Harish Chandra Chintamani. We are grateful to the Almighty, Omnipresent, Omnipotent, Omniscient, All-pervading, Ever-existing (Sat), All conscious (Cit) and All bliss (Ānanda), Infinite, Unchangeable, Unborn, Incorporeal, Immortal, Just, Merciful, Eternal, Beginningless, Incomparable, Fearless, Efficient cause of creation, its sustenance and destruction, Unconfounded and Possessor of truthful quality and action. It is through his kindness, and because of our good fortune, that our dear brethren from America (Pātāla Vāsī), with whom our interaction had ebbed away over the last five thousand years, now has restarted. The time for mutual love, affection, welfare (Upakāra), communication through correspondence and exchange of questions/answers has begun. I accept the opportunity to correspond with you, with great affection. After this, whenever you feel like communicating, please write through Mool Ji and Harish Chandra Ji. I will also be sending letters to your honourable selves through them. I will also assist to the extent possible (to my capacity).

Whatever your views about Christianity and other faiths, my views on them are similar. For example, as God is one, there should be one faith for all people. It is important for all persons to pray to one God, to obey His orders, to promote the welfare of all, one's behaviour ought to be established by the eternal knowledge of the Vedas and followed by learned persons, based on evidence and logic, and according to laws of creation, It should be just and unbiased, according to Dharma, beneficial for the soul, truthful, beneficial to all, and acceptable by all faiths, and to be followed by all. In contrast, there are people, who are low-minded, deceitful, ignorant, selfish, and full of adharma, who believe in the reincarnation of God (avatāravāda), and who propagate (false) claims like 'making dead people alive again', who 'heal people suffering from leprosy,' who 'lift mountains', who 'break the moon into pieces,' etc. which are all adharmas (hypocrisy). We have come to the definite conclusion that all these create mutual enmity and antagonism, destroy all comforts/good things in life and create all sorts of sorrows. I pray to God that with His Grace and the efforts of people, sooner or later one true dharma shall prevail among entire humankind after all the above (negative) traits are destroyed.

I was at Lahore (Panjab State) when the letter was

received from your good selves. Many learned people over there were overjoyed (to hear of it). I felt very happy after going through the content of your letter. Since I don't always stay at the same place, it will, therefore, be preferable to send letters to the address (of my stay). Although I don't find much time, due to a lot of work, yet I could find time to fulfil the wishes of your honourable selves, who are so determined to propagate true Dharma and spread love among all people. Knowing this, I feel happy to assist and correspond with good souls like you for the welfare of people and humanity at large.

Swami Dayanand Saraswati

Letter No. 58

To Kaviraj Shri Shyamal Das

(April 28, 1878)

This letter, partly written in Sanskrit (only the address part) and partly in Hindi, was sent from Lahore. The original letter is preserved in the collection of 'Rajasthan Vidyapeeth, Udaipur. This letter contains 31 lines written in black ink. Swami Ji signatures are in red ink.

My blessings to learned Kaviraj, Shyamal Dass whose surname is Dadhivadia. We are very happy here. May the Almighty keep all of you in a state of great joy. Let me narrate the news in Hindi.

Your letter of Caitra Śukla 3, Saṁvat 1935 or April 5, 1878, has reached me in timely fashion and I have come to know of its contents. The books have been sent to you by railway on March 25, and separate letters have also been dispatched to Shri Pandya Ji and Shri Kalu Ram Treasurer, Nasirabad. However, so far no receipt for the books has been received either from you or from the above-mentioned Treasurer, without any reasons for the delay being communicated. It seems that Shri Mohan Lal Vishnu Lal Pandya Ji might have been preoccupied with some work. Please send the receipt, if the books have since been received.

I am very happy to learn that Hon'ble Shri Maharana Ji of our country (Āryāvartta: India) is very wise. May God bless him with increasing prosperity day-by-day. Now I plan to proceed in a fortnight on a trip to the Eastern region of the country, after staying for some time in Lahore. There is nothing more to write.

Please convey my blessings to Purohit Padmanath Ji (of Udaipur) and Thakur Manohar Singh Ji (of Sardargarh) and other Sardars.

Swami Dayanand Saraswati

We are enjoying the full grace of God. May God shower blessings upon you.

Letter No. 59

To Pundit Sundar Lal Ram Narain

(Jyeṣṭha Śukla 13, Saṁvat 1935 i.e. June 13, 1878)

This letter, written in Hindi, was sent from Amritsar.

Be happy Pundit Sundar Lal Ram Narain Ji.

I am informing you that I am sending three hundis (money orders) amounting to Rs. 517.50 to you, one for Rs 400, another for Rs. 100 and third for Rs. 17.50, receipts for which may be kindly sent as soon as possible; and in 4-5 days, I will also be sending to you papers related to accounts received from Lazarus (Printer/Publisher). On receipt of my letter please kindly go there and settle the account. I am very happy (here).

Swami Dayanand Saraswati

Letter No. 60

To Pundit Sundar Lal Ram Narain ji

(Jyeṣṭha Śukla 14, Saṁvat 1935 i.e. June 14, 1878)

This letter, written in Hindi, was sent from Amritsar. A copy of this letter is preserved in the collection of Paropkarini Sabha.

Always be full of joy, Pundit Sundar Lal Ram Narain Ji. A letter was sent to you yesterday. Tomorrow, I will be sending the hundis through registered post. Details of the hundis are of Rs 300/-, Rs 100/-, Rs. 100/- and of Rs. 17.50. Out of the total four hundis, the first two hundis are from Sitaram Kashiram handed over by Gopinath Gokul Chandra. I am very happy (here).

Swami Dayanand Saraswati

Letter No. 61

To Pundit Sundar Lal Ram Narain

(Āṣāḍha 7, Saṁvat 1935 i.e. June 22, 1878)

This letter, written in Hindi, was sent from Amritsar.

Be ever joyful, Pundit Sundar Lal Ram Narain Ji.

I am sending four lists to you with the following details. The first list contains the number of Sandhyābhāṣya books pending with Lazarus (Printer), the second list contains the separate accounts of each volume (of Vedabhāṣya), the third list contains the accounts due to Lazarus. So now, please kindly go to Kashi to take stock of the accounts. Please keep these ledgers with you and peruse the accounts maintained by him. We are sending the accounts maintained by him as evidence. Please tell him that this account also includes Rs.20 and 14 annas (75 Paise), Rs 12 from Jawala Prasad, Rs 4 and 6 annas (36 Paise) from Raj Krishan Mukur Ji, and Rs 4 and annas 8 (50 Paise) from Pundit Jai Narain Vajpai). This amount was sent later after receipt of the memo. Please count each issue thoroughly, before receiving, or give him the hundis and the money when you go there. The balance amount will be sent to you within 10-15 days.

Thus, we have to pay to Mr. Lazarus' Press Rs. 1346, 1 anna, and 2 pais, (6 Paise) out of which Rs. 540 and 2 annas (12 Paise) is for the Pañca mahāyajña Vidhi, and Rs.805, annas 15 (90 Paise) for the Vedabhāṣya. Please receive the books as per the memo carefully. Also, tell him that Swamiji requires the bills of money spent on advertisements. Why did he fail to send it? Also, take charge of advertisements after consulting Mr. Lazarus. Please enquire from Mr. Lazarus whether Sarju Prasad Shukla has sent one hundi (money order) of Rs. 100 to him or not. Please give the balance amount from your pocket, and I will reimburse the same to you soon.

The 4th list contains the list of books, which have been kept with Brij Bhushan Dass, Nai Sarak (near Chowk). When you visit Kashi, please collect the books from him as per the list. I will be sending a letter to him to hand over the books to you. Take over the charge of the books carefully. I am fine here.

Swami Dayanand Saraswati

List of Books Kept with Brij Bhushan Dass Ji at Kashi

No. of Books	Name of Book
4	Mahābhārata &
4	Index
1	Vaiśeṣika Darśana
1	Āśvalāyana Gṛhya Sūtra
1	Viṣayavāda
3	Muktāvalī
1	Kārikāvali
1	Mahābhāṣya 3 Volumes
1	Jāgadīśī

4	Checklists
2	Upaniṣad (in Gujarati)
1	Sāṁkhya Pravacana Bhāṣya
1	Pātañjala Yoga Śāstra
1	Vedokta Dharma Prakāśaka
1	Vyāmoha Vidrāvaṇa
1	Chāndogyopaniṣad
10	Mimāṁsā Darśana
1	Bhūgola Hastāmalaka
2	Manu Smṛti
1	Didhitiḥ Jāgdīśi

Swami Dayanand Saraswati

Letter No. 62

To the Secretary and Members of Arya Samaj

(Āṣāḍha Kṛṣṇa 11, Wednesday, Saṁvat 1935 i.e. June 26, 1878)

This letter, written in Hindi, was sent from Amritsar to the secretary and members of Arya Samaj Gujranwala, present in Pakistan.

May the Secretary and Members (of Arya Samaj Gujranwala) be happy!

I would like to inform you that now I will be proceeding on July 11, 1878, to the east, meeting people at Jalandhar, Ludhiana, and other cities on the way. I may break my journey at Ambala for some days (2-4 days). Now we shall be in contact through correspondence only, and, therefore, please continue writing to me regularly. I will keep responding.

Continue your (efforts) for the progress of the country. You have taken on the responsibility of a big task. Its completion will provide you with a lot of mental satisfaction.

The Arya Samaj here (in Amritsar) is progressing day and night. Many respectable people have joined it. Pandits at this place consulted (each other) about a debate (Śāstrārtha), but it was neither discussed in the meeting, nor was a reply given to the questions put to them. They just returned after showing their face in the meeting. Some (local) people, who were supporters of Christianity, tried to lodge some fake complaints against the Arya Samaj to the government. authorities, but it was in vain. When the truth comes into the limelight, nobody dares to raise their eyes in opposition against the Arya Samaj.

Namaste to all the members (of Arya Samaj).

Swami Dayanand Saraswati

Letter No. 63

To Pundit Sundar Lal Ram Narain

(June 27, 1878)

This letter, written in Hindi, was sent from Amritsar. A copy of this letter is preserved with Paropakarini Sabha.

Have a happy time, Pundit Sundar Lal Ram Narain Ji!

It may be known that the hundis (money orders) from three or four places are likely to reach you shortly. Please let me know as soon as you have received a hundi. Please let me know soon whether Thakur Bhupal Singh resident of village Aikh Pargana, Murthal, District Aligarh has sent you a money order (hundi) of Rs 34/- or not. Please write to me when you go to Varanasi. I am fine here.

Swami Dayanand Saraswati

Letter No. 64

To Pundit Sundar Lal Ram Narain

(June 30, 1878)

This letter, written in Hindi, was mailed from Amritsar. A copy of this letter is preserved with Paropakarini Sabha.

May you be happy, Pundit Sundar Lal Ram Narain Ji!

I would like to inform you that I have sent a proof sheet to Bombay which has not reached there to date. It is negligence on the part of the postal authorities. There were also some issues of the Vedabhāṣya that have not been delivered to customers. It seems that the postman and others, who are irritated by our talks, have destroyed the dak (post) in a prejudiced manner. Our proof sheet has disappeared in a similar manner. I wish to file a complaint to the post office. Let me know what your opinion is in this regard, and in which register (at the post office) can we find the entry of proof sheets or book post, and where we should file a complaint. Since, we have incurred great losses, please advise us on how much compensation we should demand, and how to follow the matter up. Please send a reply immediately after your receipt of the letter. Also, please, let me know what arrangement has been made following the letter sent, with regard to accounts at Kashi (with Mr. Lazarus).

Swami Dayanand Saraswati

Letter No. 65

To Pundit Sundar Lal Ram Narain

(July 1, 1878)

This letter, written in Hindi, was sent from Amritsar. A copy of this letter is preserved with the Paropakarini Sabha.

May you be happy, Pundit Sundar Lal Ram Narain Ji!

I would like to inform you that I have sent you a letter about the post office complaint, as mentioned in the earlier letter. Please let me have your advice as to what should be the right course of action.

Moreover, I have written to Mr. Lazarus many times to send accounts of the balance of sixteen rupees and the advertisements, but he has failed to send any reply. Therefore, when you go there, please enquire about the accounts. Please also let me know about the schedule of your departure and arrival from Banaras.

The Vedabhāṣya will reach everyone shortly. I have noted that an M.O. (Hundi) of Rs. 34 has reached you.

Swami Dayanand Saraswati

Letter No. 66

To Pundit Sundar Lal Ram Narain

(July 8, 1878)

This letter, written in Hindi, was also sent from Amritsar. A copy of this letter is preserved at the Paropakarini Sabha.

May you be happy, Pundit Sundar Lal Ram Narain Ji!

I would like to inform you that I have received your letter and read its contents. I have sent a copy of the accounts to Mr. Lazarus, and have written to him about appointing Pundit Sunder Lal Ram Narain Ji to cross-check the accounts, to take delivery of books, and to make payments thereof. So, now you may settle the accounts with him, as you deem fit. The accounts book relating to issues of the Vedabhāṣya and the Sandhyā Bhāṣya is absolutely correct. The accounts of payments made to Lazarus records an amount of Rs. 1346, 4 annas 2 pais (Rs. 1346.25), out of which Rs. 18, and 2 pais have already been received. Thus, only a balance of Rs. 1328, 4 annas (Rs. 1328.25) are now to be paid to him. I have written to Lazarus to send you accounts through the post. Then, you can settle the accounts by personally going there after doing some homework at home. I am very happy here.

I have made payments to Lazarus for Kaśikā, and if the eighth chapter has been printed, please bring the same.

Swami Dayanand Saraswati

Letter No. 67

To Lala Mohan Lal, the President and Lala Sain Dass, the General Secretary

(Āṣāḍha Śukla 10, Saṁvat 1935 i.e. July 9, 1878)

This letter, written in Hindi, was dispatched from Amritsar. This letter is quoted by Pt. Lekhram at page 285 of the Urdu Biography of Swami Ji.

Be joyful, Lala Mohan Lal & Lala Sain Dass.

I would like to inform you that many letters from America have been received, out of which six have been read. Out of these six, three contain an admission form, a specimen, and a diploma. The fourth letter is addressed to the Arya people, and is about the fact that it has been decided that the Arya Samaj should associate with the Theosophical Society of India, and its name should be changed to the 'Theosophical Society of the Arya Samaj of India'. Further, this name should be the 'Arya Samaj of Āryāvartta of the Theosophical Society', with a stamp made with such a name. Names of good and prudent presidents and secretaries should be written in the Diploma, with the rules and regulations of the Society. Furthermore, we should write letters to all (Indian) Arya Samajs asking them to write (indicate) and enumerate prudent and wise presidents and secretaries. Also, if Kamal Nain, who knows English, comes to us during the ensuing Saturday, he may copy all the (relevant) material.

I will stay here until 15th (July), 1878. Lala Mul Raj should be informed that since the examination days are near, he should not worry a lot, but should rather concentrate on the exams. We should be thankful that we were able to establish relations with America (Americans) after five thousand years. We should make more concerted efforts. We should discard those things which are of no use to us.

Swami Dayanand Saraswati

Letter No. 68

Unknown Addressee

This letter has been quoted in Swami Ji's Biography by Pt. Lekhram (p. 416, Hindi version). It is unknown when, to whom and from where this letter was dispatched.

At this stage, I have made up my mind to visit a particular place, and can't tell you the probable date and time of my stay there and departure to my next destination. Therefore, presently, I can't commit to my visit to Roorkee. However, whenever it will be possible, I will inform you.

Swami Dayanand Saraswati

Letter No. 69

Unknown Addressee

The summary of this letter is also recorded in the Biography by Pt. Lekhram (p. 416, Hindi version). We are not able to ascertain the place of dispatch of this letter, but it is clear that this letter was written before Swami Ji's visit to Roorkee on 25th July, 1878

Due to certain constraints, I had to defer my earlier decision, and come to Roorkee. I will stay here for three days. If you find it convenient to come, please let me know. In the absence of any information from you, it will be presumed that you have no objection to my proposed visit (to Roorkee).

Swami Dayanand Saraswati

Letter No. 70

To Pundit Sundar Lal Ram Narain ji

(July 10, 1878)

A copy of this letter is preserved in the Paropakarini Sabha. This letter, written in Hindi, was sent from Amritsar.

Be happy, Pundit Sundar Lal Ram Narain Ji!

I would like to inform you that I have sent a letter (No. 153) to you on 8th July (1878), which you might have received by now. I have also sent a letter and the account details to Mr. Lazarus, he will be writing to you. In the earlier letter, I had mentioned Rs. 1328 and 4 annas (25 paise) to be paid to him. Now, today I have received a letter from Suraj Prasad Shukul from Mirzapur, saying that he has sent Rs 100 to Mr. Lazarus. So now I would like to inform you that only Rs. 1228 and 4 annas (25 paise) are to be paid to him, and I have written to him about it. Here, we have had good rains. Please keep us informed about the news at your place.

Swami Dayanand Saraswati
Amritsar

Letter No. 71

To Pundit Sundar Lal Ram Narain

(July 14, 1878)

This letter, written in Hindi, was also sent from Amritsar. A copy of this letter is also preserved in the collection of the Paropakarini Sabha.

Be happy, Pundit Sundar Lal Ram Narain Ji!

I would like to inform you that I have received a letter from Mr. Lazarus, and accordingly, he has sent the accounts to you, and you might have received the same by now. We have to pay him the balance amount of Rs. 1218 and 9 annas (56 paise). Finalise the balance amount, and also let me know when you are proceeding to Kashi, after tallying the accounts. Please get my books from Brij Bhushan Dass and bring them. The list of books has already been sent to you. Also, inform me about your return journey. We are very happy here by the grace of God.

Swami Dayanand Saraswati
Amritsar

Letter No. 72

To Shri Shyam Lal Ji Krishan Verma

(Śrāvaṇa Kṛṣṇa 1, Saṁvat 1935 i.e. July 15, 1878)

This letter, written in Hindi, was sent from Amritsar. From the date of this letter, it is evident that Swami Ji was in Amritsar until 15th July 1878, whereas Pt. Lekhram and Ghasiram write in their biographies that Swami Ji was in Amritsar until 11 July. If these letters been made available to the authors, it is probable that they would not have made an error in writing the dates of Swami Ji's stay in different cities.

I have heard that you intend to go to England to teach Sanskrit, which is an appreciable idea. But I have written to you earlier and I am also writing to you now that it would have been better if you could have stayed with us for some days and learnt about the important issues pertaining to the Vedas and Śāstras. Now, it will be proper for you to deal with only what you have already studied. You should tell others that you have not studied the whole of the Vedas and the Śāstras and that you are a modest student. Take care that nothing happens (there) which could denigrate or spoil the image of our country. People (in Great Britain.) look for scholars who can teach Sanskrit. Since, many types of people will come to meet and discuss things about the Vedas and India with you, please be prudent in your speech. Please send a reply to this letter. Convey my blessings to Pundit Mohan Lal Vishnu Lal. I am fine here.

Swami Dayanand Saraswati

Amritsar

P.S.

In addition, please be wary of Padris. Please always send a Devanagari version of any letters from America, which will facilitate early action from this side. Send the English version of the rules and sub-rules of the Arya Samajs of Bombay and Punjab, modified, wherever you deem fit and suitable, having first informed me.

Letter No. 73

To Pundit Sundar Lal Ram Narain

(July 23, 1878)

This letter, written in Hindi, was sent from Roorkee, Dist. Saharanpur, UP. A copy of this letter is available in the collection of the Paropakarini Sabha.

May you be happy, Pundit Sundar Lal Ram Narain Ji!

I would like to inform you that I have reached Roorkee from Amritsar on 18th (July). Please inform me whether you have returned from Kashi after settling the accounts (with Lazarus) or not.

Rs. 8 and 8 annas (50 paise) have been paid to Lazarus. Thus, now only Rs. 1210 and 1 anna (6 paise) is to be paid as balance. Please send an early reply to this letter.

Swami Dayanand Saraswati
Roorkee, Distt. Saharanpur

Letter No. 74

To Babu Madhava Lal ji

(Śrāvaṇa Kṛṣṇa 11, 1935 i.e. July 25, 1878)

This is the first letter we came across which mentions the number of the letter. It shows that a proper diary dispatch system was introduced by Swamiji in 1878 to his official correspondence. This letter has been given No. 216. The original letter is preserved in the collection of Arya Samaj Danapur (Bihar). This letter was also written in Hindi. From the contents of this letter, it is evident that Swami Ji also wrote a commentary on Paṇini's grammar.

Be happy, Pundit Sundar Lal Ram Narain Ji!

I am happy to have received your letter. You may send the list of customers for the book Pāṇini Aṣṭādhyāyī Bhāṣya (Commentary to Paṇini's Aṣṭādyāyī). The amount likely to be spent on its publication will be communicated to you soon. Its publication will be started when we find 1000 customers. Namaste to all members.

Swami Dayanand Saraswati
Roorkee, Dist. Saharanpur

Letter No. 75

To Henry Steel Olcott

(Śrāvaṇa Kṛṣṇa 11, Friday, 1935 i.e. July 26, 1878)

This letter, originally written in Sanskrit, was sent to Henry Olcott of Theosophical Society of America as a reply to their queries on certain points. This is a very vast letter dealing with Swami Ji's views on many aspects of Vedic philosophy, culture, Indian history, and geography. Swami Ji tries to explain many Vedic concepts in a nutshell to his new friends and followers in the USA. Here we provide the English translation of the Sanskrit letter.

Blessings from Swami Dayanand to the honourable men and women of the Theosophical Society, namely the president Shri Olcott and other members of society, who are engaged in activities of altruistic welfare, have the etiquette and manners becoming of scholars, who are ready to worship one God, are the believers in his Vedas, being residents of Pātāla loka (America), and who are willing to propagate the principles of the Arya Samaj. Here everybody is fine by the grace of God and hope for the same there. I have received all of your letters through Shri. Harishchandra Chintamani, the president of the Arya Samaj. Having known the news from your side, I, all the presidents, secretaries, and members of the Arya Samaj here are extremely happy. God, who is omniscient, omnipotent, who is the Lord and sustainer of the entire universe, may be thanked thousands of times for such good developments. After a pretty long time, He has made us, who were once in utter darkness, and who held antagonistic views about each other, due to rampant hypocrisy and vicious teachings, now instead develop a zealous inclination towards the Vedas, the true scriptures that are His utterances and which are the treasure trove of all true sciences. We are very fortunate and we pray to the Almighty to help us carry out our agenda of altruistic welfare.

1. I have signed the document of agreement on the letter pad sent by you and I have returned the same to you. I hope you will receive them soon. Moreover, the name the 'Theosophical Society: The Branch of Arya Samaj of Āryāvartta (India)' given by you is acceptable to me.

2. Everybody should worship God following the method described in the 'Introduction to the Four Vedas'. Let me briefly mention it: Everybody should take a position in a neat and clean place and after having control over his mind, vital airs, sense organs, God should be worshipped both in Saguna (qualified with positive attributive epithets) and Nirguna (unqualified with negative attributive epithets) manner. This worship has three constituents: praise, prayer, and meditation, each one of these are further divided into two parts of Saguṇa and Nirguṇa.

Saguṇa Stuti (Praise): If God is praised with His own qualities, that is called as Saguna stuti (praise).

Nirguṇa Stuti (Praise): Similarly if God is praised by negating the qualities that He does not own, the praise is called a Nirguṇa stuti (praise). Whenever we describe God by the negative term 'neti neti ... etc.' that is called as Nirguṇa stuti.

Saguṇa Prārthanā (Prayer): When God is prayed for attaining good qualities like education, intelligence, etc. the prayer is known as Saguṇa prayer.

Nirguṇa Prārathanā (Prayer): When God is prayed only for the sake of prayer without any anticipation in return of prayer, the prayer is known as Nirguṇa prayer.

Saguṇopāsanā (Meditation of Embodied God): When God equipped with attributive epithets is meditated upon, the meditation is known as Saguṇopāsanā. Similarly, if formless God, or God devoid of the qualities that He does not own, is meditated upon, the meditation is known as Nirguṇopāsanā.

3. The Meaning of the Word 'Arya': A person who is accessible to all, due to his knowledge, education, altruistic welfare, spirituality, righteousness, he is worthy of being called an Arya. According to Pāṇini: आर्य ब्राह्मणकुमारयोः-6.2.58. That is a brāhmaṇa and Kumar both are Āryas. Brāhmaṇa is a person who comprehends the Vedas and realises God and follows their instructions. Kumar is a person who observes celibacy from 8 years until 48 years and studies the Vedas and then enters into household life. There he only comes together with his wife during certain days and who never tries to have a romance or affair with another person's wife. Both these, the Brāhamaṇa and the Kumar can be referred to as being Ārya. Ṛgevda (1.51.8) mentions वि जानीह्यार्यान्ये च दस्यवो बर्हिष्मते रन्धया शासदव्रतान् Thus the Vedic scholars based upon the Ārya word registered in the Vedas, gave the name Ārya to noble persons. As soon as creation and the Vedas

appeared (Here it should be stressed that creation and Vedas appeared simultaneously in the universe. The Vedas are the knowledge of creation. So the knowledge of creation came into being as soon as creation came into being), the necessity for names arose and the seers gave two names - Ārya and Dasyu- to human beings based on their nobility and ignobility respectively. The above-quoted mantra of Ṛgveda distinguishes between 'Ārya' and 'Dasyu'. According to the mantra, a person who is endowed with the best qualities, actions, and nature should be known as Ārya and the persons with opposite traits should be known as Dasyus. Āryas are teachable. On the other hand, the Dasyus are punishable. Thus from the above mantra, it is crystal clear that 'Ārya' and 'Dasyus' have opposite natures.

We can quote one more mantra from the Ṛgveda (1.117.21). The mantra goes like this:

यवं वृकेणाश्विना वपन्तेषं दुहन्ता मनुषाय दस्रा।
अभि दस्युं बकुरेणा धमन्तोरु ज्योतिश्चक्रथुरायार्य। ।21। ।

yavaṁ vṛkeṇāśvinā vapanteṣaṁ duhantā manuṣāya dasrā
abhi-dasyuṁ-vakureṇādhamantoru-jyotiścakrathur
āryāya

Here Aśvinau have been prayed to in order to punish the ignoble (Dasyus) and to protect the Āryas (nobles) by providing them with various facilities of education, etc. In this mantra also human beings have been given two names: Āryas and Dasyus. These names were given by scholars at the beginning of the creation of human beings. Human beings were first created in the Himalayas. When the region began to become crowded, human beings were divided into two classes;

noble persons and ignoble persons. Both types of human beings started having clashes with one another owing to the differences in their nature. The Ārya (noble people) migrated to this land by coming down from the Himalayas. As this land came to be inhabited by Āryas, it was known as Āryāvartta (a place approached by Āryas from all sides). There is evidence of this in the Manusmṛti (2.1.17; 22).

सरस्वतीदृषद्वत्योर्देनद्योर्यदन्तरम् ।

तं देवनिर्मितं देशमार्यावर्त्तर् प्रचक्षते ॥ 2.1.17

sarasvatidṛṣadvatyornadyoryadantaram
tam̐ devanirmitam̐ deśamāryāvarttam̐ prachakṣate.

आसमुद्रात्तु वै पूर्वादासमुद्रात्तु पश्चिमात् ।

तयोरेवान्तरं गिर्योरार्यावर्त्तं विदुर्बुधाः ॥ **2.1.22**

āsamudrāttu vai pūrvādāsamudrāttu paśchimāt
tayorevāntaram̐ giryorāyāvarttam̐ vidurbudhāḥ.

The country sandwiched between Sarasvati and Dṛṣadvati and inhabited by Devas (scholars from the north) is called Āryāvartta. The present-day Indus river originating from the North and flowing to the West is called Sarasvati and the present-day Brahmaputra going towards the east is called Drishadvati. Similarly, a country bounded by the Bay of Bengal in the east and the Arabian Sea in the west is called 'Āryavartta'. The society of Āryas is known as the Ārya Samaj. It is a society where its members are ready to adopt noble traits by shedding ignoble qualities. For this reason it is better to name all good societies as the Ārya Samaj. We don't see any harm in this type of naming.

4. One should engage in the pursuit of true

education, knowledge, justice, nobility and conduct altruistic welfare activities, moreover also inspire his nearest and dearest to do the same. This is the brief answer to your query about the 'Purpose of Vedas'. Its explanation can be had through the study of Vedas and other Śāstras itself. The books composed by me e.g. Commentary of Vedas, Sandhyā-Upāsanā, Āryābhivinaya, Refutation of Anti-Vedic Views, Removal of Darkness enjoined by a Vedāntic Scholar, Satyārtha Prakaśa, Sanskāra Vidhi, Āryoddeśya Ratnamālā will also help you all to understand the purpose of Vedas.

5. Life symbolises the soul. Life is the nature of the soul. The soul is qualified by the qualities of desire, formlessness, indestructibility, begininglessness. It is never born nor ever dies. This idea has been discussed in the Vedas and allied literature by way of various arguments. Here due to the paucity of space, the matter has been presented very briefly. There is a mantra in Yajurveda (6.22)

Accordingly :

सुमित्रिया न आप ओषधयः सन्तु।
दुर्मित्रियास्तस्मै सन्तु योऽस्मान्द्वेष्टि ये च वयं द्विष्मः॥

sumitriyā na āpa oṣadhayaḥ santu
durmitriyāstasmai santu yo'smān dveṣṭi ye cha
vayaṁ dviṣmaḥ.

The above mantra clearly shows that the quality of a soul is a desire for comfort and aversion from discomfort. Another mantra of Yajurveda (31.18): वेदाहमेतं पुरुषम्। points out that knowledge is also one of the qualities of the soul. Because the soul is of the nature of consciousness, whatever it finds suitable to it, it considers it as comfortable and longs for the same. Whatever it finds unsuitable, it considers it as discomfort and tries to get rid of it. Several other qualities are also incorporated into these qualities. According to Nyāya philosophy (1.10), desire, hatred, effort, comfort, discomfort, knowledge is the sign of a soul[1]. According to Vaiśeṣika philosophy (3.2.4), exhalation, inhalation, blinking of eyes, life, thoughtfulness, movement, sensations, internal ailments, comfort, discomfort, desire, and effort - these are the symptoms of a soul. The other symptoms of the soul are to carry out righteous or non-righteous acts; to be conscious of numbers which are one from the point of species but many from the point of individuals (e.g. the human species is one but human-beings are many); to be able to recollect past experiences; having size (atomic) and mass; to be distinct from others; to be united and disunited.

In the Mahābhārata, in the context of emancipation, Maharishi Bhardwaja defines the soul as - मानसोऽग्निर्जीव. The soul is the light of knowledge that illumines the mind. The soul is a sort of consciousness which is different from the body, sense organs, breathing, and mind. It is because of the soul that we can combine different experiences into one. For instance, I hear whatever was audible to me with my ears. I touch with my hands, whatever I saw through my eyes. Whatever was touched with my hands is being tasted with the tongue. Whatever tasted with the tongue is being smelt

---

[1] इच्छाद्वेषप्रयत्नसुख-दुःखज्ञानान्यात्मनो लिंगमिति।

through the nose. Whatever olfactory sensation I had, I am mindful of it. Whatever I had in my mind, I remember it. Whatever I remembered, I am sure about it. On being sure about something, I accept it. This type of cognition is the quality of the soul which is different from other constituents of the body. Now one may pose a question as to how the soul is different from other constituents of the body. It is the soul only that can combine at one place and time, the different experiences had by different sensory organs at different places and timings. A thing seen by someone else cannot be remembered by the other. An ear is not able to have the experience of the skin sensation. Nor is the skin able to experience auditory sensation. But if I touch the same 'pot' that I had seen in the past, the recollection of past experiences into the present can only be the quality of the soul, which can recollect the combination of both present and past experiences into one, and can enjoy both experiences simultaneously. In this way, with regards to the nature of the soul, several Āryas were able to comprehend the past, changes in the present and also the future through the path of Samādhi as revealed in the Vedas.

The phenomenon of the soul leaving the body is called death. This can be called the separation of the soul from the body and by no means death. Having left the body, a soul stays in the atmosphere until it receives the next body in accordance with its good or bad Sanskāras/karmas under the process of Almighty God. While it remains in the atmosphere or in the state of conception or childhood, the soul does not enjoy special knowledge. Its condition is like that of a person who is asleep or in an unconscious state.

6. If the soul has the power to talk, to knock on the door, or to enter into an alien body, then why does it not reach the people and places of its choice? Some say that if we summon a soul with due meditation upon it, it will come to us. In this regard, our view is that when some near and dear one dies, we always think about him or her, but he or she never comes to visit us. If somebody says that the soul never comes to its previous relatives, but goes to others if so summoned, it doesn't seem right because the soul has more attachment towards previous relatives, compared to those who are not relatives. Creation cannot take place in the absence of its creator. Almighty God, who is the governor of all, is Just, All-knowing. It is He who provides the fruits of one's actions, in accordance with the deeds done by souls, and who remains always awake. Therefore, the photo of the dead person that you have sent to me seems to be the handiwork of some cunning and wicked person. Just as a wizard shows impossible things, as if they are possible by using tricks and tactics, it (the reviving of a dead body or the summoning of a dead body) also appears to be just like this.

In Sanskrit, the term 'Bhūta' (ghost) means the absence of a being, who no longer exists. The dead body until the time it is cremated is called 'preta'. There is a saying about God. No one similar to God neither is born (bhūta) nor will he be born (bhaviṣyati). Thus, the words bhūta and bhaviṣyata here point out the existence of a being in the past and future. There is a verse in Manusmṛti (5.65):

गुरोः प्रेतस्य शिष्यस्तु पितृमेधं समाचरन्।
प्रेतहारैः समं तत्र दशरात्रेण शुध्यति ॥

guroḥ pretasyastu śiṣyastu pitṛmedhaṁ samācharan.
pretahāraiḥ samaṁ tatra daśarātreṇa śudhyati.

When a Guru dies, his disciple should cremate him. He also gets consecrated within 10 days along with the carriers of the dead body.

Here preta denotes the dead body and pitṛmedha or nṛmedha denotes the cremation of the dead body. The conventional meanings of bhūta (ghost) and preta (spirit) are not tenable. These all are nothing more than flights of fancy.

7. Whatever education you want to learn from me, it is indeed very vast and can be divided into two parts: Paramārtha (metaphysical) and Vyavahāra (empirical). It cannot be explained through a short letter of this nature. Its explanation is available in the Vedas and its allied literature. I have appointed Sh. Harishchandra Chintamani to furnish some explanations about it to you. He will translate my book 'Āryoddeśya Ratnamālā' into English and send it to you. The book will be sent to you at the earliest date possible. Through that book, you will be able to understand me.

8. Following the method delineated in Vedas, you should cremate dead bodies. It has been explained in detail in my book called 'Sanskāravidhi'. Even then, let me briefly make this issue clear to you. When a person dies, his dead body must be washed and sprinkled with scented material. It must be carried to the crematorium dressed in scented new clothes. There a pyre is prepared with the following parameters. It should be long enough, equal to the size of a person with his hands up over his head. Its width should be equal to the size of the width of the dead person with his hands

spread out. Its thickness should be equal to the length of the knees of the dead person. Its base should be the size of 12 cubits. The dead body should be sprinkled with water. The quantity of ghee should be equal to the weight of the dead body. With every 250 grams of ghee, one rattī (weight equal to the weight of 8 grains of rice) kasturi (musk) and 1 gm. keśara (saffron) should be taken and powdered. This powder should be mixed in ghee. The pyre should be laid with wood from the sandal, palaśa tree (butea frondosa), mango tree, etc. When it becomes half full with such wood, the dead body should be placed over it. Powdered camphor, Guggulu (the gum of a pine tree called bdellium olibanum) and sandalwood should be sprinkled over it, then the pyre should be laid with the wood of the same trees until it is one cubit in height. Lightened fire should be placed among these wood pieces. Oblations of ghee should be given by reciting the mantras of the 39th chapter of the Yajurveda. When the body is consigned to the flames, the people involved should take a bath, having reached their houses and then they should engage themselves in their day-to-day activities. At the end of three days, one should go to the cremation ground and collect all of the ashes along with the remains of the bones. Ashes thus collected, should be buried in some other place. This is the exact Vedic method of cremating the dead.

9. Two letters have already been sent to the England address.

10. You should be convinced of the truth first, then only should you change the name of your society. There should be a rule laid down by the society that,

its learned members should first approve whatever new programme is to be launched. Whatever goes against the altruistic welfare of all, must be abandoned. Whatever brings happy results, should be carried out immediately, without wasting time. So, now I think that the time has come to state that there is no harm in naming the society in the USA as the Arya Samaj.

11. Send to me, whatever letters you want to send. They should however bear my name, and be sent through Sh. Harishchandra Chintamani only, as mentioned before. Mention my name on the letter, but the covering letter should have the name of Sh. Harishchandra Chintamani. Let us offer innumerable thanks to Almighty God who is Eternal, All-bliss, and All-knowing, for this friendship between you and us. Taking this precious opportunity we must seek out and strive to remove all forms of hypocrisy, corruption, prejudice, ignorance from this world and make true knowledge as reflected in the Vedas, become more prevalent. Letters serve some purpose, however until we sit face to face, the main purpose cannot be served. It is hoped that by the grace of the Almighty, we shall meet personally in the near future. The less said the better, as is the way for an intelligent person. This letter was written on 11th of the dark half of the Śrāvaṇa month in the Saṁvat 1935 i.e. 26th July 1878.

Swami Dayanand Saraswati

Letter No. 76

To Pundit Sundar Lal Ram Narain ji

(July 26, 1878)

This letter, written in Hindi, was sent from Roorkee Saharanpur. Its copy is preserved in the collection of Paropakarini Sabha.

Be happy, Pundit Sundar Lal Ram Narain Ji!

I would like to inform you that Babu Ram Narain has again sent Rs. 4/- to Lazarus, reducing his balance to Rs. 1206 and 1 anna (6 paise). In the account books sent to you, please reduce 1 each from the Mantra Bhāṣya till the 11th volume, and 2 each from the 12th and 14th volumes, which Lazarus has already sent to the customers.

Please settle the accounts early, as the goldsmiths (saraf) from Kashi and Lahore have been pressing hard that is why the hundi amounts have not been taken from them. Moreover, it is not good nowadays to take money from anybody without any proper purpose. I am fine here.

Swami Dayanand Saraswati

Letter No. 77

To Babu Daya Ram Ji

(Śrāvaṇa Badi 13, Saṁvat 1935 i.e. July 27, 1878)

This letter, written in Hindi, was dispatched from Roorkee Saharanpur. It has been quoted in the Biography (Hindi version) of Swami Ji by Pt. Lekhram at p. 865.

Be happy, Babu Daya Ram Ji!

I will be sending a (Devanāgarī) translation of the letter received from America. You might know already that the American Theosophical Society has now become a branch of Arya Samaj, and the Americans now fully recognise the (authority of) the Vedas and wish to study the Vedas. I am fine here.

Swami Dayanand Saraswati

Letter No. 78

To Lala Mool Raj Ji, M.A.

(Śrāvaṇa Badī, 13, Saṁvat 1935, i.e. July 27, 1878)

This extract is quoted in the Biography of Swami Ji by Devendranath Mukhopadhyaya.

The Americans now fully recognise the (authority of) the Vedas and wish to study the Vedas.

Swami Dayanand Saraswati

Letter No. 79

To Lala Mool Raj ji, M.A.

(Śrāvaṇa Śukla 7, 1935 i.e. August 5, 1878)

This letter, written in Hindi, was also dispatched from Roorkee. It has been quoted in the Biography (Hindi version) of Swamiji by Pt. Lekhram p. 835.

Be ever joyful Lala Mool Raj Ji!

I would like request that the diploma and enclosed letter to be found among the parcel of letters from America that may have already reached you, may be kindly forwarded to me. Also, publish it in the Lahore and Tribune (dailies) at the earliest possible date, as they are in great demand. You can get 200 copies of the same print. Please send the original letter and diploma to me, and its copies may be sent to the press for printing.

Daily lectures are being held here and people at this place are rich in ideas. I am very happy here. My namaste to all the members there.

Swami Dayanand Saraswati

Letter No. 80

To Thakur Bhoopal Singh Ji

(Śrāvaṇa Śukla 8, 1935 i.e. August 6, 1878)

This letter, written in Hindi, was dispatched from Roorkee. In fact, Thakur Bhoopal Singh, resident of village Ekh District Aligarh, was one of the staunchest devotees of Swami Ji. He served Rishi Dayanand with dedication during his last days. This letter was extracted by famous poet Nathuram Shankar Sharma from Harduaganj (Aligarh) from a heap of rubbish. When Lala Mamaraja reached his house in 1928 on his mission to trace more and more letters written by Swamiji, the Poet handed over this letter to Lala Ji at his humble request. The original letter was preserved later in the collections of Pt. Bhagvaddatta.

Be happy, Thakur Bhoopal Singh Ji!

I would like to inform you that Thakur Ranjit Singh has sent the money to me, but Thakur Mukand Singh was not able to. A while ago, two or three letters were received from him informing me that the amount was available for dispatch, He asked for the address to where the amount was to be sent. It has been written to him many times, that the amount is to be sent to me. He has however gone silent again now, for unknown reasons. It is a mystery and I am unable to understand the reasons for this. Since the amount is urgently required here, please arrange to send one hundi to me at Farrukhabad city. Take this matter as being of the utmost importance. I am very happy here.

Swami Dayanand Saraswati

Letter No. 81

To Lala Mool Raj Ji, M.A.

(Śrāvaṇa Śukla 12, Tuesday, 1935 i.e. August 9, 1878)

This letter, written in Hindi, was sent from Roorkee. It is available in the biography of Swamiji written by Pt. Lekhram (Hindi version) page 865-66.

Be joyful Lala Mool Raj Ji!

You might have received my earlier letter, no. 255, dated August 5 that was sent to you. I would like to remind you to send the two original letters and diploma to me as soon as possible, as its copy was taken by Babu Kamal Nain for safe keeping at the Arya Samaj. Half of the printing expenses will be borne by you and the remaining half by Umrao Singh and Shankar Lal of Roorkee. However, please get it printed soon at the Lahore press or Tribune-press, or as you deem fit and suitable, since the government will be holding exams at Thomson College on the 28th, and thereafter there will be two months' holidays when everyone would have gone home. They will be returning in the third month, as their results will be declared then. You are, therefore, requested to get it printed before the 28th (instant).

Swami Dayanand Saraswati

Letter No. 82

To Babu Madho Lal Ji

(Śrāvaṇa Śukla 12, Friday, 1935 i.e. August 9, 1878)

This letter, written in Hindi, was also sent from Roorkee. The original letter is preserved with Arya Samaj Danapur, Bihar.

May you rejoice Lala Madho Lal Ji!

I would like to caution you about the many people who may be exploiting and cheating you by saying that they have been sent by Swami Ji. I have not deputed anybody for the lectures so far, however when I do depute someone I will send a circular to all Arya Samajs under my seal, endorsing a copy with the seal to the deputed person(s). Please don't get cheated by any such people. Please send me the list of customers of the Aṣṭādhyāyī, as the book is now ready.

Swami Dayanand Saraswati

Letter No. 83

To Pundit Sundar Lal Ram Narain Ji

(Śrāvaṇa Śukla 12, Friday, 1935 i.e. August 10, 1878)

This letter, written in Hindi, was dispatched from Roorkee. Its copy is available with Paropakarini Sabha.

Be joyful Pundit Sundar Lal Ram Narain Ji!

It may be known that one money order for the Banaras treasury from Jabalpur has been sent to you. Please keep that amount in your safe custody after getting its proceeds.

Further, you might have received the books from Shri Bhiki Mal of Kashi. Please prepare the account sheet and send the same to me. Also, please inform me whether Bhiki Mal has received the (amount) from Braj Bhushan Das or not. Please send the receipt.

Swami Dayanand Saraswati

Furthermore, since the money order is in the name of Lazarus, please get his signatures and receive the amount.

Letter No. 84

To Maulvi Mohd. Kasim Ali

(August 10, 1878)

This letter, written in Urdu, was dispatched from Roorkee. It has been quoted in the Biography of Swamiji by Pt. Lekhram (p. 736 of Urdu edition and p. 761 of Hindi edition).

Dear Mr. Maulvi Mohd. Kasim,

I would like to inform you that your letter was received yesterday at 6 p.m. Since this letter did not have your signatures, despite the cover and the advertisement bearing them, it is being sent through our clerk for your signatures. Hence, we request your kind signatures on the letter to enable me to send my duly signed letter through registered post to you. Everything else is fine here.

Swami Dayanand Saraswati

Letter No. 85

To Maulvi Mohammed. Kasim Ali

(August 11, 1878)

This letter, written in Urdu, was dispatched from Roorkee as a reply to the letter of Maulvi Mohammed. Kasim dated 9 August 1878. This letter is quoted by Pt. Lekhram (Hindi edition, p. 762-764)

Dear Mr. Maulvi Mohd. Kasim, the leader of Islam,

May Almighty God keep your good self and us steady on the path of truth. I am sorry to learn that you are not keeping physically well presently, but I do hope that God will bless you with good health. I am grateful to you for visiting our place, despite your ill health. Now, after making a mention of rightful duties, my reply to your kind letter is as follows:

After my arrival in this city, I started discussions on various religious subjects to which I have become accustomed. But, it pains me to say that some people have wrongly interpreted my debates and lectures as being, (with regards to their content) specifically opposed to Muslims. I accept this much in every respect that I criticise Islam, as per my understanding, but it is wrong to say that I have singled out Islam specifically for such criticism. As I criticise Islam, criticism of Christianity is no less evident in my lectures. I do not even spare our Hindu brethren.

I hope that you are aware that debating during lectures absolutely defeats the object and diminishes the importance of learning. The reality is that no work can be accomplished nicely without being properly organised and managed. Therefore, I had clarified before my lectures that if anyone has reservations and wants clarifications, he should note down such sentences with the context; and after the lectures, the points can be argued. Being a learned person, will you not agree that unless someone has completed the lecture series, by citing evidence in support of his claims, as per his understanding, based on truth, and until he has clarified thoroughly the disputable topics, how can anyone offer criticism on certain observations?

This is the reason that I have kept debates separate from my lecture programme. After the conclusion of my lectures, I had an advertisement issued, calling on gentlemen to engage in discussion i.e it was a call to those who desire discussion, or those who ask warranted questions worthy of consideration, on subjects related to my lectures. Although there was a mention of one day only being arranged, if no further advertisement against it was published, such an arrangement should be extended for another day. But, during these two days, no one appeared for debate or discussion, nor sent any written observations on that score. The second point to be stated is that, for the purpose of debate, I wish to debate in a respectful decent manner with learned people who have an excellent grasp of their sect or religion's principles. I consider highly such gentlemen who are unique in their mannerisms and knowledge (about their sect). Due to my prior knowledge, I was fully satisfied with your capabilities on both these points. That is the reason why your name came to my mind many times whenever discussions on religious matters occurred.

With regards to Maulvi Ahmed Ali Saheb and Hafiz Rahimullah Saheb, I have certainly heard about the ability and knowledge of the former regarding his religion. However, I am sorry (to say) that no satisfactory information about Hafiz Rahimullah Saheb's style of debating has been received. Instead the type of information that has reached me, does not inspire me to start a debate with him. I am sorry to say that I take issue with him, and it is not wrong for me to present the real situation before people who love fairness (like you).

Now please understand what I have to say about Hafiz Rahimullah Saheb. I have learnt from very reliable sources that he does not possess adequate knowledge about his religion in order to debate. The main reason for this is, that he is ignorant of the Arabic language in which, in addition to the Quran and Hadis, many great dependable translations (Bhāṣyas) and other religious books are composed. The people who informed me (about him) are ready to furnish proof to support their contention. Not only this, but I also want to inform you that if a question is placed before Hafiz Saheb on Hadiths, etc. even by his co-religionists (not by outsiders), the authenticity of his replies are doubted. While it can be undoubtedly said that Hafiz Saheb holds the title of a 'Hafiz', it is impossible 'to get the solution to mathematical problems from a scholar of literature'. In brief, this was the reason why I didn't find these gentlemen worthy for debate.

No wise person can accept what you say about

your own ability. It is because, as everyone knows, wise people ought to talk about themselves with humility, just as the branches of a tree laden with fruits bend towards the earth. I myself am not capable enough to be counted among the scholars of Arya Dharma (religion), as I don't have the calibre to take part in any debates. However I am forced to debate by dint of circumstance. There is no need to trouble gentlemen such as Lala Kanniah Lal Alakdhari, Munshi Inder Mani Ji, Babu Harish Chandra, Gopal Rao Hari Deshmukh, and Pundit Hevat Ram Ji, etc. to take part in smaller debates. I was greatly surprised when you came specifically to me to discuss matters, having announced it through an advertisement in the paper. If you consider that having a chat with a lowly person like me is below your dignity (for a hermit, every place at night is a resting place), then the purpose could have been served through correspondence. But I fail to understand the objective behind putting out an advertisement. Although I was not obliged in any way to send a reply to your advertisement, especially since some people attempted to reply off their own back, and sent their replies with mine, I am now taking action in accordance with their advice.

Now about the debate for which the day and time have already been specified, my request is that the appropriate rules for the debate should be sent in writing. Similarly, whatever rules I find appropriate, will be communicated to you. I am sorry that a lot of time has been wasted on this communication through registered posts. If handwritten paper would have served the purpose, the matter could have been resolved. But, I could not understand your farsightedness in sending letters by registered posts.

You are also talking about the mismanagement during Chandpur (fair) in your letter. You are probably aware of the cause of the mismanagement. Relevant details can very well be understood through reading the reports of the Manager of the Chandpur fair, Rais Mukta Prasad and Munshi Pyre Lal Saheb which were published in a magazine. What more can I write about this? It will be better, however if this letter is taken as a final reply to your letter. You say that I should not forget the firm stand taken by you in the first debate while initiating the current debate. I am not surprised that you have clarified your firm stand. May God help you recover from your cold and cough, in the event that you have no further new excuses to rely on.

This letter dated August 11, 1878, is dispatched by registered post no. 927 to Maulvi Saheb.

Swami Dayanand Saraswati

Letter No. 86

To Maulvi Mohd. Kasim Ali Saheb

(Bhādra Kṛṣṇa 1, Tuesday, 1935 i.e. August 13, 1878)

This letter, written in Urdu, was dispatched from Roorkee in reply to Maulvi Mohd. Kasim's letter. It was dated August 12, 1878 and it is quoted by Pt. Lekhram (Hindi Edition of Biography, p. 770-771)

Mr. Maulvi Mohd. Kasim Ali Saheb, the leader of Islam!

May God lead us all to the right path. I received your kind letter. Yesterday, I had an opportunity to go through it. The language and contents of this letter had such a high standard that I considered it foolish to reply to it without much consideration. But as of today, however, I send the briefest possible reply.

The reality is that I have an objection to each and every word of your letter and I have a reply to each of them. But I consider sending a detailed reply to it as a waste of time. The reason is that I did not receive a proper reply to my queries. I never expected such replies from you. I never believe in behaving with any person in an uncultured way and using abusive language, as you do in your writings. Therefore, ignoring such remarks (of yours) I attempt to write replies to only the essential points made.

Four points were decided between you and me in the presence of Captain Stuart and Colonel Maunsell Saheb.

1) The number of people to be present during the

debate

2) The venue of the debate

3) The time of the debate and

4) To record the proceedings of debate.

But, now I fail to see in your letter, our agreement on the above points. It is my humble view that wise persons don't backtrack from their promise. If some point or plea does not appear right, one should not agree at the beginning to it. But to back out from a promise does not behove a gentleman. Thus, in my view, I can't go against the above four points. It is up to you whether to accept it or not. Apparently, you can't be forced to debate, if you don't want to. There is no way out, if every time you back out from the settled agreement. From my side, I don't consider it proper to change my stand, which has already been agreed upon, and I don't support any change on that score. If you have any doubts about laying down rules, you (better) ask Captain Saheb and others before whom such matters were decided.

I don't know the basis for your contention. I believe only in the Veda. May I know kind sir, which of my lectures or writings led you to reach this conclusion? I have a firm belief that there is not even a single sentence in it that exists in any of the four Vedas. Moreover, regarding what you are saying about the translation (Bhāṣya) of the Vedas, you need to clarify what particular Bhāṣya you are referring to as you have not done so. There are no translations of the Vedas in Urdu, Persian, or Arabic so far, but English translations for some parts have appeared. I have many doubts about the ability of the translators who have done the translations of the Vedas in English. We don't accept their academic and religious credentials, and this is the reason why some brief English translations are not found to be consistent with the ancient translations (Bhāṣyas) of the Vedas.

To sum up, it is humbly submitted that you may let me know what other rules you want included. I will send my opinion on such rules very promptly. Greetings!

Swami Dayanand Saraswati

Letter No. 87

To Maulvi Mohd. Kasim

(Bhādra Kṛṣṇa, 2, Thursday, 1935 i.e. August 15, 1878)

This letter, written in Urdu, was dispatched from Roorkee. This letter has been quoted by Pt. Lekhram (pp. 775-782, Hindi edition of Swamiji's Biography).

Mr. Maulvi Mohd. Kasim Ali Saheb, Leader of Islam!

May God lead you and everyone to the right path. I received your kind letter yesterday in reply to my letters dated 13 August and the one dispatched last Sunday. I feel the need to correct you at the outset, especially your misunderstanding regarding the complaint about the advertisement. From the language of the advertisement, two points clearly emerge as bones of contention. But, you have spelt out some different meanings in your kind letter. In my view, despite the limitations of the written language, it does not appear good to lodge complaint after complaint. While demands for discussions and debate did not come from me, any desire on my part, to engage in any future debate, would be based on the wish to throw a light on the truth, without highlighting any particular religion. Despite that, I don't consider this as being the right place to criticise or denounce your letter that is full of love. From this angle there is nothing meaningful in it.

Again, in your kind letter, as always, it appears that

you respect me as before. But since I find the knowledge of Islam possessed by Munshi Kannaiha Lal, Munshi Inder Mani and other gentlemen (about whom you are not acquainted with) to be far better than mine, I feel only embarassment on reading your full praise, which I don't deserve.

But I am sorry to say that whatever you have written about Munshi Inder Mani Saheb, is not acceptable. Moreover, no evidence has been found anywhere in your letter to support the two reasons cited by you. Firstly, Munshi Inder Mani Saheb never disagreed with me on that occasion, but he disagreed with you. You requested him before the commencement of the debate to meet you alone to decide something. Munshi Saheb accepted your request and went with you near Padre Naval's place. Although your discussion with him in writing has been going on for a long time and will continue in the future, you asked him in private to keep silent, so that your discussion with others may ensue. Munshi Ji said in his reply that he will comply with your request, as much as he can, however, it will be difficult to keep silent when it may become necessary to interject during such debates. Thus, if you have formulated some view about the ability of Munshi Inder Mani Saheb based on your discussions with him, it is worth accepting by all wise people.

Secondly, you seem more truthful while levelling allegations against me than when you wanted to debate me. According to you I made an excuse at that time that I needed to eat and that in order to stop me leaving you had to hold me back, You claim that I got out of your hold and I slipped away. Kind sir! you better ask Munshi Pyare Lal and other gentlemen who were present at the meeting. They were not very far away and can say whether your statement is truthful or not. If they don't corroborate your statement, your allegations will be proved to be baseless.

Regarding your statement that despite Munshiji's name being listed for debates, he kept silent from start to finish during the two days debates, I fail to understand your purpose in saying that here. If Munshiji was not involved in talks during the two days, one cannot give him a certificate of incompetence. If you want to prove this from his silence, then you should also not accept the competence of Sayed Abdul Mansoor Saheb, because he, too, sat silently during the two day discussion. On the other hand, you maintain that calling Munshi Saheb to debate was futile. Rest assured, I would not have called Munshi Saheb as I understand very well the responsibility attached to making statements. While it was and is up to Munshiji whether to attend or not, my only fear is that the people who have decided to be present in the debate, may from now on rethink their decision which may lead to different outcomes.

This issue aside I would like to reiterate in this letter that I have never declined to accept (the authority) of the four Vedas, nor have I ever only accepted one Veda and rejected the remaining three. I can never doubt your ability to misunderstand my statement about the sacred Vedas. This is a very surprising state of affairs as because even Captain Saheb, who is unable to speak the languages of this nation, was able to understand the real meaning of my statement. Contrastingly you, who are a native of this country and residing in Western Uttar Pradesh, an area considered to be full of learned people, have interpreted my statement wrongly, ignoring its real intended sense. I used the following words in my talk, 'I will limit my criticism only to the Quran, and you may also do so to only the Veda'. Here, the word 'one' which has come twice did not signify the number, but it has been used to signify the meaning of 'only'. And that is the reason why while expressing this sentence, the lesser emphasis was given on the term 'one' as compared to other terms. The day before yesterday, when I discussed this matter with Captain Saheb, he felt sorry that Maulvi Saheb misunderstood the simple sentences out of context.

Further, you complained that I have cited Colonel Saheb as a witness to our decision. I still put forward Colonel Saheb to be my witness. When I complained to Captain Saheb, he said that undoubtedly Colonel Saheb was a witness to the decision. If you have any doubt about it, you may immediately contact Colonel Saheb and Captain Saheb and enquire from them, citing this letter. This will also make you aware of whether 'I have proved Captain Saheb to be a liar', as alleged by you, or you have proved both gentlemen to be liars.

Then, you say that it does not look nice on my part to complain about the lack of decency (on your side) and cite the following couplet in defence,

'जरा इन्साफ तो कीजे , निकाला किसने शर पहले। (*jarā insāf to kīje nikālā kisane śara pahale*) (Please decide who has taken out the arrow first). I consider this (itself) as an adequate defence. In this context please read my first article and also your advertisement and decide (as to who started it). Further, with regard to your statement about a sentence which you have termed as being 'uncultured', all I can say is kind sir, the meaning should be ascribed as per the context. However, if you wish to say something different i.e. in such a manner that it goes against the purpose for which it was intended, then the meaning and purpose of such a statement or writing can only be understood by someone if you had informed him beforehand. I am thankful however that you have, in your letter yesterday, at last, expressed your doubts about whether the meeting was in actual fact uncultured. However, from a 'cultured' person's perspective whatever you have said is 'full of faults'.

Turning to your statement in which you said that I have made another advancement, as I have mentioned only three rules etc. in my letter of yesterday. To that I would like to say respected Maulvi Saheb, please refrain from doing injustice with your hands when writing! I request that you also please see the intention behind such words. In the previous letter, a mention was made about the three rules, while in the letter preceding the previous letter, there was a discussion about four matters decided earlier. It was neither written in the previous letter that only three rules will be decided, nor was there any mention in the letter preceding the previous letter that only the four issues will be decided. Out of the decided issues in the first letter, only the need for the discussion of three rules was felt, and in the preceding letter, the fourth rule was also written. This was because in your reply to the first letter you objected to the fourth rule. In addition to these four rules, there are many other rules, which have already been decided, but it was felt that there was no need to repeat them time and again to you. But, if it appears that you are backing out from certain rules, or if you feel compelled to maintain that some other rules be incorporated, they will undoubtedly be highlighted in future correspondence.

For example, you may please recall, that it was decided first of all, that during debates, both sides should take care that discussions be done in a decent or cultured manner and that no-one would use harsh words about any one's ancestors or leaders. Secondly, during our debates with each other, it was decided that no-one else, except ourselves, would enter into the discussion. Thirdly, that I would defend the Vedas and criticize the Quran, and you will defend the Quran and criticize the Vedas. Now, you please tell me whether these three rules at least, out of the four decided, have been decided or not? I have not mentioned them in any of my letters, because no such need was felt. Besides, your complaint might have been justified if it would have been said that these three rules have been decided, and the fourth one is still to be decided. I don't know whether you accept the decision about the fourth rule or not. Again in reply to your comment that Captain and Colonel Saheb were the witnesses (to the proceedings), I would like to inform you that this is not only what I say but that there are witnesses to the proceedings who accept this. These gentlemen are not very far away from here, so why don't you visit them or ask them through correspondence and satisfy yourself.

Then you mention the letter which Captain Saheb had written to Munshi Ahsan Ullah Saheb. I also went through your reply to Captain Saheb's letter. In the former it is said that, people have made the wrong interpretation of his writing and have arrived at different meanings. He further said that had he been there, he would have said to Munshi Ahsan Ullah Saheb, that his words were being misinterpreted, and moreover, that a note had been received from Munshi Ahsan Ullah Saheb, indicating that Maulvi Saheb (yourself) wished to talk to him about matters relating to the debates. It was Sunday, and he didn't have time then to do so, as Captain Saheb had written in his reply. Further more I accept that what Captain Saheb has said is true, given his view that Maulvi Saheb should look into the need for further discussion on the subject with Pundit Ji, which he acceded to doing at a later stage. For this reason, my statement that 'rules were decided in the presence of Captain Saheb and that he has been witness to the known decisions' cannot be at variance with what Captain Saheb has said. Rather there is a consonance of views between Captain Saheb's views and mine, on that score. I am not saying that any rule should be found acceptable only on my bidding, or it should be certified if only Captain Saheb says so or it should be decided on someone else's suggestion. However, the reality is that the rules which were framed with great effort, and which you agreed upon after lengthy discussions, are justifiable and important, in my opinion; and Captain Saheb and Colonel Saheb also were of a similar view and they were satisfied with the decision taken by them, and are witnesses to the decisions taken so far. If this is so, then why did you write that I have now accepted that the decision has been taken? Good Sir! If the decision was not taken, you should not accept that it was. Don't worry about me, but please at least have trust in Colonel Saheb and Captain Saheb, who were the very respectable dignitaries present in the Camp, where the decisions were taken.

Then you say, "If such criticism is prohibited, let it be so." Please write judiciously and explain in which of the Vedas such criticism is prohibited. No doubt, it is our religious belief that is wrong and what is not supported by any authority or evidence cannot be accepted. That is the reason why, I have had to put a lot of effort into framing the many necessary and essential rules, so as to prevent great problems arising in the absence of such rules. More information or details about this matter may be referred to in the enclosed appendix, where I have refuted what you have proferred in support of your contention with regards to non-framing the number (of rules).

You further complain that I object to each and every word of yours. I understand that probably here also you might have misinterpreted my words, like you did with regards to my faith in the Vedas. You missed the real sense behind my intentions there as well. While understanding the meaning of this sentence please keep in mind that in articles or writings, there are certain situations where the unreal meaning is also accepted. This is very clear from the language of a sentence as it shows the strength of the relationship between the real and unreal meaning. I would have, no doubt, explained in detail my objections to the whole article or writing, but since it will defeat the real purpose, I am ignoring it.

Now your comments in which you say that I 'saying something at one place and saying another thing at another place', etc. it is advisable for the gentleman to think before he speaks, and writes. I have already explained in detail about 'the decisions taken before Captain Saheb, and about my faith in the Vedas. However, if you have forgotten the contents of this detailed letter by now, please kindly refer to it again.

Furthermore, you say that as per the advertisement taken out in Kanpur, I expressed faith in 21 scriptures, etc. I am truly surprised by your understanding. Firstly, please ask someone for the meaning of the word 'debate' or 'disputation', before condemning me. Suppose, I ask you for some proof to support the statement that you have made, what will your reply be? Kind sir! In that debate I accepted the truth as laid out in twenty-one different lectures on the holy Vedas, and I still maintain my acceptance of the same. There are only six scriptures (Śāstras) of an Arya, and there is no relation between those lectures and the six scriptures. Please tell me where have I rejected the Brāhamaṇa and Mantra portions? (I have certainly not rejected them at all). I don't accept any claim without valid support, and probably you might consider it to be a sign of scholarship.

With regards to your earlier statement that I (Swami Ji) was capable of changing the circumstances, please explain why I (Swami Ji) am not capable of accepting the humble submission of your devotee (Maulvi) etc.

What a drama! Firstly, you write that in reality no one has control over external factors, and nobody can make real what is unreal and vice versa; but then you say that I am capable of changing the aforesaid external factors. Kind sir, had you inquired about my faith from myself beforehand, would that have been a sin? The reality is that the religious (dharmic) principles, which are the foundation of trust and faith, are fixed, and probably no change can happen to them. But we can say that when two people study a particular aspect of religion, and there is a difference in their knowledge-related ability, they may give different meanings to it. In reality, none of them will ever know if those meanings (held by each of them individually) may be different from the real intended sense. This is a situation beyond their capacity. One of these may, of course, find fault with the other's mind. For example, if someone with weak eyesight sees things shorter in size than their normal size, it should be considered as being as a result of his eyesight and not because the thing is a shorter size. Secondly, I have never said that I can't increase the number beyond two hundred people. I have only said that until there is a valid reason to increase the number, I don't consider it right to do so. I was very well aware of what you had said at Captain Saheb's residence on this aspect. But I am sorry to say that you have either forgotten my response, or you didn't understand it at all. Now the matter will be clarified by the detailed explanation made in the enclosed appendix. However it remains to be seen whether you will accept it despite it being correct. Adhering to appropriate rules is the prerequisite for discussions or debates, so any efforts by you to avoid them and to keep hovering around superficial points will prove futile. If you were not ready to follow the rules framed for the debate, then why did you accept them. By now it is very clear that you avoid discussions, as much as possible.

As for your statement, 'Suppose, I back out from the promise, then as per the rules it will be deemed that you refuse to engage in debate', you have not used the word 'suppose' correctly, as you are definitely backing out from your promise (to debate). Now, regarding your accusation about me, firstly, let me assure you that I am not going to back out from the debate. Undoubtedly, I prefer framing rules in order to initiate the debate. Now your argument that an 'agreement' should be laid down in such a way that none of the parties become the loser or winner. Here, the question must be asked: who is the winner, and who the loser? Probably you wish to say that there cannot be an agreement about the framing of the rules for the debate. If I raise the issue of agreement, you will ask me the justification of such an agreement and if there is no justification, an agreement, you will say is not possible. But you shall have to enter into an agreement for the proper management of the debate. Compliance with the rules of the agreement will be termed as victory and non-compliance as defeat. There has been a tradition of agreements between kings and agreements for sale and purchase. It is also not considered good to back out from agreements. However, it is a different matter if you think that one can back out from other agreements except those that are signed between two kings or signed for sale and purchase. There is a dictum:

चो कुफ्र अज काबा वर खेजद कुजा मानद मुसलमानी। (*cho kufra aja kaaba var khejada kujaa maanad musalmaani*). That is, If Islam and God are not believed in Kaba (place of worship), then where will the Muslim religion remain?

Please be judicious, give up your stubbornness, and consider the right rules as being 'right'. And if you don't wish to debate, say it clearly instead of being elusive. Then there won't be discussions on many matters, and our time will not be wasted, and your admirers' aspirations (of you winning the debate) will not be fulfilled. If Captain Stuart and Colonel Maunsell also become hostile witnesses, then God's witnesses may be required. Witnesses are still available, and, therefore, it is possible to decide the matter.

Regarding the translations (bhāṣyas) of the Vedas, mine are not a new discovery. The word 'destruction' for something is used only when its existence is proved. For example, so long as the Quran has not been translated into Sanskrit, you cannot ask who has destroyed and made the Sanskrit translation of the Quran disappear? During the period of Akbar and Dara Sikoh, no translation of the Vedas was done. Dara Sikoh translated the Upaniṣads in Persian naming it as 'Sirr-e- Akbar'(Great Mystery). But what is the purpose of your statement (about the Vedas)? Perhaps, you are ignorant of the Vedas and Upaniṣads; the authors of Upaniṣads and Vedānta. What is the relationship of the Upaniṣads with the Vedas? Whose statements are the Vedas? Kind sir! We consider only the Vedas to be the word of God.

To conclude, please be judicious, fair and don't back out from the agreed rules, and inform me of your views today. If you don't find time today, you may do it by tomorrow morning, so that all arrangements for the debate can be finalised. For the rest, it is up to you to decide. However in the case of disagreement, please inform me about your views.

Swami Dayanand Saraswati

Letter No. 88

To Babu Madho Lal ji

(Bhādra Kṛṣṇa 4, Saturday, 1935 i.e. August 17, 1878)

This letter, written in Hindi, was sent from Roorkee. Its original copy is preserved in the collection of Arya Samaj Danapur, Bihar.

May you be happy Babu Madho Lal Ji.

I would like to inform you that your letter has arrived, through which one Rs 10 note and stamps worth Rs. 28 were received. As per your request, I am sending the following books:

4 Satyāratha Prakāśa	Rs.	10
3. Pañca Mahāyajña Vidhi	Rs.	12 Pai
1. Āryābhivinaya	Anna	8
	Total: Rs.11 Annas 8 Pais 2	
Postal Charges	Annas 8	

Please acknowledge receipt. Keep up with the progress of the Arya Samaj. The commentary of Aṣṭādhyāyī has commenced. Everything is fine here and I am very happy here.

Swami Dayanand Saraswati

Letter No. 89

To Lala Mool Raj ji, M.A.

(Bhādra Kṛṣṇa 4, Saturday, 1935 i.e. August 17, 1878)

This letter, written in Hindi, was sent from Roorkee. It has been quoted by Pt. Lekhram (p. 832-33, Hindi edition of Biography).

May you rejoice Lala Mool Raj Ji.

I would like to inform you that your letter was received on August 14 and a parcel containing a Diploma along with two printed letters has arrived. Please send me information about expenses incurred when getting these letters printed, as the same is to be paid by people at Roorkee. It is hoped that the Arya Samaj will be set up here.

Swami Dayanand Saraswati

Letter No. 90

To Secretary(Mantri) Arya Samaj Multan

(Bhādra Kṛṣṇa 4, Saturday, 1935 i.e. August 17, 1878)

This letter, written in Hindi, was sent from Roorkee to Multan. It has been quoted by Pt. Lekhram (p. 784, Hindi edition of Biography).

Secretary Arya Samaj Multan,

Lectures are being delivered daily at Roorkee. We are very much hopeful that an Arya Samaj will be set up here. Maulvi Mohd. Kasim has also come for a debate with us, for which the date of the 18th August has been fixed, but nothing is sure. I will inform you when it is finalised. I am very happy, fit and fine here. Convey my namaste to all the members there.

Swami Dayanand Saraswati

Letter No. 91

To Maulvi Mohd. Kasim

(Bhādra Kṛṣṇa 4, Saturday, 1935 i.e. August 17, 1878)

This letter, written in Urdu, was sent from Roorkee. It has been quoted by Pt. Lekhram (p. 784, Hindi edition of Biography).

Maulvi Mohd. Kasim,

We are very (thousand times) grateful to God that you have at last agreed to the rules related to the debates. Unfortunately, however you still did not write in your kind letter whether I will assist in the recording of the proceedings of the debate. Instead, you have written that I have the right to record it if I am able to and that you will sit only after you have finished your lecture. This shows that you will try to go against my wishes. When someone gives a lecture slowly, it is not difficult to record it. But if someone delivers lectures with the intention that the other side is not able to record it, then nobody can really record it. The rule regarding maintaining a record of the debate is very important, as without it there can be never an agreement about the debate. It means that when a question is asked by one side, the other side should not reply until it has been recorded, and till the reply is written, the second question should not be put. The speech should be delivered slowly so that it can be recorded without any difficulty. The period for the 'Question-Answer' session will be decided tomorrow, before the commencement of the debate. If you agree to these points, please inform me through the bearer of this letter.

Swami Dayanand Saraswati

Letter No. 92

To Maulvi Mohd. Kasim

(Bhādra Kṛṣṇa 4, Saturday, 1935 i.e. August 17, 1878)

This letter, written in Urdu, was sent from Roorkee. It has been quoted by Pt. Lekhram (p. 784, Hindi edition of Biography).

Maulvi Mohd. Qasim,

In reply to your kind letter, I am submitting some more points to enable you to think over the matter in a judicious way. No wise and justice-loving person will deny the advantage of this arrangement that during debates, one writer each from both sides will continue to record the proceedings. Afterwards, by comparing both the notes, signatures of both of us should be ascribed, so that there is no doubt about the veracity of replies of both sides. If you don't accept this justifiable rule, it is up to you. This shows that you have no intention to debate. I can never back out from important points that need to be made. I have now received another letter. Some of my friends have written to Captain Saheb, and when the reply is received from him, you will be duly informed.

Swami Dayanand Saraswati

Letter No. 93

To Captain W. Stuart

(Bhādra Kṛṣṇa 4, Saturday, 1935 i.e. August 17, 1878)

Although this letter was not written by Rishi Dayanand, due to its reference in the previous letter (No. 92) it is being given here. This letter was written in English by Umrao Singh, one of the followers of Swamiji, from Roorkee. It has been quoted by Pt. Lekhram (p. 785, Hindi edition of Biography).

Captain W. Stuart, R.E.Roorkee

Sir,

We beg to state that some Muhamedans of the station applied to the Cantonment Magistrate for permission for a religious discussion between Maulvi Mohd. Qasim and Swami Dayanand. The Magistrate said in reply that he could not sanction such a meeting to be held in the civil or cantonment station. A similar reply was received by the Muhamedans on their application to Colonel Maunsell. The Muhammadans, in this case, propose to us the holding of the assemblage in the jungle out of the station where all could attend, but we believe that that it would be inconvenient, and request the favour of being allowed to hold a meeting in the place where Swami Dayanand Ji presently stays.

We beg to remain Sir,

Yours obediently,

Umrao Singh

Letter No. 94

To Maulvi Mohd. Kasim

(Bhadra Krisna 5, 1935 or August 18, 1878)

This letter, written in Urdu, was sent from Roorkee. It has been quoted by Pt. Lekhram (p. 786, Hindi edition of Biography).

Maulvi Saheb, the leader of Islam!

May God lead you, us, and others to a good path!

I am sorry to say that the meeting near Idgah does not appear right, the reason being that without deciding the number of people to be present, proper arrangements cannot be done there. Moreover, you also cannot take the responsibility for this illegal activity both on your own part and on behalf of others. Therefore, my house or Captain Saheb's residence only appears to be the right venue (for the debate). Yesterday, we dispatched a letter to Captain Saheb, to which a reply has been received. Copies of both are being sent for your kind perusal and decision in the matter.

Swami Dayanand Saraswati

Letter No. 95

To Lala Mool Raj, M.A.

(Bhādra Kṛṣṇa 7, Tuesday,1935 i.e. August 20, 1878)

This letter, written in Hindi, was sent from Roorkee, Dist. Saharanpur. The original letter was preserved by Rai Bahadur Moolraj.

Lala Moolraj Ji M.A

Be Rejoiced!

I would like to inform you that on August 18, 1878, Babu Harish Chandra and Shyamji Krishna Varma have proceeded from Mumbai to Aligarh to have a meeting with me, and they will be reaching that place by 21st or 22nd August, and I will also be reaching Aligarh on August 22.

It is desirable, therefore, that you also kindly reach Aligarh on August 22 or 23, but please come alone. When you reach there, please enquire about the garden of Thakur Mukand Singh Ji, where I am presently staying. I am very happy here.

Please don't circulate or give any publicity about this letter and your visit to Aligarh.

Swami Dayanand Saraswati

Letter No. 96

To Lala Mool Raj ji, M.A.

(Bhādra Kṛṣṇa 12, Sunday, 1935 i.e. August 25, 1878)

This letter, written in Hindi, was sent from Aligarh. Here it is worth informing the reader that Swami Ji reached Aligarh on 22, August 1878. The original letter is with Rai Bahadur Moolraj.

Lala Mool Raj Ji,

Be joyful!

It may be known that on August 16, 1878, Babu Harish Chandra Chintamani and myself will start from here for Meerut, and Babu Harish Chandra Chintamani, Shyam Ji Krishna Varma, and Mulji Thakurshi shall start on August 27 (Tuesday) by mail train to reach Lahore on 28th August 1878 at 8 a.m. Therefore, all Arya people should be present at the railway station to welcome and serve them well and take them to your meeting place or Arya Samaj or some other good resting place where they may stay and may be given hospitality.

Harish Chandra Chintamani will deliver one lecture, and Shri Shyamji Krishan Verma two lectures (one in English and one in Sanskrit). Afterwards they will be going to Amritsar. So, please welcome them nicely. The Arya Samaj has been set up at Roorkee. I am very happy here. Please convey my namaste to all the members there.

Swami Dayanand Saraswati

Letter No. 97

To Lala Mool Raj ji, M.A.

(Bhādra Kṛṣṇa 14, Tuesday, 1935 i.e. August 27, 1878)

This letter, written in Hindi, was sent from Meerut. Swamiji reached Meerut on 26 August 1935. It has been quoted by Pt. Lekhram (p. 866, Hindi edition of Biography).

May you rejoice Lala Mool Raj Ji, M.A.

You have written that you will be sending a letter dated August, 24, but it has not been received as yet. If you have not already sent it, please send it now to Meerut.

Swami Dayanand Saraswati

Letter No. 98

To Pundit Ram Narain ji

(September 1, 1878)

This letter, written in Hindi, was sent from Meerut. It has been preserved by Propakarini Sabha.

May you rejoice Pundit Ram Narain Ji!

I would like to inform you that in your last letter you mentioned that Lala Bhiki Mal has sent books to Prayag (Allahabad) after receiving the same from Lazarus. But you have not written a further letter about their safe arrival, and whether you have carefully checked the books prior to their receipt.

Please send an early reply to this letter, and also inform me about the reply of Brij Bhushan Dass that has been sent to you. The Arya Samaj has been set up at Roorkee and hopefully, it will be founded at Meerut also. I am very happy here.

I have sent you Rs. 100 through Babu Shyam Lal, who is an employee of the Post Office at Saharanpur. Please confirm whether you have received the amount or not.

Swami Dayanand Saraswati

Letter No. 99

To Pundit Ramadhar Bajpai ji

(Bhādra Śukla 6, Monday, Saṁvat 1935 i.e. Sept. 2, 1878)

This letter, written in Hindi, was sent from Meerut. The original letter is preserved by Arya Samaj Lucknow in its collection.

May you rejoice Pundit Ramadhar Bajpai Ji!

You are requested that whatever amount is present with you, or received from some customers, or received as proceeds of books sold and realised from customers, may kindly be sent to me at Meerut. It is because I am in urgent need of finance, and therefore, I am writing to you that the total amount may kindly be sent to me soon. Please also write about the whereabouts of Swami Gangesh nowadays. Please send a quick reply.

Swami Dayanand Saraswati

Letter No. 100

To Maulvi Abdullah

(Bhādra Śukla 11, Saturday, Saṁvat 1935 i.e Sept. 7, 1878)

This letter, written in Urdu, was sent from Meerut. It has been quoted by Pt. Lekhram (p. 436, Hindi edition of Biography).

Salamat! Maulvi Abdullah Saheb.

This letter is being written in reply to your letter. It will be better that you write about what you require from respectable rich people of the city and the Sadar (town) area, to which I have no objection. The debate should be written and not oral. Everything else is all right.

Swami Dayanand Saraswati

Letter No. 101

To Lala Mool Raj, M.A.

(Bhādra Śukla 15, Wednesday, Saṁvat 1935 i.e. Sept. 11, 1878)

This letter, written in Hindi, was sent from Meerut. This letter shows that Shyam Ji Krishna Varma was chosen by Swamiji as his heir apparent, so far as his scholarship was concerned.

May you rejoice Lala Mool Raj Ji, M.A.

It may be known that Pundit Shyam Ji Krishna Varma started from here on August 9 for Lahore and might have reached there by now. Please arrange for his stay at your residence or a comfortable place there. He will deliver lectures in Sanskrit and English. Babu Harish Chandra Chintamani has returned to Mumbai due to some urgent work. Lectures are being delivered here daily, and I am very happy here. My namaste to all the members there. Probably an Arya Samaj will also be set up here.

Swami Dayanand Saraswati

Letter No. 102

To Pundit Ram Narain

(Bhādra Śukla 15, Wednesday, Saṁvat 1935 i.e. Sept. 11, 1878)

This letter, written in Hindi, was sent from Meerut. A copy of this letter is available in the collection of Paropakarini Sabha.

May you rejoice Pundit Ram Narain Ji!

I have received your letter and known its contents. It was with great difficulty that Braj Bhushan Dass released the books. It was difficult to take the books out from there. Now, please get them, and, if Lala Bhikamal Ji has no time to handle them, keep them somewhere else with someone who could later send them onto you. Now, since he has agreed somehow to release the books, please don't delay in getting them; and when he hands over the books, please inform me by letter. I am very happy here.

Swami Dayanand Saraswati

P.S.

Please go also on Saturday to collect the books from Brij Bhushan and return on Sunday with the books or send someone else for that purpose. I have already sent a letter to you about (the further disposal of) the books. Expenses incurred upon this trip may be debited from my account.

Letter No. 103

To Babu Madho Lal ji

(Āśvina Kṛṣṇa 2, Friday, Saṁvat 1935 i.e. Sept.13, 1878)

This letter, written in Hindi, was sent from Meerut. The original letter is preserved in the collections of Arya Samaj Danapur.

Babu Madho Lal Ji, Be joyful!

I would like to inform you that your letter along with Rs. 10 6 annas, and 2 pais (Rs.10.40) have been received, receipt of which is being sent. I have written to Mumbai and you may receive two copies of the Vedabhāṣya Bhoomika in 10-11 days from there.

Presently, I am staying in Meerut and intend to proceed to Delhi from here. When I proceed towards the eastern side I will let you know. Lectures are being delivered daily. It is hoped that the Arya Samaj will be set up here also. I am very happy here. My namaste to all the members there.

Swami Dayanand Saraswati

Letter No. 104

To Lala Kishan Sahai ji Saheb

(Āśvina Kṛṣṇa 6, Wed.Saṁvat 1935 i.e. Sept. 18, 1878)

This letter, written in Urdu, was sent from Meerut.

Lala Kishan Sahai Ji Saheb,

Be joyful!

Yesterday, As desired by you, rules for the meeting were dictated by Pundit Man Singh and other gentlemen. I will fully abide by these rules. If you truly, wish to decide between truth and untruth, please consider the rules carefully and comply with them. Non-compliance with the rules, both orally and in writing, may give the offending party a bad name. Everything else is fine.

Swami Dayanand Saraswati

Letter No. 105

To Pundit Ram Narain ji

(Āś vina Kṛṣṇa 6, Wed. Saṁvat 1935 i.e. Sept. 18, 1878)

This letter, written in Hindi, was sent from Meerut. Its copy is preserved in the collection of the Paropakarini Sabha.

May you rejoice Pundit Ram Narain Ji!

I would like to inform you that a letter was sent to you earlier, its reply is still awaited. Therefore, I am writing to you again so that you can get the books from Brij Bhushan Ji, compare them with the list of books already sent to you, and inform me through a letter (about the situation).

Moreover, I need the services of a Munshi, who knows English, Hindi, and Urdu, and who can, send the copies of the Vedabhāṣya from Mumbai to all customers and do the proof reading and correction work as well. Furthermore, he should be able to correctly draft a reply for any correspondence coming to me. His monthly remuneration will be in the range of Rs. 20 to Rs. 30. But he should be a confident person and have also some good references from a respectable person, as some money will also remain in his custody. Please send a reply soon. I am very happy here.

Swami Dayanand Saraswati

Letter No. 106

To Lala Kishan Sahai

(Āśvina Kṛṣṇa 7, Thursday, Saṁvat 1935 i.e. Sept. 19, 1878)

This letter, written in Hindi, was sent from Meerut. It was a long letter, but its summary is quoted by Pt. Lekhram (p. 445, Hindi Edition of the Biography of Swamiji).

It is not becoming of you to write in such a way at the request of Pandits, who do not know the Vedas. Now if you feel it will be suitable, I could send two of my students to the meeting, and they could, with your permission, ask some questions of the Pandits about the Vedas. This will enable you to know the reality about them (knowledge of the Vedas). If you don't agree with this suggestion, please enable us to join the Pandits at my residence or at the house of Babu Chedi Lal, to get all their doubts cleared.

Swami Dayanand Saraswati

Letter No. 107

To Babu Madho Lal ji

(Āśvina Kṛṣṇa 12, Monday, Saṁvat 1935 i.e. Sept. 23, 1878)

This letter, written in Hindi, was sent from Meerut. Its original copy is preserved in the collection of Arya Samaj Danapur, Bihar.

May you be joyful Babu Madho Lal Ji!

Further to your letter No. 164 dated September 20 I have received it and read its contents. A reply to your query is that I will be staying at Meerut and Delhi from October 1 to 15. If you can come to Meerut after October 1, we can then go together to Delhi.

Here, the Arya Samaj has been set up, and lectures are also being held. Everything is fine here. I am very happy here. Namaste to all the members.

Swami Dayanand Saraswati

Letter No. 108

To Pundit Sunder Lal ji

(October 5, 1878)

This letter, written in Hindi, was sent from Delhi. From letter No. 109, it is clear Swamiji reached Delhi on 5th Oct. 1878. He stayed in the area of the Sabzi Mandi in the garden of Lala Balmukunda Kesrichand. He used to deliver lectures in the area of Chhatta Shah at the residence of Mr. Yahun which also housed a Govt. school. A copy of this letter is preserved in the collection of Paropkarini Sabha.

May you be happy Pundit Sunder Lal Ram Narain Ji!

You may aware that 15-16 copies of issue No.1000 of the (Vedabhāṣya) Bhūmikā have been sent to you. Please inform me when these are received at your end.

For a long time, no letter has been received from you. Please do so now, informing me whether you have carefully checked the books received from Kashi, and whether the books have been received from Brij Bhushan Dass or not. If not, please get them through somebody, and inform me, after carefully checking them (with the list of books).

I am very happy here.

Swami Dayanand Saraswati

Letter No. 109

To Pundit Shyam ji Krishan Varma

(Āśvina Śukla 11, Monday, Saṁvat 1935, i.e. October 7, 1878)

This letter, written in Hindi, was sent from Delhi. According to Pt. Bhagvaddatta, the original letter was preserved by Prof. Dhirendra Varma.

May you be joyful Pundit Shyam Ji Krishan Verma!

I have received your letter from Mumbai and apprised myself of its contents. You might have observed the work there. This time like the last, the cover of the Vedabhāṣya did not bear the addresses in the Devanāgrī script (Hindi). If there is no English knowing person among the villagers, how will the issues reach there? As there are many Hindi knowing people in the villages? Please ask Babu Harish Chandra Chintamani, immediately after the receipt of this letter, to depute a Hindi knowing Munshi so that the work can be done nicely. Otherwise, you should get the addresses of customers conveyed in Hindi by a Hindi knowing person, as per the entries in the register. Also, please kindly supervise the work well there. Along with the accounts of issues already sent to customers the issues still available there, should also be sent to customers. Please tell Babu Saheb to send the title page along with proofs of the Vedas.

Please inform me soon by letter about the news there. The Arya Samaj has been founded in Meerut. I have come to Delhi on October 3. Everything is fine here. **Swami Dayanand Saraswati**

Letter No. 110

To Pundit Shyam ji Krishan Varma

(Kārtika Kṛṣṇa 3, Saṁvat 1935 i.e. Oct. 14, 1878)

This letter, written in Hindi, was sent from Delhi. The original letter was preserved by Prof. Dhirendra Verma.

May you be happy Pundit Shyam Ji Krishan Varma!

I would like to inform you that a letter was sent to you. Hopefully you would have received it by now. Today, I am writing again, as I thought it was necessary to do so. The letter which was discussed in Meerut, I hope it can be sent soon. While you are still in Mumbai, please manage the work relating to the Vedabhāṣya in consultation with me through correspondence, because without you this work can't be done. Please delegate the work there to a person who is well versed in the Hindi language, because Babu Harish Chandra Chintamani has been seen to transcribe 'Chedi Lal' as 'Shadi Lal', in English and he also fails to write the customer number. I have already written to you in detail about this matter, so please do whatever is necessary to resolve this it quickly. And please keep me informed about all the developments and the management of work there. Please also send a book on the 'Kāmasūtra' to me from there. I am very happy here.

Swami Dayanand Saraswati

Letter No. 111

To Babu Madho Lal ji

(Kārtika Kṛṣṇa 4, Tuesday, Saṁvat 1935 i.e. Oct. 15, 1878)

This letter, written in English, was sent from Delhi to Babu Madho Lal Ji of Arya Samaj Danapur of Bihar. This letter has been marked as No. 597. By that time Swami Ji was staying in the garden of Lala Kashmiri Chand & Balmukund at Kaboolee Gate near Subzimandi. It's a pity that the Arya Samaj made several temples afterwards, but neglected these historical places utterly. In fact, all such places where Swamiji used to stay should have been purchased and converted into Vedic Research Institutes-cum-Arya Samajs in the memory of this great man of India.

From

Delhi Kabuli Gate, Near Subzi Mandi
In the Garden of Lala Kashmiri Chand
& Balmukund

To

Babu Madho Lal
Arya Samaj Danapur

I received your letter No. 181 of 31st October today. I shall be glad to see you at Delhi at the address written above. I have founded an Arya Samaj in Meerut, and I have been delivering lectures here on Vedic reform. I am well and hope you are too.

Swami Dayanand Saraswati

Letter No. 112

To Babu Ramadhar Bajpai

(Kārtika Kṛṣṇa 4, Saṁvat 1935 or Oct. 15, 1878)

This letter, written in Hindi, was sent from Delhi. The original letter is preserved in the collection of Arya Samaj Lucknow. This letter has been wrongly marked as No. 588 in place of 598.

May you be happy Babu Ramadhar Bajpai Ji!

I would like to inform you that a letter was received here, at Meerut, from you, in which you wrote that you would be sending money for the books. But it has not been received so far. Therefore, I would like to kindly request you to please send the amount through a Hundi (money-order) to me here in Delhi. This is being written due to some urgent need for finance.

I have already written to you in my previous letter about the setting up of an Arya Samaj at Meerut and about my present stay in Delhi. I am very happy here.

Swami Dayanand Saraswati

Letter No. 113

To Munshi Samarth Dan

(Undated letter)

This letter, written in Hindi, was sent from Delhi to Ajmer. The summary of this letter is available from the Hindi Biography of Swamiji by Pt. Lekhram (p. 452-453) and by Devendra Nath (p. 505).

I accept (the invitation) to come to Ajmer. Please make arrangements for the house, etc. I will be coming there, after finishing work at Delhi, and till then make arrangements for a house, etc. and write to me about the arrangements. I will be writing a letter to you in 3-4 days before my departure from here and will send a telegram after boarding the train.

Swami Dayanand Saraswati

Letter No. 114

To Pundit Ram Narain

(October 16, 1878)

This letter, written in Hindi, was sent from Delhi. A copy of this letter is preserved with the Paropkarini Sabha. This letter has been marked as No. 603.

Pt. Ram Narain Ji,

Be joyful!

I would like to inform you that your letter dated October 13, 1878, has been received and all its contents read. Furthermore, you should known that a 1000 copies of Issue No.s. 15 and 16 of the Veda Bhāṣya Bhūmikā have arrived. Please let me know when you have taken charge of all the books. I am also sending a list of the remaining books with Brij Bhushan Dass. Please kindly take it from there. I have also sent a letter along with the list of books to Lala Bhika Mal Ji. Do also write about the books. I have also written to Brij Bhushan Dass. I am very happy here by all means.

Swami Dayanand Saraswati

List of Books available with Brij Bhushan Dass

Name of Book	**No. Of Books**
Copy of Mahābhārata	8

Index of Mahābhārata	4
Viṣyavāda	1
Muktāvalī	1
Copy of Mahābhāṣya	3
Vyāmohavidrāvaṇa	1
Didhīti Jāgadīśī	1
Kārikāvalī	1
Jāgadīśī	1
List of Books	5
Upaniṣad in Gujarati	1
Pātañjala Yogaśāstra	1
Vedoktadharmaprakāśa	1
Bhūgolahastāmalaka	1

Letter No. 115

To Pundit Sunder Lal Ram Narain

(October 18, 1878)

This letter, written in Hindi, was sent from Delhi. A copy of this letter is available in the Paropkarini Sabha. This letter has been marked as No. 611.

May you be joyful Pundit Sunder Lal Ram Narain Ji!

I would like to inform you that Babu Makhan Lal and Bhola Nath are reaching your place. Please give them one copy of the Bhūmikā (S. No. 13), and they will give you its price of 6 Annas (36 paise). Also, give them 10 copies of the Bhūmikā. I have already informed you about everything in my previous letters.

Everything is alright here. Whoever asks for a copy of the Bhūmikā, please supply them with it after receiving a payment of Rs. 5.

Swami Dayanand Saraswati

Letter No. 116

To Babu Ramadhar Vajpai

(Kārtika Kṛṣṇa 9, Sunday, Saṁvat 1935 i.e. Oct. 20, 1878)

This letter, written in Hindi, was sent from Delhi. The original letter is preserved in the collection of Arya Samaj Lucknow. This letter has been marked as 623.

Babu Ramadhar Vajpai, Be happy!

I would like to inform you that your letter was received and its contents were read. The Hundi (Money-order) of Rs 46 has not been received as yet. It may reach us tomorrow or the day-after-tomorrow, and then its receipt will be acknowledged. I have already written to Mumbai to send 7 copies of the Ṛgveda and 6 of the Yajurveda. You can receive them from there now as well as in the future.

Furthermore, only the Bhūmikā can be had for Rs 5. You can charge 8 Annas (50 Paise) more from customers who paid Rs. 4.50 last year. For only one Veda charge Rs. 4, and for customers who paid Rs.4.50 last year and wish to buy both (two) Vedas, charge Rs. 7, and Rs. 4 for only one Veda. From new customers, who wish to have both the Vedas along with Bhūmikā, charge Rs.11.50, and for those who want only one Veda with the Bhūmikā, charge Rs. 8.50, and Rs. 4 only for one Veda.

Lectures are being delivered here daily. I am happy and alright here.

Swami Dayanand Saraswati

Letter No. 117

To Babu Samarth Dan Charan

(Kārtika Kṛṣṇa 10, Saṁvat 1935 i.e. Oct. 21, 1878)

This letter, written in Hindi, was sent from Delhi to Ajmer. This letter was published by Pt. Lekhram (Hindi Biography, p. 453) and Bharat Sudasha Pravartak, Dec. 1881 issue (p. 23). This letter has been marked as No. 628.

May you be joyful Babu Samarthdan Ji Charan!

Just to let you know that today a letter has been received from Jugal Kishore Sharma, indicating that no arrangements have been made for the collection of subscriptions there. Please don't worry. If we don't meet now, we will meet later. Don't feel sad about it. I very well know your love for us, and there is nothing to feel sad about. Here also lectures are being delivered blissfully. Everything is alright here. I am very happy here.

Swami Dayanand Saraswati

Letter No. 118

To Pundit Shyam ji Krishan Varma

(Kārtika Kṛṣṇa 11, Saṁvat 1935 i.e. October 22, 1878)

This letter, written in Hindi, was sent from Delhi. The original letter was preserved by Prof. Dhirendra Varma. From this letter and other letters, it is quite evident that Swamiji was convinced by the scholarship of Shyam Ji Krishna Varma. He was keen to give him the full responsibility for the Hindi translation of the Vedabhāṣya. This letter has been marked as No. 630.

May you be joyful Pundit Shyam ji Krishan Verma!

I would like to tell you that your letter dated October 18, 1878, has been received and its contents read and understood. I am writing the following with happiness. Please take the responsibility for the Vedabhāṣya work and do it with great diligence as long as you are in Mumbai. Furthermore, I am giving you the complete authority to spend Rs. 30 on servants as you deem fit, and I have no objection even if expenses are incurred up to Rs. 35 on that score. This limit is due to our small work load at the moment, but when the number of our customers reaches 2000, there will be no need to count numbers and put limits on expenses. If you will organise the work well, progress will be made every day.

Today, I have written to Babu Harish Chandra Chintamani and I have asked him to meet you and to hand over the work to you with a glad heart. Please don't doubt his sincerity. He is not the type of person to feel bad about such things. Consider what has happened to be a small domestic matter and believe that he is always very happy with you.

This is the first letter of mine in our mutual correspondence, so please keep it safely and similar letters in the future as well. I will also be keeping your letters safely too. Furthermore letters sent to you and books, etc. should also be kept carefully. Please always use good quality of paper as used this time and not lower quality paper. I will also be sending Rs. 500 next month to you. Please show this letter of mine to Babu Harish Chandra. Convey my blessings to Gopal Rao Hari Deshmukh. From next month your name will also be printed on the title cover, so that customers may send letters and money (subscriptions) in your name. I am very happy here.

Swami Dayanand Saraswati

Letter No. 119

To Babu Ramadhar Vajpai

(Kārtika Kṛṣṇa 11, Tuesday, Saṁvat 1935 i.e. Oct. 22, 1878)

This letter, written in Hindi, was sent from Delhi. The original letter is preserved in Arya Samaj Lucknow. This letter has been marked by Swami Ji as No. 632.

Be joyous Babu Ramadhar Vajpai Ji!

I hope, you have received my earlier letter. The need to write this letter has arisen now as a Hundi (M.O) of Rs.46 written in your last letter has not been received so far. This is for your information. Everything is alright here.

Swami Dayanand Saraswati

Letter No. 120

To Babu Ramadhar Vajpai

(Kārtika Kṛṣṇa 12, Wednesday, Saṁvat 1935 i.e. Oct. 23, 1878)

This letter, written in Hindi, was sent from Delhi. The original letter is preserved in the collection of Arya Samaj Lucknow.

May you be happy Babu Ramadhar Bajpai Ji!

I would like to assure you that the money order of Rs. 46 sent by you has been received today. Please send also the balance amount soon, as there is a great squeeze on my finances nowadays.

Please also write the details of the amounts received for each book and the name of the customer on whose name it should be credited. Seven copies of the Ṛgveda and six of the Yajurveda shall reach you from Mumbai, the information regarding this has already been sent there. Lectures are being delivered here daily. I am very happy here.

Swami Dayanand Saraswati

Letter No. 121

To Babu Madho Lal

(Kārtika Śukla 1, Saturday, Saṁvat 1935, i.e. Oct. 26, 1878)

This letter, written in English was sent from Delhi to Arya Samaj Danapur, Bihar. The original letter is in the collection of Arya Samaj Danapur.

I have received your letter just now and read its contents. You must send the accounts of the books to me. You will, hopefully, ask Babu Harbans Sahi for the subscription of the Vedabhāṣya, when you reach Agra.

Here I am delivering Vedic lectures over three days. It is hoped that the Arya Samaj will be set up in Delhi. I am happy and fine and hope the same for you.

Swami Dayanand Saraswati

Letter No. 122

To Pundit Shyam Ji Krishna Varma

(Kārtika Śukla 2, Sunday, Saṁvat 1935 or October 27, 1878)

This letter, written in Hindi, was sent from Delhi. The original letter is available in the collection of Prof. Dhirendra Varma. Through this letter Swamiji allows Shyam Ji Krishna Varma to take over the charge of the Vedabhāṣya from Harish Chandra Chintamani.

Be happy Pundit Shyam Ji Krishna Varma!

I would like to infom you that an earlier letter sent to you should have been received by you by now. Furthermore, I have written three letters to Babu Harish Chandra Chintamani about handing over the work to you, and another letter has been written today. He has probably called on you and handed over all the work to you. From November 1, 1878, all the work should be done by you, including the sending of the Vedabhāṣya to customers. Please learn about all of the work relating to the (maintenance of) the register of issues of the Vedabhāṣya, making correspondence, etc. If he allows it, keep the books at his residence, keeping the keys with you. If he does not, keep the books wherever you like, but keep them in an organised way, so that no loss may occur. Whatever money is required for the postage or for the despatch of the Vedabhāṣya, may be taken from Babu Saheb, and later we will make separate arrangements for the same. When you have taken over the work and confirmed the position to me, then I will be writing to you about all the arrangements necessary for your future work.

Please write soon about whether you have taken complete charge or not, and write all the news about that place. I am very happy here.

Swami Dayanand Saraswati

Letter No. 123

To Col. H.S. Olcott

(October 1878)

This letter, written in Hindi, relating to the Theosophical Society, New York was not sent by Babu Harish Chandra Chintamani to New York but was published in a special advertisement by Rishi Dayanand. In this letter, Swamiji makes the clear distinction between members of the Arya Samaj and members of the Theosophical Society in the USA. Only people who follow the rules of the Arya Samaj can be considered as the members of the Arya Samaj. This letter is also very relevant today. We find that a huge number of people in Arya Samajs are not in reality following the rules of the Arya Samaj.

Dear Col. Olcott,

As there are many people in India (Āryāvartta) who don't accept the rules of the Arya Samaj, and very few follow them, it is not a surprise that many people in America also don't accept the rules. Therefore, the people who accept the rules of the Arya Samaj and happily follow the Vedic faith, (are to be considered as members of the Arya Samaj), and those who don't follow them should be considered as members of the (Theosophical) Society, although the latter's separate entity is not desirable.

Swami Dayanand Saraswati

Letter No. 124

To Munshi Samarth Dan

(Kārtika Śukla 3, Saṁvat 1935 i.e. October 28, 1878)

This letter, written in Hindi, was sent from Delhi to Ajmer. This letter is found quoted by Pt. Lekhram (Hindi edition, p. 453), Bharat Sudasha Pravartak (p. 23, Dec. 1878 issue) and Devendra Nath Mukhopadhyay (p. 506).

I will definitely come to Ajmer. I have understood that here some Brāhmaṇa in the name of 'Jugal Kishore' has done some damage. Although there are many such deceitful people, nothing can be achieved by such actions.

Swami Dayanand Saraswati

Letter No. 125

To Pundit Ram Narain

(October 29, 1878)

This letter, written in Hindi, was sent from Delhi. A copy of this letter is available in the collection of Paropkarini Sabha.

May you be joyful Pundit Ram Narain ji!

I would like to let you know that your letter of Kārtika Śukla 1 has been received and its contents apprised. I am grieved to know about the sad demise at Pundit Sunder Lal's home, but we are helpless and can't do anything. This is the outcome of marriage in childhood, which everyone should be aware of by now.

As you know, we don't have a place where all the books can be sent to. This time, it is only your home, where, with concerted effort, these can be kept safely. Moreover, when you go to Agra, then these books can be kept with people like Bal Mukand or someone else who can keep them properly. Keep me informed about his name and address, so that we can make requests for whatever books we require from there. Some books have been sent to you from Mumbai. Please tell me whether you have received them or not.

Please send the following numbers of books to Babu Samarthan Dass, student Govt. College, Ajmer: Vedabhāṣya Bhūmikā 20, Satyāratha Prakāśa 378, Sandhyopāsanādi 50, Sanskāra Vidhi 30. I will come to Pushkar on Kārtika Śukla 11 and 12, Saṁvat 1935. Otherwise, it is joyful here in every respect.

Swami Dayanand Saraswati

Letter No. 126

To Pundit Shyam ji Krishna Varma

(Kārtika Śukla 5, Saṁvat 1935 i.e. October 30, 1878)

This letter, written in Hindi, was sent from Delhi to Mumbai. The original letter is available in the collection of Prof. Dhirendra Verma. From this letter, it is evident that the Arya Samaj in Delhi first started functioning in Nov 3, 1878.

May you be joyful Pundit Shyam Ji Krishna Varma!

I would like to let you know that the three or four letters written to you earlier on, should have reached you by now, and I have also written many times to Babu Harish Chandra Chintamani also to hand over complete charge to you. It is hoped that he might have handed it over to you by now. Please keep me informed quickly about whatever transpires between you and him. After taking charge, kindly start the work from November 1. Also please write about what expenditure is likely to be incurred upon purchasing one printing press machine along with letters and type, etc. Do you know the whereabouts of Mohan Lal Vishnu Lal Pandya? Is he in Mumbai or not?

I will be proceeding to Pushkar on November 6 (Wednesday), and, therefore, all correspondence after this date should be sent to me to Ajmer. Yesterday, the president, etc. of the Arya Samaj have also been appointed here and the Arya Samaj will start here from November 3. The date from which you take charge should be kindly intimated to me at the earliest. From that date, our mutual correspondence will commence regularly and joyfully.

Swami Dayanand Saraswati

Letter No. 127

To Sardar Ganda Singh, Granthi Ropar, District Ambala

(Kārtika Śukla 6, Saṁvat 1935 i.e. October 31, 1878)

This letter, written in Urdu, was sent from Delhi to Ropar, Dist. Ambala, Punjab. Ganda Singh was an accountant at the Military Works, Ropar. A photocopy of this letter was received by Pr. Bhagvaddatta from Sardar Narain Singh Bimbhrao, Subedar Head Clerk, son of Late Sh. Ganda Singh.

May you be happy Ganda Singh Ji.

Your letter in Hindi has been received. Its reply is that expenditure outweighs income, therefore, I can't do anything. However, if you spend your own money, then I have no objection to teach, because the world will benefit more if you are taught than a Brāhamaṇa. I will teach very gladly. If you can make some arrangements for expenses, teaching will be possible. However, please come after 5-6 months, as I will be proceeding for Pushkarji on November 6, and on my return from there, I will go to the Kumbh Fair at Haridwar or to Delhi, etc. It may be possible to teach you there, but not at this juncture, as there will be additional costs to bear and this will affect your studies and also teaching will not be able to be done properly. That is why I am writing to you so that the actual position is known to you.

Lectures are being delivered here daily. The Arya Samaj has also been set up here and many respectable people have joined it. Progress is happening in leaps and bounds. Similarly, Arya Samajs have been set up at Roorkee, Saharanpur, Meerut, Ludhiana, etc. Now, darkness is slipping away from the world, and the light of truth is gaining ground.

Swami Dayanand Saraswati

Letter No. 128

To Pundit Gopal Hari Deshmukh

(Kārtika Śukla 8, Thursday, Saṁvat 1935 i.e. November 2, 1878)

This letter, written in Hindi, was sent from Delhi to Allahabad. The original letter was preserved by Prof. Dhirendra Verma in his collection. This letter has been marked as No. 648.

May you be happy Pundit Gopal Hari Deshmukh Ji!

I would like to inform you that ever since work arrangements, relating to the Vedabhāṣya, have been assigned to Babu Harish Chandra Chintamani, customers have not been receiving the relevant issue of the Vedabhāṣya properly on time. What can this poor fellow do when there is no able person to help him with this work?

I am now happy that Shyam Ji Krishna Varma has been accepted for this work. This gentleman is quite capable of doing this work. I wrote to Babu Ji to hand over the work to him, and he has written that he would be sending a reply in a day or two. Let us see what he writes to me about it. Firstly, it is hoped that he will not quarrel, and if he makes an issue out of it as he probably would, you may on your visit to Mumbai or through correspondence, convince him to facilitate the handover of all duties and responsabilities to Shyam Ji Krishna Varma. You are the presiding officer for this work, and Babu Ji may also remain so too, but all the work will be done under your supervision properly by Shyam Ji Krishna Varma, who may be writing to you for advice, as the need may be.

Here, the Arya Samaj has been set up at Delhi. I will be proceeding to Pushkar on November 6. I am very happy here in all respects.

Swami Dayanand Saraswati

Letter No. 129

To Pundit Shyam ji Krishna Varma

(Kārtika Śukla 8, Saṁvat 1935 i.e. November 2, 1878)

This letter, written in Hindi, was sent from Delhi to Mumbai. The original copy of this letter was kept safe in the custody of Prof. Dhirendra Varma.

May you be happy Pundit Shyam Ji Krishan Verma!

I received your letter yesterday and read all of its contents. Yesterday, I also received a letter from Babu Harish Chandra Chintamani, who has indicated that he will be writing to me in a day or two, after deliberating over the matter carefully. So, when he writes something to me, I will convey it to you. He will not quarrel with you in handing over the work to you, as there appears no loss to him on that score. If he writes that his reputation has been ruined by not writing his name on the cover, then we may continue writing his name until Māgha as before. We will change it (to your name) from the next year. I will be writing to him accordingly.

I have written a letter to Leela Dhar Hari Dass so that he may assist you in the Vedabhāṣya work after consultation. He has indicated in his reply that he will be definitely consulting you when he meets you next time. Thus, you along with Sunder Dass and Purshottam, etc. may do the work together - the main work will be done by you, and they will assist you. Along with this letter, I am sending you a letter addressed to Gopal Rao Hari Deshmukh, and the same may be delivered to him wherever he is, or given to him when he comes to Mumbai. Furthermore, I have written more letters to Babu Ji. Please do write whatever transpires between both of you.

The Arya Samaj has been set up here. Now, I will be proceeding to Pushkar on Kartik Śukla 12 (November 6), and for two-three months I will be visiting the cities of Jaipur, Ajmer, etc. before going to the Kumbh Fair at Haridwar. When I am in far-off places, and if you need something urgently, please contact Leeladhar Haridass for assistance, and do the work well. Please also meet Babu Harish Chandra, whose second letter is expected shortly. When this letter will come, some different arrangements may have to be made. I will only be able to write to you after these are made. Please continue writing all the news from your end. Please also write about the whereabouts of Gopal Rao Hari Deshmukh nowadays. I am very happy here.

Swami Dayanand Saraswati

Letter No. 130

To Pundit Sunder Lal Ram Narain ji

(Kārtika Śukla 10, Saṁvat 1935 I.e. November 4, 1878)

This letter, written in Hindi, was sent from Delhi. It has been marked as No. 655. A copy of this letter is preserved in Paropakarini Sabha.

May you be happy Pundit Sunder Lal Ram Narain Ji!

I wrote a letter to you before about sending 38 Satyārtha Prakāśa, 30 Sanskāra Viddhis, 20 Bhūmikā, and 50 Sandhyopāsanās to Babu Samarth Dan Charan, student of Govt. College, Ajmer. It is hoped that you might have already sent the above books to the above address. If you have not sent them so far, please send them very soon, as at the ensuing Pushkar Fair many of the books will be sold. Furthermore, please keep 18 issues of the Bhūmikā with Mantra Bhāṣya ready in sequence, so that when I request for its despatch to a particular place, the same may be sent to that destination.

Please keep all the books well-protected so that these are not spoiled by termites. I will also need a rupee or two for my monthly expenditure but this will be taken care of. Keep them (the books) with someone like Bal Mukand and inform me that you have done so, so that when I request for some books to be sent to some address, he can do so. Postal charges may be debited to my account. As there is no other house except yours, where these books can be kept, therefore their protection and arrangement are your responsibility. The Arya Samaj has been set up here. Now, I will proceed to Pushkar on November 6. I am very happy here.

Swami Dayanand Saraswati

Letter No. 131

To Pundit Sunder Lal Ram Narain ji

(Kārtika Śukla 15, Saṁvat 1935 i.e.November 8, 1878)

This letter was written in Hindi and sent from Pushkar. It was marked as No. 674. A copy of this letter is also preserved in Paropakarini Sabha.

May you be joyful Pundit Sunder Lal Ram Narain Ji!

You may have received my earlier letters ent to you from Delhi. I reached Pushkar on November 7, after starting from Delhi on November 6, and I am staying at Nath Ji Ka Dulicha here. After Purnima, I will go back to Ajmer. Now, you may send the following numbers of books to me at Ajmer: Sanskāra Vidhi 30, Bhūmikā 20, Satyārtha Prakāśa 39, Āryābhivinaya 50, Veda Virudha Mata Khaṇḍana 50, Vedantidhvānta Nivāraṇa 50.

Also, write whether you have received books from Mumbai or not. Now, please send the above books quickly to me at Ajmer. I am very happy here.

Swami Dayanand Saraswati

Letter No. 132

To Pundit Shyam ji Krishna Varma

(Kārtika Śukla 15, Saṁvat 1935 i.e. November 10, 1878)

This letter No. 676, written in Hindi, was sent from Pushkar to Shyam Ji in Mumbai. The original letter is preserved in the collection of Prof. Dhirendra Varma.

May you be happy Pundit Shyam Ji Krishan Verma!

I would like to let you know that one letter has been received from Babu Harish Chandra Chintamani, in which he writes that he can't leave this work at the end of the year, as it would bring his name into disrepute. I have sent the reply to him that there will be no damage to his reputation, as up to the end of the year, the cover page will bear only his name, and correspondence from customers will also be received by him, and that the rest of work will be looked after by Shyam Ji. Now let us see how he replies.

Yes, please correct the 4th issue, and send it to all the customers properly, and do all the work well. Make arrangements for good quality paper, which looks nice, as you have done for the 2nd issue. I have reached Pushkar safe and sound and from here we will go to Ajmer. Please write all the news from there to the same place (Ajmer). Continue your interaction with Babu Ji.

Swami Dayanand Saraswati

Letter No. 133

To Pundit Sunder Lal Ram Narain ji

(November 13, 1878)

This letter No. 692, written in Hindi, was sent from Ajmer. The original letter is preserved in Paropakarini Sabha.

Be blessed Pundit Sunder Lal Ram Narain Ji!

Today I received your letter and I read its contents in their entirety. The total amount of Rs.300 and 12 annas (Ps. 75) is due to me. Please kindly arrange each type of book separately, and also the Bhūmikā issues from 1 to 16 in sequential order, so that when I write to you to send books to me, you may send them. I am very happy to know that the books are being kept safe by you. I have learnt that the books have been received by you from Mumbai. After reaching Ajmer safe and sound, I am staying now at the garden of Seth Ramanand, outside Nayā Darwājā, Pushkar Road, Ajmer. So, please send the following number of books to me urgently: Satyāratha Prakāśa 15, Sanskāra Vidhi 20, Bhūmikā 10, Sandhyopāsanā 100, Aryābhivinaya 50, Veda Virudha Mata Khaṇḍana 50, Vedanti Dhvānta Nivāraṇa 50. And also send 20 copies of Bhūmikā and other books that they want. I am very happy here.

Swami Dayanand Saraswati

Letter No. 134

To Pundit Sunder Lal Ram Narain

(November 16, 1878)

This letter No. 698, written in Hindi, was sent from Ajmer. The original letter is preserved in the Paropakarini Sabha.

Be happy Pundit Sunder Lal Ram Narain!

I have received your letter today and read its contents. You may now send the following number of books to me quickly: Aryābhinaya 25, Vedāntī Dhvānta Nivāraṇa 11, Veda Virudha Mata Khaṇḍana 38, Satyāsatya Vicāra 50. I have learnt that you have sent the books to Babu Samarath Dan. Lectures are now being delivered here. If there is any further news I will write to you. I am very happy here.

Swami Dayanand Saraswati

Letter No. 135

To Pundit Sunder Lal Ram Narain

(November 20, 1878)

This letter No. 702, written in Hindi, was sent from Ajmer. The original letter is preserved in Paropakarini Sabha.

May you be happy Pundit Sunder Lal Ram Narain Ji!

I have received two boxes of books sent by you, and received the following books in the two boxes:

Satyāratha Prakāśa	38
Sanskāra Vidhi	30
Vedabhāṣya Bhūmikā	20
(along with Mantra Bhāṣya)	
Sandhyopāsanā	50

Please send the following books immediately:

Name of Book	No. Of Books
Aryābhivinaya	25
Vedāntī Dhvānta Nivāraṇa	11
Veda Virudha Mata Khaṇḍana	38
Satyāsatya Vicāra	50
Vedabhāṣya Bhūmikā	

(Along with Mantra Bhāṣya)	10
Sandhyopāsanādi,	
Pañca Mahāyajña Vidhi	50

Please send these books urgently. And keep all the issues of the Vedabhāṣya in a proper sequence, so that when I request you to send them to someone, you can then send them there. Lectures are being delivered here daily. I will be writing to you if there is any further news. I am very happy here.

Swami Dayanand Saraswati

Letter No. 136

To Pundit Shyam ji Krishna Varma

(Mārgaśīrṣa Kṛṣṇa 11, Wednesday, Saṁvat 1935 i.e. November 20, 1878)

This letter No. 704, written in Hindi, was sent from Ajmer. The original is preserved in the collection of Prof. Dhirendra Verma.

December 11, 1878)

This letter No. 780, written in Hindi, was sent from Nasirabad, Ajmer.

May you be joyful Pundit Shyam Ji Krishna Varma!

My opinion is that instead of 3100 copies of the Vedabhāṣya presently being printed, we may get printed only 1500 copies so that printing expenses remain low. Therefore, let me know the estimate of expenditure for the printing of 1500 copies, and to what extent expenses can further be reduced on the printing and papers, etc. Please write in detail about all of this. Also, please write the whereabouts of Rao Saheb Gopal Rao Hari Deshmukh, and whether he has met you or not. Further, what is the news from America? And where is Keshav Lal Nirbhay Ram?

Please send a reply to this letter to Jaipur, because I will be proceeding there on December 15 via Ajmer. I am very happy here.

Swami Dayanand Saraswati

Letter No. 141

To Pundit Sunder Lal Ram Narain ji

(December 16, 1878)

This letter No. 799, written in Hindi, was sent from Jaipur.

May you rejoice Pundit Sunder Lal Ram Narain Ji!

I felt delighted on receiving your letter from Nasirabad. Now, I have reached Jaipur on December 15 via Ajmer and am currently staying at Sada Sukh Dhadda's garden, outside Sanganer Darwaza in Jaipur.

Today, with this letter I am sending a hundi (M.O.) of Rs 200, receipt of which please send soon. Please credit this amount of Rs. 200 against the total amount of Rs. 300 and Annas 12 (Ps. 75). I am very happy here. Reply to me soon.

Swami Dayanand Saraswati

Letter No. 142

To Babu Pyare Lal, Member, Arya Samaj, Lahore

(Pauṣa Śukla 14, Saṁvat 1935 i.e. January 7, 1879)

This letter, written in Urdu, was sent from Rewari Dist. Gurgaon to Lahore. The original letter has been quoted by Pt. Lekhram (Hindi edition, pp. 580-581)

I was very glad to receive your letter from Rewari. I came to Jaipur from Ajmer and stayed there for 8 days. During this period, Thakur Fateh Singh Saheb, Babu Shri Prasad Mohtamim Bandobas, and G. Akhtiar, and respectable people, such as the Captain, etc. came to meet me. It was a great pleasure (to meet them). But no meeting could be held with Raja Saheb. After departing from there on December 24, I reached Rewari District Gurgaon on December 25th and delivered lectures there. Now, the programme of lectures here has concluded. Therefore, the day after tomorrow on January 9, 1879, I will be proceeding to Delhi, and staying in the garden of Babu Keshari Lal, near Subzi Mandi, Delhi. Further details will be sent to you from there. Everything else is all right here. I am very happy. Convey my namaste to all the members (of the Arya Samaj).

Swami Dayanand Saraswati

Letter No. 143

To Pundit Shyam ji Krishna Varma

(Māgha Kṛṣṇa 10, Saṁvat 1935 i.e. January 17, 1878)

This letter No. 937, written in Hindi, was sent from Meerut. The original letter is preserved in the collection of Prof. Dhirendra Verma.

May you be joyful ! Pundit Shyam Ji Krishan Verma,

You might have already received my earlier letter. I will let you know again as to why the fourth issue of the Vedabhāṣya has not come out so far, and what work is being done at the printing press nowadays. What is Babu Saheb doing? The issue is getting published later and later and seemingly every two months. This has caused the customers to press us hard. That is my reason for writing to you. Please reply promptly about the reason for the delay in bringing out the fourth issue.

Yesterday, I came to Meerut from Delhi and will be staying here for 8-9 days, proceeding on to Muzaffarnagar, Saharanpur, Roorkee, reaching in the Chaitra month at Hardwar. Please reply as soon as possible. I am keeping fine.

Swami Dayanand Saraswati

Letter No. 144

To Pundit Shyam ji Krishna Varma

(Māgha Kṛṣṇa 12, Friday, Saṁvat 1935 i.e. January 19, 1878)

This letter No. 942, written in Hindi, was sent from Meerut. The original letter is preserved in the collection of Prof. Dhirendra Verma. Through this letter, we come to know of the pressing circumstances under which Swami ji had to replace Harishchandra by Shyam ji Krishna Varma as the editor of Vedabhāṣya which was published in instalments from Mumbai.

May you be happy Pundit Shyam ji Krishan Varma!

You might have already received my earlier letter of January 17. Again I am writing to ask that you find out and write to me very soon about the situation there and about whether Harish Chandra has got the fourth issue printed or not. Kindly inform me too whether he has just dumped it after getting it printed, in order that our cause is defeated.

The Māgha month is now going to end, and as per Babu Ji's wishes, therefore, you should now take over the work of the Vedabhāṣya, and bring out the fifth issue yourself. You should also sign an agreement with the printing press owner to undertake our work with due regard to deadlines and time constraints. We will also be sending money in the second and third months. Please don't worry about funds, as it will be arranged.

Please write in detail about the extent to which, costs will be reduced if 1500 to 2000 copies are printed. Babu Ji has written that we can save Rs. 100 if 1500 copies are printed, out of which only Rs 77.50 will be reduced with regards to the cost of papers and no further reduction will be possible regarding the cost of printing and binding. Therefore, you should calculate all the details and let me know. Even if you have a thousand engagements, leave them and reply soon to each and every word of this letter. Here, in Meerut, some rich people would like to arrange a printing press. So please decide on its feasibility and indicate what amount will be required for purchasing fonts, etc.

Swami Dayanand Saraswati

The photographs are ready. You can collect them on the payment of Rs. 5.

Letter No. 145

To Lala Ram Shran Dass Jiva

(Māgha Kṛṣṇa 13, Saṁvat 1935 i.e. January 20, 1879)

This letter, written in Hindi, was sent from Meerut. The original letter was preserved by Pt. Bhagvaddatta. Lala Mamraj helped to procure this letter from Seth Dhanpat Rai, who was the son of Lala Ram Sharan Dass.

May you be happy Lala Ram Shran Dass Jiva Saheb!

As advised, a printing press should be arranged on behalf of the Arya samaj, and it was agreed that every member would contribute Rs. 100 each towards it. Therefore, two shares of Rs 100 each may also be added from my side, and the requisite money may be taken from me, whenever desired.

Swami Dayanand Saraswati

Letter No. 146

To Kripa Ram Swami

(Māgha Śukla 10, Saṁvat 1935 i.e. February 2, 1879)

This letter No. 1000, written in Hindi, was sent from Saharanpur.

May you be joyous Shriyut Kripa Ram Swami!

I was glad to receive your registered letter dated February 1. Having gone through its contents, I am sending this reply. Please convey my blessings to the people over there. I will be happy to visit your place. I may be able to come at the beginning of Vaiśākha, Saṁvat 1936. From here (Saharanpur), I will proceed to Roorkee on February 6, and after a halt of 8 to 15 days there, I will be going to Hardwar, and stay there for one and a half months in the gardens of Moola Mistri, which is located near the bridge of the canal on the main road between Kankhal and Jawalapur. I may be coming to your side afterwards. Is it possible that I can skip meeting you?

Swami Dayanand Saraswati

Letter No. 147

To Pundit Shyam ji Krishna Varma

(Phālguna Śukla 8, Saturday, Saṁvat 1935 i.e. March 1, 1879)

This letter, written in Hindi, was sent from Saharanpur. According to Pt. Bhagavaddatta, the original letter was preserved in a dilapidated condition by the sister of Swami Samarpananada.

May you be happy Pundit Shyam ji Krishna Varma!

I have received your letter of February 24, and all its contents have been read. Please extend my sincere blessings to the American gentlemen and enquire about their health, and also for how long they want to stay here and which places they want to visit. When they visit places like Lahore, etc. please let me know in advance, so that it may be ensured that they are given a warm welcome everywhere. What do they mean when they say that they will set up a new Samaj and Theosophical Society at Mumbai, when a Samaj already exists there? The case for a new Samaj and Theosophical Society has not been made out by me. Please give me further details so that I can understand this matter clearly. Further, regarding financial contribution by them, it is advisable that this funding be spent for the Vedabhāṣya work, etc. if they so desire. I don't see any better, more beneficial work than this. The rest may be done as decided by the majority.

Further, one Munshi Samaratha Dan will perform the work of the Vedabhāṣya there. He is a thorough gentleman who knows Hindi and Persian very well, and a bit of English also. He is a reliable and dependable person from a respectable family. He will be proceeding from Hardwar to Mumbai after a few days. Please give him training about all the works related to the printing press and paper, etc. and also about the rules and how to deal with people related to them. He should not feel any inconvenience of any kind. Make arrangements for his stay, and introduce him to everyone there. Also depute a peon, preferably a dependable elderly one, or a new one, who has been tested earlier. Make all the arrangements perfect and do them well.

Swami Dayanand Saraswati

Letter No. 148

To Pundit Shyam ji Krishna Varma

(Phālguna Śukla 11, Saṁvat 1935 i.e. March 4, 1879)

This letter, written in Hindi by Swamiji in his own handwriting, was sent from Saharanpur. The original letter is preserved in the collection of Prof. Dhirendra Verma. The letter shows that during Swamiji's lifetime, mischievous elements had infiltrated the Arya Samaj, who were taking the Samaj for a ride and causing a lot of damage to the Arya Samaj. There is also no dearth of these type of elements in the Arya Samaj nowadays. This is the main reason why the Arya Samaj like other once leading movements, has fizzled out and become irrelevant in spite of its great contribution to Indian society and the world at large.

May you be happy Pundit Shyam ji Krishna Varma!

I have received your letter of the 24th February and all its contents have been read. I regret very much that I am not in a position to come and meet our American friends in Mumbai. It is because of that that we have already made arrangements on Phālguna Sudī 6 for me to stay at Hardwar until the end of Chaitra, and all the publicity in this regard has already been done here, and this arrangement now can't be changed. When they come to see Arya Samajs at places like Lahore, then I may meet them with great love there or some other place, and have proper discussions with them. Please extend my warmest greetings to them.

Furthermore, you have written that the 'Arya Samaj here will be dismantled, if I fail to visit this place'. It is strange that you set up the Arya Samaj by depending only upon Harish Chandra Chintamani. And, if the stability of Arya samaj depends only on my visits, how many places can I realistically visit? If a president of the Arya Samaj is incompetent anywhere, then he should be replaced (with a competent person) so that the Samaj may function smoothly.

Munshi Samartha Dan will start from here tomorrow for Mumbai for the Vedabhāṣya work.

He will meet you. Please train him with regards to the rules and regulations relating to the printing press and introduce him to paper suppliers. Also, allow him to have all the books and relevant papers from Babu Harish Chandra Chintamani, and also brief him about accounts etc. quickly He should not face any difficulty on account of accommodation, etc.

Swami Dayanand Saraswati

Letter No. 149

To Pundit Shyam ji Krishna Varma

(Phālguna Śukla 12, Wednesday, Saṁvat 1935 i.e. March 5, 1879)

This letter was written in Sanskrit by Swami Dayanand in his own handwriting from beginning to end at Saharanpur. This letter was sent through Munshi Samartha Dan and delivered by hand. The original letter is preserved in the collection of Prof. Dhirendra Verma.

Many many blessings to a nobleman like Shyamji Krishna Varma! Everything is fine here and wishing you the same there. Just to let you know, I am sending a gentleman Samaratha Dan, today to Mumbai for the management of the Vedabhāṣya work there. He will be reaching you at the proper time. Please make arrangements so that he won't face any difficulty there. He should be trained perfectly in the Vedabhāṣya work. Please don't delay this work. Introduce him to all the members there. Extend my warmest blessings to the visiting American gentlemen and enquire about their health on behalf of me. Please have the same love for Samaratha Dan as you have for me. Please assist him in his studies, and arrange a proper place for his stay.

Swami Dayanand Saraswati

Letter No. 150

To Munshi Samartha Dan

(Chaitra Śukla 2, Monday, Saṁvat 1935 i.e. March 10, 1879)

This is a summary of the letter, written in Hindi, sent from Hardwar. The original letter is quoted by Lekhram (Hindi edition, p.867) in the Biography of Swamiji.

Upon reaching Mumbai, please meet the American gentlemen and let me know the developments there.

Swami Dayanand Saraswati

Letter No. 151

To Col. Olcott

(Date not known)

This is the summary of the letter, written in Hindi, sent from Hardwar to Mumbai. The original letter is quoted by Pt. Lekhram (Hindi edition, p.817). This letter informs the reader that during those days there were also a lot of crowds in Hardwar on the occasion of Kumbh Melas.

To avoid inconvenience at the fair (Kumbh fair) you should not come to Hardwar.

Swami Dayanand Saraswati

Letter No. 152

To Lala Madho Lal

(Chaitra Kṛṣṇa 9, Sunday, Saṁvat 1936 i.e. March 16, 1879)

This letter, written in English, was sent from Hardwar to the Secretary, Arya Samaj, Danapur, Bihar. The original letter is preserved in the collection of Arya Samaj Danapur.

Dear Sir,

I have the pleasure to acknowledge receipt of your letter of the 13th instant, containing three currency notes, aggregating to Rs. 20 and postage stamps amounting to five Annas (30 Paise), for the books mentioned therein.

I am very glad to hear that efforts are being made for establishing an Arya Sanskrit Pathshala and until now more than Rs. 102.30 has been raised to help. I shall be happy to hear about further progress at your end.

There are 10 copies of Satyārath Prakash available, and 5 copies of Vedbhāṣya.

Always your well-wisher

Swami Dayanand Saraswati

Letter No. 153

To Munshi Samartha Dan

(Chaitra Śukla 3, Saṁvat 1936 i.e. March 26, 1879)

This is a summary of a letter, written in Hindi, sent from Hardwar to Mumbai. The original letter is quoted by Pt. Lekhram (Hindi edition, p. 651-52) in the Biography of Swamiji.

Please convey my warmest greetings to the visiting American gentlemen. Do enquire about their health. Please also let them know about the status of the preparations made in Arya Samajs at Lahore and other places for their visit. Find out when they would like to go there, and whether they have started learning Sanskrit or not. Further, please write to me as to what their opinion is about me. Even if I don't write, please continue writing about their health and well-being. Here, the fair is attended predominantly by Sadhus, as very few householders (Gṛhasthis) are in attendance.

I have written another letter to Colonel Olcott on 24th, from whom you may receive a written reply. Please, convey my namaste to Shyam Lal Khanna.

Swami Dayanand Saraswati

Letter No. 154

To Munshi Samartha Dan

(Chaitra Śukla 5, Saṁvat 1936 i.e. March 27, 1879)

This is a summary of the letter, written in Hindi, sent from Hardwar to Mumbai. The original letter is quoted by Pt. Lekhram (Hindi edition, p. 651) in the Biography of Swamiji.

About two lakh Sadhus and Sanyasis, etc. have attended the Kumbh Mela. The Fair has now been concluded. Five people have died within three days due to an outbreak of cholera.

Swami Dayanand Saraswati

Letter No. 155

To Munshi Samartha Dan

(Chaitra Śukla 11, Saṁvat 1936 i.e. April 2, 1879)

This letter, written in Hindi, was sent from Hardwar to Mumbai. The original letter is quoted by Pt. Lekhram (Hindi edition, p. 651) in the Biography of Swamiji.

I have been suffering from dysentery for the last 15 days, with a frequency of 10 to 12 motions daily. Now, for the last few days, I am feeling better, but I feel greatly weakned (due to dehydration). Therefore, I will be going to the hills of Dehradun on 12th April, from where I will make a move to Mumbai if my health allows. Please tell the American gentlemen about this. Please tell them that I may not be fit to travel for about two months, especially by rail due to the intense heat. It will be very difficult for me to undertake journeys to and from these places of a duration of 8 days each. Please assure them that I will definitely come when I am fit to travel. I feel very sorry that the Americans have come at such a time when I am not in a position to meet them.

Swami Dayanand Saraswati

Letter No. 156

To Swami Vishuddhananda

(Saṁvat 1936 i.e. 1879)

The summary of this letter, written in Hindi, is quoted in Swamiji's Biographies written by Pt. Lekhram (Hindi version, p. 653) and Devendranath Mukhopadhyaya (p. 531). This letter was also sent from Hardwar.

You know whatever I am saying is absolutely right, but despite being a learned and reputed person, why are you hesitant to express it publically?

Swami Dayanand Saraswati

Letter No. 157

To Pandits for Debate

(Vaiśākha Śukla 1, Saṁvat 1936 i.e April 7, 1879)

The summary of this, written in Hindi from Hardwar, is quoted by Pt. Lekhram in the Biography of Swamiji (Hindi version, p.663).

I never back out from debates, as I am always ready for them. However, the debates should be arranged in such a way that the organiser of the debate should be a Government Officer (viz. a Magistrate), and there should only be Pandits (learned people) and no uneducated people present. Furthermore, there should be a neutral venue for debate. I perceive there to be a threat to my life at the venue (i.e. Junagarh Akhara) selected for debate. Although I am the least bothered about my life, I am more concerned about the work I am doing and for which I must continue to defend my life. As such I don't find that place safe for the debate.

Swami Dayanand Saraswati

Letter No. 158

To Pandits desirous of a debate

(Date not known)

This summary of the letter, written in Hindi, was sent from Dehradun. It was quoted by Pt. Lekhram in his Biography (Hindi edition, p. 655).

If Swami Vishuddhanand Ji recommends you as capable of understanding the Vedas like me, and capable of debate, then I am ready for the debate and I appoint Vishuddhanand Ji as a mediator.

Swami Dayanand Saraswati

Letter No. 159

To Munshi Samaratha Dan

(Vaisākha Śukla 2, Saṁvat 1936 i.e. April 8, 1879)

This is a summary of the letter, written in Hindi, sent from Hardwar to Mumbai. The original letter is quoted by Pt. Lekhram in the Biography of Swamiji (p. 651 of Hindi edition).

In your absence, my health has deteriorated. I had more than four hundred motions due to dysentery, because of which my body has become very weak. I was thinking that if I could perhaps become physically fit, I could proceed from Hardwar to Mumbai. But, now I am planning instead a visit Dehradun. By spending time there I may become physically fit in a few days. Only then will I be able to write about my arrival plans in Mumbai.

Please convey my namaste to the people from the American Mission, and they should not think that I am ignoring them as I will definitely meet them upon reaching Mumbai.

Munshi Inder Mani is also staying with me here (at Hardwar). The Kumbh Fair did not attract a huge gathering this time.

Swami Dayanand Saraswati

Letter No. 160

To Lala Madho Lal

(Vaiśākha Kṛṣṇa 4, Thursday, Saṁvat 1936 i.e April 10, 1879)

This letter, written in English, was sent from Hardwar to Lala Madho Lal, the secretary of Arya Samaj, Danapur, Bihar.

Dear Sir,

I have been informed that the American Mission (Col. H.S. Olcott and Countess H.Blavatsky) is coming to see me at Dehradun about the 14th current (instant) and I hope (they) will stay with me for some months.

Swami Dayanand Saraswati

Letter No. 161

To Munshi Samaratha Dan

(Vaiśākha Śukla 12, Saṁvat 1936 i.e. April 18, 1879)

This letter, written in Hindi, was sent from Hardwar to Mumbai to Munshi Samartha Dan. He was the son of Mangal Dan Charan. He was the resident of village Natheva, Ramgarh, Sikar near Jaipur.

In Hardwar, Omkar Mal and Sunder Raj have not met me. Many charming well-wishers from Ramgarh also arrived at Hardwar. I had discussions with many people at Hardwar. Sadhus also benefited by listening to our sermons. Cholera has broken out here but only to a limited extent. When we will have a chat with the people of the American Mission, their doubts will be addressed.

At Hardwar, I had about four hundred motions, and it is still continuing to some extent; but due to the cold climate of this place, I am now gradually feeling better. But, my body has become weak. Today, it seems that the loose motions have stopped. When it stops altogether, the body will also recover in a span of 15 to 20 days.

Swami Dayanand Saraswati

Letter No. 162

To Babu Madho Lal

(Vaiśākha Śukla 3, Thursday, Saṁvat 1936 i.e. April 24, 1879)

This letter, written in English, was sent from Dehradun to the Secretary, Arya Samaj, Danapur, Bihar.

Dear Sir,

I am very glad to receive your letter of 20th instant by today's post. You were quite right in remitting the payment for the Vedabhāṣya Bhūmikā to Pundit Sunder Lal at Allahabad, who can supply you with as many copies as you wish. I have also received the payment for the books that you had taken from Delhi.

I am pleased to hear that you are planning to opening a Sanskrit School, but before you go ahead, I should be informed as to what arrangements you have made with regards to the standard of various sciences to be taught at the School. Have you got all the necessary books ready yet? I think not. (What) I mean to say is that before you start work, you should have all the books printed first. The 'Quran' in Nagri is ready but has not been printed yet.

We have not been able to find a sufficient number of subscribers for Aṣṭādhyāyī; the four chapters (adhyāyas) of this book have recently been completed. The work is going on satisfactorily, though not a (single) copy (has) reached the press till date.

The great dishonesty and misconduct on the part of Babu Harish Chandra Chintamani have been the cause of the delay in the printing of the Vedabhāṣya. The man has been fired now and another man has been appointed to replace him. It is hoped that he will carry out the work very efficiently.

I intend to set up a press at Moradabad under the auspices of Munshi Indra Mani. For this purpose a subscription to the tune of Rs. 5,000/- is necessary to be raised by shares of Rs. 100/- each. Of this sum Rs. 2,500 has already been raised. I hope it will greatly help our cause. You are free to buy as many shares as you can. In that case, you should apply to Lala Ram Saran Das of Meerut, who is authorised to deal with this matter.

Yours truly,

Swami Dayanand Saraswati

Letter No.163

To Munshi Samaratha Dan

(Vaiśākha Śukla 14, Saṁvat 1936 i.e. May 5, 1879)

This letter, written in Hindi, was sent from Meerut to Munshi Samaratha Dan who was appointed Manager of the Vedabhāṣya by Swamiji. This letter clearly shows that Harishchandra Chintamani played a duplicitous part in the eventual break up of the alliance between Swami Ji and Theosophists.

Please meet the American Mission people, after reaching Mumbai and write to me about them. After my departure from Dehradun, I reached Saharanpur, where I met Olcott Saheb, Lady Blavatsky, and Mool ji Thakur Singh, who has come from America and has had interactions with them. After a break of two days there, I am now in Meerut, where I will stay for five to six days. Later, they will come to Mumbai, but I will take a break for a few more days. Olcott Saheb and I share common ideas and there is no difference of opinion between us. Furthermore, the doubts that Harish Chandra created in his mind, have now been removed. Olcott Saheb is a gentleman of a very clear conscience, with no deceit in his mind whatsoever. I am sorry to say that Harish Chandra has done a lot of damage. However, now we should be more alert.

Swami Dayanand Saraswati

Letter No. 164

To Munshi Samarathadaan

(Vaiśākha Śukla 14, Saṁvat 1936 i.e. May 5, 1879)

This letter, written in Hindi, was sent from Meerut to Mumbai. The original letter is quoted by Pt. Lekhram in the Biography of Swami ji (Hindi version, p. 871).

Yesterday, Olcott Saheb and Lady Blavatsky visited the Arya Samaj and today they will deliver lectures in the city centre of Meerut and are likely to depart from here to Mumbai in a day or two. They have no problem with our Samaj i.e. they are in unison with us, in so far as their conduct and behaviour are concerned. On the basis of our talks for the last four-five days with them, it appears that they are people possessing pure consciences. Had you sent the letter of my consent for including my name in the 'Theosophical Society,' I would have given the copy of the same to Mr. Olcott. But when the subject was discussed in detail, he informed me that up till now the objective of their Theosophical Society was to permit people from all faiths to join it and for them to voice their opinions. Now after understanding the objectives of Arya Samaj, the Theosophists will follow our directions. Furthermore, he also assured me that in the future such things will not be allowed to happen, and a person who is not ready to follow the rules of the Arya Samaj will also not be able to become a member of the Theosophical Society. These details shall be further explained to you when Moolji Bhai comes to Mumbai.

Swami Dayanand Saraswati

Letter No. 165

To Secretary, Arya Samaj, Shahjhanpur

(Jyeṣṭha Kṛṣṇa 2, Saṁvat 1936 i.e. May 8, 1879)

This letter, written in Hindi, was sent from Meerut to the Secretary, Arya Samaj, Shajahanpur. This letter is quoted by Pt. Lekhram in the Biography of Swamiji (Hindi version, p. 869-70).

May you be happy Secretary, Arya Samaj, Shahjahanpur!

I am happy to inform all of you that there have been several rounds of talks on May 1, 1879, at Saharanpur with Colonel Olcott and Madame H.P. Blavatsky, who have been corresponding with our Arya Samaj. The views expressed by them in their letters seem to be true, and we noticed that they were very gentle. We had many rounds of talks with them for two days at Saharanpur. All of our people extended a warm welcome to them and listened to them attentively for five days. Their audience comprised of wealthy people and celebrities, government officials, and English people alike. During these lectures, the doubts of listeners were cleared up and their enquiries about the availability of relevant literature related to the truth were answered. In other words, the people from the American Mission confirmed that all principles of altruistic welfare and knowledge have emanated from Vedas, and all the faiths which are anti-Vedic are hypocritical. They later left for Mumbai on May 7, 1879, but I will continue to stay here for some more days. It seems that our interaction with these people may result in the progress of the people of Āryāvartta (India) and other countries. In the way that a good medicine, if administered with proper diet, cures the disease, similarly, such meetings will facilitate the propagation of the Vedas in India and elsewhere, eliminating the disease of untruth completely. The conduct and behaviour of these gentlefolk appear to be very good, as they are ready to render assistance for the Vedic faith by all means (physically, mentally, and financially) at their disposal.

The rumour spread by Babu Harish Chandra Chintamani about these gentlemen that they know magic and talk like cheats is definitely false propaganda. This is because, whatever is termed 'magic' is knowledge of physical or material science, which they have acquired to impress foolish people and to lead them to the path of truth. So, there is no fault in it, but to people like Harish Chandra, even 'gold' appears also to be base metal. This Harish Chandra has created such huge misgivings about us in their mind, it cannot be expressed in words. But all these doubts have been cleared after we met each other. Just look at the dishonesty of Harish Chandra, he who has created a lot of hurdles on the way to the Vedabhāṣya work, and still continues to do so. Therefore, all the Arya people should consider him expelled from the Arya Samajs, and should not, entertain him in any way in the future.

Just look at how our Saints (Rishis and Munis) in ancient times, knew the spiritual sciences and with their spiritual strength, were able to quickly read the minds of other people. Similarly, with the combination of 'inner spiritual matter,' yogis can perform great wonders, just like with the aid of physical, material sciences, the technology of the rail, the telegraph, etc. is being developed (which only a fool would consider to be 'magic'). It is unsurprising that whatever is performed with the help of physical sciences, is augmented many more times with the help of the inner spiritual sciences. Just like the outer material is used from the outside, similarly, the 'inner material' is used from the inside. For instance, the actions of macro or physical materials can be seen through naked eyes from the outside, but the actions of micro or subtle materials cannot be seen with the help of the eyes. This explains why people are amazed on learning about these things. It is however also true that certain deceitful people don't know this knowledge, but they bring a bad name to it by using unfair means. As such truthful people should be honoured and liars discouraged.

Harish Chandra's fraud was exposed after a long period, and so he was expelled from the Arya Samaj. Similarly, whosoever is found guilty of exaggeration is to be treated on a par with Harish Chandra. The integrity of a person should always be monitored carefully. This process is called reformation which is the quality of gentlemen. When you find something wrong, it should be 'exposed', and immediately abandoned. There should be no hitch in imposing a ban on falsehood. In the absence of such actions one can neither reform oneself nor reform others.

Now, I conclude this letter with the comment that the previous correspondence of these gentlemen (the

American Mission people) and the recent discussions over the seven days, confirm that they want to propagate truth and mitigate falsehood. They also want to contribute to the cause of the welfare of all people, with all their might (physical, mental, and financial) like our people (people from Arya Samaj).

Swami Dayanand Saraswati

Letter No. 166

To Babu Madho Prasad and others

(Jyeṣṭha Kṛṣṇa 3, Saṁvat 1936 i.e. May 9, 1879)

This letter, written in Hindi, was sent from Meerut. It was quoted by Pt. Vibhumitra Shastri in his leaflet titled 'Dānāpura Ṛṣi Dayanand Kā Padarpaṇa Aur Prabhāva' (Arrival and Influence of Rishi Dayanand in Danapur).

Rejoice Babu Madho Prasad Ji and others!

It is a matter of pleasure to inform all of you that a meeting took place on May 1, 1879, at Saharanpur with Colonel Olcott and Madame H.P. Blavatsky, whose letters from America were received earlier by our Arya Samajs. It was noticed that they are more meritorious than what was reflected in their letters. We had meetings with them for two days at Saharanpur. All our Samaj people extended a warm welcome to them and listened to their talks attentively. Later on, they accompanied me to Meerut. Here also they were given a warm welcome by all our Samaj People. Their talks for five days were appreciated by one and all present there. The rich, people of name and fame, government officers as well as the British formed part of their audience. During these talks, all doubts or enquiries were addressed beautifully. In other words, the American Mission people supported our view that the Vedas are the source of all good things and knowledge. All faiths which are anti-Veda are nothing but trash. Later on, they left for Mumbai on May 7, 1879. I may continue to stay here for some more days. Further, our interactions with these people will serve the cause of the progress of the people of Āryāvartta (India) and other countries. Like good medicine, if administered along with a proper diet, cures the disease, similarly, such meetings will facilitate the propagation of the Vedas and Vedic ideas in India and elsewhere, as a result of which the problem of falsehood will be eliminated within no time. The conduct and behaviour of these good people appear to be appreciable, as they are ready to render assistance to the establishment of the Vedic faith by all the means (physically, mentally, and financially) at their disposal.

The rumour spread by Babu Harish Chandra Chintamani about these noble people that they know magic and talk like spies in a disguised manner is definitely false, because, whatever is termed as 'magic' is only but knowledge of the physical and material sciences, which they have acquired to impress fools and to lead them to the path of truth. So, it should not be considered a weakness. People like Harish Chandra would even regard 'gold' to be a base metal. This Harish Chandra has created great misgivings about us in their minds, which cannot be expressed in words. But all these doubts have been cleared up after rounds of talks. Just look at the dishonesty of Harish Chandra, who has created a lot of obstacles on the way of the Vedabhāṣya, and still continues to do so. Therefore, all Arya people should consider him expelled from the Arya Samajs, and should not, in the future, trust in him in any way.

Just look at how in ancient times, our Saints (Rishis and Munis) were knowledgeable about the spiritual sciences and with their spiritual strength, they could quickly read the minds of other people. Similarly, with the combination of 'inner spiritual mastery,' yogis can perform wonders, just like with the aid of physical or material sciences, technologies like the rail, the telegraph, etc. are being developed (which fools consider to be 'magic'). It is not surprising that whatever is performed with the help of the physical sciences, can also be performed on a larger scale with the help of the inner spiritual sciences. Just like external material is used from the outside, similarly, 'inner material' is used from the inside. For instance, the actions of macro or physical materials can be seen through naked eyes from the outside, but the actions of micro or subtle materials cannot be seen with the help of the eyes. People are amazed when they hear about these things. This is also true of certain cunning people who do not know this knowledge, so bring a bad name to it by using unfair means. Truthful people should be encouraged and liars discouraged.

Harish Chandra's fraud was exposed after a long period of time, and he was eventually expelled from Arya samajs. Similarly, whosoever is found guilty of exaggeration, is to be treated on a par with Harish Chandra. The integrity of a person should always be monitored carefully. This process is called reformation which is the quality of gentlemen. When you come across something wrong, it should be exposed and immediately banned. It is, therefore, not unethical to ban falsehood. The absence of such an action can neither help in the reformation of oneself nor in the reformation of others.

Now, I conclude this letter with the comment that

the previous correspondence of these good people (the American Mission people) and the recent discussions over seven days, confirm that they want to promote truth and denigrate falsehood. They also want to contribute to the all round welfare of humanity through every means possible (physical, mental, and financial) like our people (from the Arya Samaj).

Swami Dayanand Saraswati

Letter No. 167

To Munshi Samaratha Dan

(Jyeṣṭha Vadi 14, Saṁvat 1936 i.e. May 20, 1879)

This summary of this letter, written in Hindi, was sent from Meerut to Mumbai. It was quoted by Pt. Lekhram in the Biography of Swamiji (Hindi version, p. 871-872).

The American Mission's letter through you has not been received so far. Please convey my namaste to them and enquire about their health. Please continue to tell them about the benefits of a daily routine. They visited the residence of Babu Chedi Lal and Shiv Narain, Gumashta, Commissioner, Meerut. They told them (Chedi Lal) to send the printed copy of the lecture, which has not been printed so far. Please remind them. It is quite likely that they have forgotten about it. I will proceed to Aligarh the day after tomorrow.

Swami Dayanand Saraswati

Letter No. 168

To Munshi Samaratha Dan

(Jyeṣṭha Śukla 4, Saṁvat 1936 i.e. May 25, 1879)

This letter, written in Hindi, was sent from Aligarh to Mumbai. This part of the letter was published by Devendra Nath Mukhopadhyay in the Biography of Swamiji (p. 767).

Harish Chandra had once written to me that the American mission people wanted to send some money. I told him to circulate this news in public and especially in Arya Samajs that they want to extend their financial help to the Arya Samaj, and whatever amount is received from them should be published in newspapers along with the names of the donors. He, then, replied that he will do that in accordance with the wishes of the Americans. I advised him to spend the amount received along three lines:

1. Towards the promotion and propagation of Vedic knowledge and for the marketing of Vedic books.

2. Towards the provision of grants to institutions teaching morality and ethics.

3. Towards helping the poor and destitute.

But, now it appears that he has not even undertaken one of these tasks.

Swami Dayanand Saraswati

Letter No. 169

To Pranji Das

(Undated)

This is a part of a letter, written in Hindi, sent from Aligarh to Mumbai. We find mention of this letter in the letter written to Shyam Ji Krishna Varma by Pran Ji Dass Kahan Dass on June 29, 1879.

Please get details of the whereabouts of Babu Harish Chandra in England by writing a letter to Shyam Ji.

Swami Dayanand Saraswati

Letter No. 170

To Munshi Samaratha Dan

(Āṣāḍha Śudi 4, Saṁvat 1936 i.e. June 23, 1879)

This is the part of a letter, written in Hindi, sent from Chalesar, Aligarh to Mumbai. It is quoted by Pt. Lekhram in the Biography of Swami Ji (Hindi version, p. 795).

I am staying at Chalesar, Tehsil, District Aligarh. I have now stopped taking purgatives, but weakness to some extent persists. I will go to Moradabad after seven to eight days. Munshi Indra Mani has also come here.

Swami Dayanand Saraswati

Letter No. 171

To Munshi Samarath Dan

(Āṣāḍha Śudi 5, Tuesday, Saṁvat 1936 i.e. June 24, 1879)

This is the part of a letter, written in Hindi, sent from Chalesar, Aligarh to Mumbai. It is quoted by Pt. Lekhram in the Biography of Swamiji (Hindi version, p. 795).

The intended sense of the letter of the American people is difficult to write here. When it is comprehended properly, a reply will be sent.

Now my health is improving.

Swami Dayanand Saraswati

Subscriptions of the Vedabhāṣya will be collected by Munna Singh.

Letter No. 172

To Pt. Shyam ji Krishna Varma

(Ā1ṣāḍha Śudi 5,Saṁvat 1936 i.e. June 30,1879)

This letter, written in Hindi, was sent by Munshi Samaratha Dan, Manager of the Vedabhāṣya, Mumbai to Pundit Shyamji Krishna Varma, Oxford (England) on behalf of Rishi Dayanand, as desired by him.

OM Dated June 30, 1879

From

Vedabhāṣya office, Marwari Bazar,
Muvakshey, Veeka Chali, Mumbai

To

Panditvar Shyam ji Krishan Verma,
Oxford (U.K.)

Kind Sir Namaste!

It is humbly submitted that your letters have been received by your Master Pran Jiwan Dass. We are very glad to know that you are hale and hearty there. It is good news that you have got admission into the College (at Oxford) for the Barrister's examination. I am writing this letter as directed by Swami ji.

I am writing about the developments concerning Babu Harish Chandra, the American Mission people, and Keshav Lal Nirbhey Ram. This has also been done through Master Pran Jiwan Das' letter enclosed herewith, which will make everything known to you. The above mentioned Babu (Harish Chandra Chintamani) has misappropriated a lot of money.

Consequently, the American people intend to file a lawsuit against him. Please find out where he is and let us know the city and address where Babu is located. There is an urgent need for this information. If he is in London, please tell us his address. Please send letters to me at my residential address which is appended below. Please put an advertisement in the newspapers there that Babu (Harish Chandra Chintamani), who was president of Arya Samaj, Mumbai, has been expelled, and Rao Bahadur Gopal Rao Hari Deshmukh has been appointed the new president to replace him. Many letters from England in the name of Swami Ji are still coming addressed to Babu. Now, please publish a notice in the newspapers there that all correspondence in the name of Swami Ji should, in future, be addressed to his secretary Munshi Samaratha Dan, giving my name and Mumbai address (as given above). This is very important. The expenses incurred, if any, on that score, will be paid to Dhan Ji, after hearing from you.

Today, issue No. 516 of the Vedabhāṣya, one Pañca Mahāyajña viddhi and one Pancāṅga are being sent by book post, on receipt of which please send an acknowledgment. The (Vedabhāṣya) issue is for Professor Monier Williams, and the book and Pancāṅga are for you, which may be collected from the Professor. You have written that the professor has not received the (Vedabhāṣya) issues. Please let us know which issues have not been received by him, so that we may send the same again. The price of the Vedabhāṣya has been published in the notice as Rs. 5, Annas 6 (36 paise), and accordingly, please kindly send the amount. Extra charges for England on the issue should also please be realised. Please get the costs for sending these, from both Professor Max Mñller and Professor Monier Williams, also inform us about their views regarding Swamiji and his Vedabhāṣya, as well as their reaction to the critique of Swami Ji about them and their Vedabhāṣya. Also, write to us about their opinions on the people from the American Mission. What type of books are being taught in the Sanskrit College there? Please enrol more members for the Vedabhāṣya, if possible. Please tell people there that if they can't read the Vedabhāṣya, they could request that such books be kept in libraries. What about the popularity of Sanskrit there? What do people there think about Arya Samaj? I know that your time is very precious, but please bear with us. We are very eager to know the news from your end. If a cultured gentleman like you will not write to us, who else will?.

Swami ji is very happy and your brother Dhan Ji is also very happy here. I am enclosing a letter from Dhan Ji for you. Please look for and let us know Babu's address as soon as possible. Keep me informed about anything you need from here. We feel that Babu might be criticising Swami Ji and Arya Samaj. Please share his activities with us. If he writes something against us in the papers, please publish rebuttals and true facts. If you are not aware of some facts, don't hesitate to ask us. If Babu asks for some help from you, please remember that he does not deserve it.

Your Well-wisher,

Samaratha Dan,
Manager, Vedabhāṣya Office, Mumbai

Letter No. 173

To Sahu Shyam Sunder Das

(Undated)

This is the summary of a letter, written in Hindi, sent probably from Moradabad. This summary is quoted by Pt. Lekhram (Hindi edition, p. 472). The time and location of this letter are untraceable. This letter sheds ample good light on the management of Gurukulas during Swamiji's lifetime. The letter also points out Swamiji's views which were against child marriage.

Please get (your) son's Yajñopavita ceremony done and teach him at home. The gurukula is not well-managed nowadays and don't get him married soon.

Swami Dayanand Saraswati

Letter No. 174

To Colonel H.S. Olcott

(Śrāvaṇa Kṛṣṇa 9, Saṁvat 1936 i.e. July 13, 1879)

This letter, sent from Moradabad to the Theosophical Society, America, was written in Hindi and translated into English by Thakur Singh alias Bhup Singh. Thakur Shankar Singh of Moradabad was a great devotee of Swamiji. He translated letters of Swamiji into English very often. This letter was procured by Lala Mam Singh from the house of Thakur Shankar Singh.

13th July 1879

Dear Colonel Olcott,

Your letters of 10th June and 5th July is duly in hand. Also of Madame H.P.Blavatsky of probably 30th June in Hindi.

You have acted very wisely in negotiating with the Governor of Bombay, so that the British Government has no more suspicions regarding your stay in India and your movements to different places on the sacred duty of preaching the Vedic religion.

The Kunte brothers are fickle-minded, I know. I am glad to hear (that) you have started reading 'Nāgari'.

Your proposal for publishing a monthly journal is very sound. I only want to add a little to the name that you have already proposed. My hope (in altering the name) is that it will convey to the subscribers that a joint effort is being made in compiling the paper - this may perhaps greatly increase subscribers. Call the journal 'Theosophist or Ārya Prakāśa.'

The date of the foundation of the Arya Samaj you

can get from the Bombay Samaj. The objects of the Samaj are that all mankind-

(1) Give up bad ideas, deeds, and habits

(2) And inculcate good ideas, deeds, and habits. Guṇa, Karma, and Svabhava through the ancient (Sanatana): (1) Veda Vidyā, (2) God's creation.

(3) The question regarding my life story, I should say that at present I am not quite prepared to undertake such a long business. I shall give you a brief account of my life after some time. I shall do this work myself or have it done directly under my own eyes. The certificate will follow.

Yours truly,

Swami Dayanand Saraswati

Letter No. 175

To M. Blavatsky

(Śrāvaṇa Kṛṣṇa 9, Saṁvat 1936 i.e. July 13, 1879)

This letter, written in English, was sent from Moradabad to the American Mission of the Theosophical Society, Mumbai. This letter was also procured by Mam Raj from the house of Takhur Shankar Singh of Moradabad.

Dear Madam Blavatsky,

After death, man's or anyone's 'atma' (soul) lives in the air (vāyu) according to the moral and immoral acts committed by the departed soul. God allows transmigration or new life. When the proportion of (an atma's) moral acts is higher than those of immoral acts, the soul occupies a body of a highly knowledgeable man or high-spirited yogī called 'Deva' (Swarga Loka) which corresponds to his or her moral values and knowledge attained in a previous life. It may attain mokṣa or become free from sorrow and troubles. When the proportion of moral acts and immoral acts is equal, then the soul attains a human body. When the proportion of immoral acts is higher than moral acts, the soul occupies the species of lower creatures and the vegetable world (called a naraka loka).

The 'Jiva' or soul suffers when due to the increase in immoral acts performed, the body of a lower animal or tree or plants etc. is obtained. However with the lapse of time, when moral acts (puṇya) and immoral acts (pāpa) again kick the beam equally, the soul occupies a human body.

In the same manner 'a spiritualist or a scholar' after

the enjoyment of blessings in the 'Deva-life', transgresses to human life again, when his or her moral acts and immoral acts remain equal in proportion.

Moral acts and immoral acts are of various kinds and degrees.

The inferior or superior body is given according to their proportion both, in the brute creation and in human beings as well as of deva.

The mukta jīva (emancipated soul) enjoys eternal happiness till mahākalpa (31,10,40,00,00,00,000 years i.e. 311 trillion years which is equal to 36,000 time creation period 4,32,00,00,000 years plus 36000 time decreation period i.e. 4,32,00,00,000 years of the world) and thereafter relegated into the human species again. The transmigration into different species continues, according to the proportion of moral or immoral deeds.

The first Ṛṣis were Āditya, Vāyu, Agni and Aṅgirā.

The Omnipresent (sarva vyāpaka), God inspired the sacred Vedas into their ātmā. It was nothing like a heavenly book coming from heaven and sent by God through his messenger. This is detailed at length in my Vedabhāṣya (Bhūmikā) from the very beginning (vide Vol. I etc.). You can have it read to you. All such things are discussed at length in my books both in Sanskrit and Bhasha (Hindi), which (you may please) see.

The verbal prayer, as well as practice, is meant to teach others but for one's own benefit it should be done silently.

(a) In order to obtain the advantage of dikṣā and

yoga, a company of the learned (vidvān), purification of the soul (ātmā kī pavitratā), and the means of cognition like perception, etc. (pratyakṣādi pramāṇna), one needs to do a lot of practice.

The practitioners are recommended to perform only such actions as are favourable to their cause; the contrary ones must be dropped- (Upāsanā Prakaraṇa of the Veda Bhūmikā, No. 9).

(b) The soul in the human body can work wonders. By knowing the properties and formations of all the things in the universe (right from God down to the bhūmi or earth) - a human being can acquire the divine power of seeing, hearing, etc. of far distant objects which generally is not possible in normal circumstances.

You can write articles on any subject, but first, consult my books and write cautiously in the light of them (engaging the right perspective). Contrary (views) or conjectures if made by you, will have to be responded to by you, if subjected to criticism.

Yours

Swami Dayanand Saraswati

P.S. I received the letter of Colonel Olcott of 9th July - from Peter Davidson Scotland (13th June 1879).

I shall send the answer to Peter Davidson in English as you say. The others will be replied to in Hindi.

In these matters, I shall follow your suggestions. So far as your inquiry regarding translating the Vedabhāṣya into English and regarding its publication in your journal, I am of the opinion that:

1. It is an uphill task to translate faithfully one language into another - and if at all possible the translator should be equally learned in both languages. My bhāṣya version is not like the common vernacular; word to word Sanskrit is translated into bhāṣā (Hindi). A most competent man well versed both in English and Sanskrit is required to translate my Vedabhāṣya - and that too may not stand (up) to the mark.

Unless I hear the gist of the translation thus made in English myself, I cannot be satisfied with its accuracy and I don't have enough time for this.

If you can manage to keep the translator with me, it is possible that during leisure time he can read it over to me and have it rectified wherever necessary. He can also get clarifications in case of any doubt.

Supposing all these arrangements are successfully made - the greatest drawback of it is that the Aryan (English speaking student) community of India will, due to the availability of an English translation of my Vedabhāṣya, may give up the Sanskrit and Hindi studies which they are so passionately pursuing nowadays in order to enable themselves to read the Vedabhāṣya, and which is the chief objective of mine, so, of course, an English translation will greatly help European scholars only.

This will lead to the fall in the number of subscribers to the Hindi Edition of the Vedabhāṣya causing a great deterioration in its publication. There is all likelihood that this may stop the publication of the Hindi version altogether. The treasure whence you wish to take will exhaust. This may also result in the total elimination of both Hindi and Sanskrit boosting the popularity of the English issue. This never means that I want to discourage you from translating it into English, as without the English translation the European nations cannot get the true light. But before taking any step, you may keep the above facts in your mind.

First of all, all four Vedas should be expeditiously translated. I have estimated that it will take 10 years for me to translate all the Vedas at the present pace of translation. It is most important to finish the translation work first.

Please address all the issues.

Yours

Swami Dayanand Saraswati

Letter No. 176

To Munshi Samaratha Dan

(Śrāvaṇa Śukla 13, Saṁvat 1936 i.e. July 31, 1879)

This is the summary of the letter, written in Hindi, sent from Moradabad to Mumbai. It is quoted by Pt. Lekhram in the Biography of Swamiji (Hindi edition, p. 837).

Please convey my namaste to the American Mission delegation. I have already sent a reply to their letter regarding the translation of the Vedabhāṣya into English, to which their reply has not been received yet. If you happen to meet them, please inform them that I (Swami Ji) have not been well, I couldn't reply to their letters received from abroad. I will now be replying to their letters, as I am feeling a bit better now. I can't come to Mumbai now but will instead be going from Patna to Danapur.

Swami Dayanand Saraswati

Letter No. 177

To Munshi Samaratha Dan

(Bhādra Śukla 4, Saṁvat 1936 i.e. August 21, 1879)

This is a summary of the letter, written in Hindi and sent from Bareilly to Mumbai. It is quoted by Pt. Lekhram in the Biography of Swamiji (Hindi edition, p. 872).

I have not been well for many days. Physically, I have become very weak. Please go and tell the American Mission delegation that they should not be under any misunderstanding (about my not coming to Mumbai). For the last two days, I have been feeling a bit better, and if I make a good recovery, I will reply to their letters as soon as possible. Furthermore, I will also be sending a short biography in Hindi of myself along with its English version, and also the replies to letters received from abroad. The American Mission delegation will be undertaking the publication of a newspaper, so guide them properly.

Swami Dayanand Saraswati

Letter No. 178

To Munshi Samaratha Dan

(Bhādrapada Śukla 11, Saṁvat 1936 i.e. August 27, 1879)

This letter, written in Hindi, was sent from Bareilly to Mumbai. The original letter is quoted by Pt. Lekhram in the Biography of Swamiji (Hindi edition, p. 479). Through this letter and others, it is quite evident that Swamiji used to suffer a lot from loose motions due to overwork.

Colonel Saheb (Colonel Olcott) has written to me to ask me to send my biography. As I am not yet physically fit, I have not been able to send the same. Since I have been getting a little bit better over the last few days, I am sending the biography along with this letter, so, please get it sent to them as soon as it reaches you, as the time has come for them to publish it in a newspaper. Please clarify to Colonel Olcott that my intention is not to name the newspaper as 'Arya Prakash' or 'Theosophist', but rather it should be a name that comprises both. Please also, tell him that the two letters sent by him have been received. Due to loose motions, my body had become very weak. Now it is all right.

Swami Dayanand Saraswati

Letter No. 179

To Pundit Ramadhar Vajpai

(Bhādrapada Śukla 13, Saṁvat 1936 i.e. August 29,1879)

This letter, written in English, was sent from Bareilly.

My dear friend,

My friend Munshi Ram Indermani requires the address of Munshi Har Prasad, copywriter. I hope you will send it to him as soon as possible.

Yours ever

Swami Dayanand Saraswati

Letter No. 180

To Pundit Ramadhar Vajpai

(Bhādrapada Śukla 13, Saṁvat 1936 i.e. August 29, 1879)

This letter, written in Hindi, was sent from Bareilly.

Be happy Pundit Ramadhar Vajpai Ji!

Why didn't you reply to Munshi's (Samartha Dan's) letter? Please send whatever information he wants to him quickly. A lot of lectures are being delivered here. There were debates with Padari Scott Saheb over three days, and all his views were challenged. I will be sending you also a copy (of what transpired between us) when this is published. On reaching Shahjahanpur and having rested there for a while I will write to you in 4 to 5 days. Please arrange a site for my lectures like the one arranged for my accommodation, as I will have a short stay there.

Swami Dayanand Saraswati

Letter No. 181

To Pt. Angad Shastry and others

(Āśvina Kṛṣṇa 11, Saṁvat 1936 i.e. September 12, 1879)

This letter, written in Hindi, was sent from Shahjahanpur as a counter reply to Angad Shastry and other Pandits. The original letter was published in Arya Darpaṇa, Shahjahanpur, Sept. 1879, p. 14-16, 261-262.

Om Namaḥ Sarvaśaktimate Parmeśvarāya!

[Meaning] Salutations to Almighty God!

Are you not fulfilling your selfish motives by resorting to anti-Vedic activities like idol worship, by disregarding the worship of one Almighty God and dharma (values) as sanctioned in the Vedas; and by misleading others on the wrong path?

Do I undertake any work pertaining to Dharma, Artha, kāma, and Mokṣa that is opposed to Vedas?

Had you been sincere enough about the debate, I would have never declined it. I will not even now decline such a debate if it is based on principles and carried out in a civilised and dignified way.

Had you been sincere enough about the debate, you could have stayed at the place where I was staying. By choosing a separate place for your stay you have proved that you don't want to engage yourself in the debate, but are merely play acting. It also raises doubts as to whether you actually came here with the intention to debate.

Of course, where there are disruptive people

present, I don't even stand up to debate there. Your statement that 'wherever you go I try to avoid you', is absolutely false. I have never feared you in the past, neither do I in the present, nor will I in the future, because you lack all the qualities, that could create fear in my mind.

Moreover in Bans Bareilly, as you were accompanied again by rowdy people and were high-handed, treasurer Laxmi Narain and others prevented you from entering his residence. This is all due to your arrogance. I had only heard about you in Bareilly and Shahjahanpur and nowhere else. Now whoever runs away from this encounter (getting together for debate) will be proved to be a liar. So please conserve whatever strength you have for the impending debate. We should never forget that learned people put in the effort to expose the truth and eradicate falsehood. So please never forget this.

I am definitely sure that, as per my knowledge and to the best of my ability, I will follow and make others follow the Ancient Sanātana Dharma based on the Vedas. As you are opposed to the Vedas and you have doubted them to a certain extent, we can have a debate to clarify all issues. Yes, in Mathura many students went to Shri Swami Ji, and you might have also gone there sometimes. But had you been a student of Swami Ji, you would not have behaved contrary to his teachings. Seniority or juniority is determined on the basis of good or bad actions and qualities.

The following rules for this debate shall be binding upon both parties:

1. In this debate, the four Vedas are the main

arbiters i.e. whatever is opposed to the Vedas will be considered as unauthentic and whatever conforms to the Vedas will be considered as authentic.

2. During this debate, if there is disagreement about the meaning of a mantra or pada, then the ancient seers' literature starting from Brahmā to Jaimini Muni, will be considered as evidence, and not otherwise. Furthermore, conformity with the Vedas, the laws of creation, evidence from practical life, experts' views, and knowledge and purity of one's own self, will be the main tools to determine truth or falsehood.

3. From each side 50 cultured, spiritual and intelligent scholars can be present in the debate.

4. 100 persons from both sides shall be issued entry passes for entry to the venue of the debate, and only authorised persons shall be allowed to enter and no one else.

5. Each of the (two) parties will submit its claim with supportive evidence in writing, and explain it to the other side orally as well as in written form.

6. Both sides can take up one issue each in their respective turn. It should be in written form and not otherwise.

7. During this debate, the statements of both sides will be recorded by three scribes. After verifying each one's submissions, all the three records shall finally be signed by both the parties and one such signed copy will be given to each party, the third copy will be handed over to the government for the record so that none could tamper with it.

8. I accept the suggestion of 'ten minutes' as

written in your letter, but it will be proper if these ten minutes are assigned for answering and only two minutes for putting a question.

9. Only both of us will be entitled to talk, to dictate, and to ask for the written statements to be read out, and no one else. The other members shall only listen to the debate attentively.

10. The bungalow of Khazanchi Ji, where I am staying, should be the venue for the debate. Because this place is neither mine nor yours.

11. For this debate, I will support the criticism of mūrtipujā (idol worship) and Purāṇas, etc. based on evidence from the Vedas and other ancient literature and you will oppose it.

12. Adherence to truth and abhorrence of falsehood, to the exclusion of unconstitutional language, stubbornness, obstinacy, wrong persistence, anger, bias, fear, shame, etc. should be the motto of both the parties, as this principle is followed by scholars.

13. Until we arrive at some decision, the debate will continue, and it will continue every day. This is because the main aim of learned scholars is to make the tasks initiated reach their logical end. The debate thus carried out for days or months together will also satisfy your eagerness for debate, otherwise not.

14. Both sides should ask for police arrangements, lest some uncultured people create obstacles during the debate.

15. The timings for such a debate should be daily from 5 pm to 8 pm, from the date of its commencement.

16. If I speak on one day, you will speak on the next day, and whoever speaks first on a particular day, will also sum up the debate at the end of that day. The listeners or readers of published documents should have the freedom to decide between right and wrong by themselves, in accordance with their knowledge and intelligence. So, they will be able to choose the right or wrong path.

Your letter was received yesterday by noon, and, therefore, the reply has been written today. Had it come in the morning, the reply would have been dictated by the evening itself. There are many mistakes in Sanskrit and Hindi in your letter, and the same will be highlighted when we meet.

Swami Dayanand Saraswati

Letter No. 182

To Pt. Angad Shastry

(Aśvina Kṛṣṇa 13, Saṁvat 1936 i.e. September 14, 1879)

This letter, written in Hindi, was sent from Shahjahanpur, as a counter reply to Pundit Angad Shastri and others. The original letter is quoted by Pt. Lekhram in his Urdu Biography of Swamiji (Hindi Edition, p. 515).

Om Namaḥ Sarvaśaktimate Parmeśvarāya!

[Meaning] Salutations to Almighty God!

Sub: Counter reply: Sh. Angad Shastri and others.

Your letter was written on Āśvina Kṛṣṇa 12, Saṁvat 1936 (Saturday) received on Āśvina Kṛṣṇa 13, Saṁvat 1936, (Sunday) at 11.30 AM. Its purport is clear. I am sure that the studies of the Śāstras can only be taken as a result of good deeds done in many past lives. If I come to the places of your choice, it will be an opportunity for you to create a lot of trouble. Now, if you wish to talk or listen to me here along with 50 high-minded religious and wise people chosen by you, I don't want to stop you. With regards to the rest, please do whatever makes you feel happy.

Swami Dayanand Saraswati

Letter No. 183

To Munshi Samartha Dan

(Āśvina Śukla 1, Saṁvat 1936 i.e. Sept. 17, 1879

This is the summary of a letter written in Hindi from Shahjahanpur. This letter is quoted by Pt. Lekhram in his Urdu Biography of Swami Dayanand (Hindi edition, p. 872).

I will write a letter to the Americans, touching upon all the points. I have already told them that it was an unconfirmed report that someone used to live on poison at Abu. That is why I have not mentioned it in my biography. Furthermore, regarding impossible things like, saying that a Sadhu (hermit) used to walk on the sea, I would never write things like that.

Swami Dayanand Saraswati

Letter No. 184

To Munshi Samaratha Dan

(Āśvina Śukla 1, Saṁvat 1936 i.e. September 17, 1879)

This is the summary of the letter written in Hindi from Shahjahanpur to Mumbai. This letter is quoted by Pt. Lekhram in his Urdu Biography of Swami Dayanand (Hindi edition, p. 518).

Reassurances have been given that Kunwar Munna Singh of Chalesar will raise subscriptions. Therefore, you should make your own efforts to raise as many subscriptions as you can. I will depart for Lucknow after eight days. Now I am feeling better.

Swami Dayanand Saraswati

Letter No. 185

To Babu Madho Lal of Danapur

(Āśvina Śukla 1, Saṁvat 1936 i.e. September 21, 1879)

This is the summary of the letter written in Hindi from Lucknow to Danapur. It is also quoted by Pt. Lekhram in the Biography of Swami Dayanand (Hindi edition, p. 518).

I reached Lucknow on September 18, 1879, in the evening from Shahjahanpur, and will proceed to Kanpur in the morning of September 24, 1879, Wednesday, and will further proceed to Furrukhabad the same day, and having rested there for a week to ten days, I will move to Kanpur. After a 2-4 days halt there, I will move to Danapur via Mirzapur, Kashi and Prayag by Kārtika Purṇamāsī. Nowadays, I am feeling much better than before.

Swami Dayanand Saraswati

Letter No. 186

To Pundit Sundar Lal Ram Narain

(September 21, 1879)

This letter, written in English, was sent from Lucknow. The original letter is preserved in Paropakarini Sabha.

Lucknow 21-9-1879

My dear Pundit Sundar Lal Ram Narain ji,

Please send all other books to Munshi Indermani Ji, Mohalla Deendarpura Moradabad, but keep one book, the Mahābhārata with you.

I arrived here on the 18th and will depart for Furrukhabad via Kanpur on the 24th by morning train and most probably will arrive there on the morning of 25th. I think I shall break my journey there for a week or ten days after which I shall go back to Kanpur and thence start to Allahabad of which I shall give you notice in due time.

You must in the meantime arrange my stay.

Yours sincerely

Swami Dayanand Saraswati

Letter No. 187

To Munshi Samaratha Dan

(Āśvina Vadi 11, Saturday, Saṁvat 1936 i.e. October 11, 1879)

This letter, written in Hindi, was sent from Kanpur to Mumbai. This letter is quoted in the Biography of Swami Dayanand by Pt. Lekhram (Hindi edition, p. 530).

For the printing press, Rs.1,000 has been raised from Furukhabad. Now we shall have our own printing press. You may also start raising subscriptions from Mumbai. My intention is to have our own printing press by Mārgaśīrṣa.

I will proceed for Prayag on Aśvina 2, Śukla 1 (Thursday) or October 16, 1879.

Swami Dayanand Saraswati

Letter No.188

To Babu Madho Lal

(Aśvina 2 Kṛṣṇa 12, Saṁvat 1936 i.e. October 12, 1879)

This letter, written in Hindi, was sent from Kanpur to Babu Madho Lal, Mantri, Arya Samaj Danapur, Bihar. This letter is quoted in the Biography of Swami Dayanand by Pt. Lekhram (see Hindi edition page 533).

Be happy Babu Madho Lal Ji, Mantri (Secretary) of the Arya Samaj!

I received many letters from you, but I have failed to reply as I have been busy travelling. Please prepare the advertisement, for which a specimen is enclosed. I will also go to Prayag on October 16, after which, I will write another letter to you. I will not go to Banaras (Kashi) now. From Mirzapur, I will proceed directly to Danapur, without breaking my journey anywhere in between. On receipt of my other letter, dispatch your letter to Mirzapur.

From Moradabad, you might have received a letter bearing an advertisement for a printing press, and accordingly, you might be making arrangements for raising funds for that purpose. From Furrukhabad Rs. 1,000 may have been raised. It may be known that this donation amount may be needed in Banaras in Mārgaśīrṣa when I go there. On my return from Danapur, I will be staying at Arra or some other place, as required by the prevailing circumstances. I will be returning to Banaras by Mārgaśīrṣa. So, I have left some space blank in the advertisement for the place, which you may fill in as soon as the final decision is taken for issuing the advertisement. Leaving a blank space for the date, will enable it to be filled on my arrival.

My place of stay should be one mile away from the city, and no further. For discourses, the place should be within the city. Please ensure that the area where I will reside is clean and free from disease. I will also attend the fair at Harihar, for which necessary arrangements for my stay should be made. I will write to you from Mirzapur afterwards.

Having reached Banaras next month, I will make a proposal for our own printing press, for which you should also raise funds from people you know in your area. For the time being, arrangements have been made for a six month stay at Banaras, and I feel that during this period the Vedabhāṣya and other pending books will be cleared for printing.

Swami Dayanand Saraswati

Letter No. 189

To Pt. Sundar Lal Ram Narain

(October 14, 1879)

This letter, written in Hindi, was sent from Kanpur to Allahabad. The original letter is preserved in the Paropakarini Sabha.

Be blessed Pundit Sundar Lal Ram Narain Ji!

I would like to inform you that I will be leaving this place (Kanpur) for Prayag on October 16. Kindly arrange my stay. I have already requested that some central place be chosen for my stay in the city and cantonment. near the railway station. The venue for lectures can be in the city. Also issue an advertisement(about my forthcoming visit), and space for a date should be left blank. If my accomodation is decided, the date should also be included, if not this can be filled in upon my arrival. I will be able to stay there for not more than seven days and the same period will be utilised for delivering as many lectures as possible.

Convey my blessings to all the members.

Swami Dayanand Saraswati

Letter No. 190

To Babu Madho Lal

(October 23 to 29, 1879)

This letter written in Hindi was sent from Mirzapur to Danapur, Bihar. The original letter is preserved in Paropakarini Sabha.

May you be happy Babu Madho Lal Ji!

I would like to inform you that having started from Prayag on October 13, 1879 (Aśvin Sudi 9, Thursday, Saṁvat 1936), I have reached Mirzapur, and am now staying in the garden of Seth Ram Rattan. What is your opinion (about my visiting your place)? I am not keeping well, but I have promised you that I will visit your place and so I must come. After my arrival the matter of holding lectures there will be decided. Even if lectures are not held, this will be an opportunity to hold discussions with the people like yourself. You told me that your people will come to receive me. They are free to come to receive me at the above-mentioned address within six days, because it is decided that on Kartik vadi Pratipada i.e. October 30, I will proceed to Dumrao or Arrah or Patna.

Please convey my blessings to all the people.

Swami Dayanand Saraswati

Letter No. 191

To Munshi Samaratha Dan

(Kārtika Kṛṣṇa 7, Saṁvat 1936 i.e. November 6, 1879)

This is the summary of the letter written in Hindi, sent from Danapur, Bihar to Mumbai.

(Probably) Colonel Olcott is not aware of the present condition of my health, that for the last ten months I have suffered from diarrhoea, and furthermore, that I have been attacked three times by severe fever, which subsided later. Although I have fully recovered now, the weakness still persists. Moreover, I am busy with many important assignments, which has left me with no spare time. Had there been only the work of writing my brief biography, I would have completed it and sent it by now.

Swami Dayanand Saraswati

Letter No. 192

To the Press Manager

(Kārtika Kṛṣṇa 7, Saṁvat 1936 i.e. November 6, 1879)

This is the summary of the letter, written in Hindi, sent from Danapur, Bihar to Mumbai. This letter is quoted by Pandit Lekhram in his Urdu Biography of Swami Dayanand on page 499.

Nowadays, lectures are being held daily in Danapur. Today is the fifth day of my stay. The (Arya) Samaj of this place and the people are very good. The arrangement of the Samaj is also excellent. From here on, I will proceed to the fair of Hariharkshetra. Afterwards, I will make it to Kashi to arrange for a printing press. I will be staying there (in Kashi) for up to a half or for the whole of the Chaitra month.

Swami Dayanand Saraswati

Letter No. 193

To Babu Madho Lal

(Kārtika Śudī 8, Saṁvat 1936 i.e. November 21, 1879)

This letter, written in Hindi, was sent from Kashi to Danapur. The original letter is preserved in Arya Samaj Danapur. Its copy has been published in Śrimad Dayanand Chitravali (3rd edition).

Be blessed Babu Madho Lal Ji!

I have joyfully and safely reached Kashi, and staying at Maharaja Vijay Nagar's Anand Garden, which is very good. The water and air here are fresh. It is well known that the residence in this garden is also excellent. On receipt of my letter, Lazarus Saheb made this arrangement for my stay. There is no garden in Kashi comparable to it.

Further news, if any, will be written to you, in due course. You may also please continue writing. Convey my namaste to all.

Swami Dayanand Saraswati

Letter No. 194

To Babu Ramadhar Vajpai

(Kārtika Śudī 11, Saṁvat 1936 i.e. November 24, 1879)

This letter, written in Hindi, was sent from Banaras to Lucknow. The original letter is preserved in the collections of Arya Samaj Lucknow.

May you prosper!

I have returned from Danapur and am lodging now-days in the garden of his late Highness the Maharaja of Vijyanagar at Banaras. I will write about the books that you told me about, which are located in Bombay and Moradabad. Try your best to treat the son of Munshi Indra Man, Narain Das, well. He wishes to go to Lucknow from Muradabad, to look for a copywriter, who uses printed lithographic paper. Please make such a copywriter available, if you can find one, as such a scribe is urgently required.

Swami Dayanand Saraswati

Letter No. 195

To Babu Madho Lal

(December 3, 1879)

This letter, written in Hindi, was sent from Kashi to Danapur. The original letter is preserved in the collection of Arya Samaj Danapur.

Be blessed Babu Madho Lal ji!

Till date, no material has been received from the printing press nor any reply from Pundit Sunder Lal. Please write to me about the rates, and send me a sample of the typeface and the cost of the royal press. This should be done as quickly as possible. We may have to take three to four samples of different typefaces from all the presses. Also get the rates of the case, wood, etc. in quotations from them.

Munshi Bhaktawar Singh, Secretary, Arya Samaj, Shahjahanpur has agreed to join us after quitting his government job. He will organize the entire press work, at a salary of Rs. 30 per month. He is a gentleman and well versed in three languages. He is also familiar with all the printing press work. Advertisements have been printed, and these are being sent to you.

Swami Dayanand Saraswati

Letter No. 196

To Babu Madho Lal

(Mārgaśīrṣa Śukla 2, Monday, Saṁvat 1936, i.e. December 15, 1879)

This letter, originally written in Urdu, was sent from Kashi to Danapur. The letter is quoted by Pandit Lekhram in his Urdu Biography of Swami Dayanand on page 838.

The following English Sahebs will be staying with me in the Garden of Raja Vijay Nagar (near Mahmood Ganj) at Banaras on 15th December 1879. If you wish to meet them, please reach here by the 16th. Please also inform Mahabir Prasad and others at Chhapra about it.

The names of the English Sahebs who shall visit Banaras on 15th December are:

Colonel H.S. Olcott Saheb (American),

Madame H.P. Blavatsky Sahiba,

A.P. Sinnett Saheb,

Manager Pioneer, Allahabad.

In addition to the above people, some of their colleagues (two or three) may also come.

Swami Dayanand Saraswati

Letter No. 197

To Munshi Samartha Dan

(Mārgaśīrṣa Śukla 4, Wednesday, Saṁvat 1936 i.e. December 17, 1879)

This summary of the letter, written in Hindi, was sent from Banaras to Mumbai. This summary is quoted by Pt. Lekhram in the Biography of Swami Dayanand (Hindi edition, p. 873).

Colonel Olcott and other American people came to see me on 15th December 1879 and my discussions with them have commenced.

Swami Dayanand Saraswati

Letter No. 198

To Mr. Bal, the Magistrate, Kashi

(Mārgaśīrṣa Śudī 8, Sunday, 1936 i.e. December 21, 1879)

This letter, written in Hindi, was sent to the Magistrate of Kashi, Mr. Bal. It is quoted on page 559 of the Biography of Swami Dayanand edited by Pt. Ghasi Ram. This letter is evidence that the British used to impose a ban on the lectures of Swami Dayanand from time to time.

Sir,

Would you please inform me of the grounds on which you passed an order prohibiting me from delivering lectures until your further order. A copy of the order is enclosed herewith for your information. I shall be obliged if you could also inform me of the period for which this ban on lectures will continue. Anticipating your reply at your convenience.

Swami Dayanand Saraswati

Letter No. 199

To Shri Jaisraj Goti Ram

(Mārgaśīrṣa Śudī 10, Tuesday, 1936 i.e. December 13, 1879)

This letter, written on a postcard in Hindi, was sent from Banaras to Kolkata. The original letter is preserved in the collection of Yudhisthir Mimansaka.

To

Jais Ram Goti Ram

C/O Kothi of Jugal Kishore Vilas Rai,

Afim Ka Chauraha, Kolkata.

Be blessed Jaisraj Goti Ram Ji!

Munim Bhaktawar Singh has left for Kolkata. Upon his arrival, please hand over my letter to him.

Munshi Saheb!

You are procuring one Royal Printing press, but a small printing press for the setting of initial proofs is also required. Please purchase these materials in consultation with the editor of the Amrit Bazar Patrika, as he is well conversant with this subject. He will also help you get a good quality product at reasonable rates. One Bengali gentleman here wishes to sell his printing press, fonts, etc. which I will be inspecting in a day or two, and will purchase it, if found suitable for our work.

Swami Dayanand Saraswati

Letter No. 200

To Pt. Sundar Lal Ram Narain

(Mārgaśīrṣa Śukla 12, Saṁvat 1936)

This letter, written in Hindi, was sent from Banaras to Allahabad. The original letter is preserved in the Paropakarini Sabha.

May you be happy Pt. Sundar Lal Ram Narain Ji!

Pundit Mandan Ram expressed his desire to work with me due to his poor financial condition. Therefore, please ask him if he is willing to join me at Kashi, where he will be most welcome. Please inform me also, if type fonts for the printing press are readily available, as these are urgently required here.

As you might have met Colonel Olcott and Madame Blavatsky, please tell me about your meeting with them.

Swami Dayanand Saraswati

Letter No. 201

To Munshi Inderman Jiva

(Pauṣa Kṛṣṇa 13, Saṁvat 1936 i.e. January 10, 1880)

This letter, written in Urdu, was sent from Banaras to Muradabad. The original letter is in the custody of Lala Bhagvat Sahaya, the grandson of Munshi Ji in Muradabad. A copy of this letter was procured by Mamraj Ji on Nov. 10, 1926, from him.

Be blessed Inderman Jiva Saheb! Namaste!

599 copies of Sandhyā Bhāṣya have reached you. As per your request, I am searching for the Chandrikā, and I will be dispatching it to you as soon as it is available. News from here is that all materials for a printing press, including papers, ink and proof sheets, etc. have been received from Kolkata. Five mann (2 quintals) of type materials have also been shipped by Raja Saheb from Muradabad, and eight mann (3 quintals and 20 kg) more materials have been purchased from Kolkata. In brief, all arrangements for the printing press shall be completed in a month's time.

It is proposed that firstly we should first get the śikṣā book (book on phonology) printed. It is small and has been prepared very recently. Later on, we shall take up other books, which are still under preparation. When the printing press becomes fully functional, then the printing work of the Vedabhāṣya will be shifted from Mumbai to Banaras.

We are facing financial hardships here. This printing

press has been set up in anticipation of financial help from you. A beginning has been made, with the hope that the end will be taken care of. Therefore, you are all requested to approach Lala Shyam Sunder to raise funds from possible sources, and transfer these funds to me in a lump sum, so that the setting up of a printing press becomes an easy endeavour.

Now, what is the proposal for starting a newspaper? In my opinion, it will be good if we can have a trilingual paper published, or whatever you prefer. Please write to me about your opinion on starting the newspaper. Everything else is as usual here. Until now the Pandits of this place have not come forward for the debates. I shall inform you about further developments in due course.

Swami Dayanand Saraswati

Letter No. 202

To Col. Olcott and Blavatsky

(Mārgaśīrṣa Vadi 6, Saṁvat 1936 or November 23, 1880)

This is a summary of the letter, written in Hindi, which was sent from Banaras to Mumbai. We find mention of this letter in a notice published by the Oriental press Mumbai on 31 March 1872 exposing the irregularities of Theosophists.

I do not accept, nor ever accepted, or will ever accept the rules of any other Society or Samaj (institution) other than the Veda-based ancient (Sanātan) Indian (Āryavartīya) Dharma. This is a firm resolve of my soul. I cannot break away from (Vedic) Dharma even if I have to risk my life.

Please exclude my name, wherever you have incorporated it, out of your own sweet will, in the list of members (of the Theosophical Society).

Swami Dayanand Saraswati

Letter No. 203

To Chaudhary Laxman Das

(Māgha Kṛṣṇa 1, Saṁvat 1936 i.e. January 28, 1880)

This letter, written in Hindi, was sent from Banaras. The Urdu copy of this letter was discovered by Pt. Mamraj from the collection of letters of Lala Ram Sharan Das of Meerut. The copy is preserved in the collection of Pt. Bhagavadatta.

May you be happy Chaudhary Laxman Das ji!

Namaste!

The shoes sent by you earlier were also of a big size, and the ones which you have just sent now, are even bigger, so are of no use. It might have cost you eight annas for the parcel and four annas to register. Probably it would have cost you less, had they had been sent by the goods train. Good quality shoes are available everywhere. In the future, unless I ask for something, please don't take the trouble of sending anything to me. Nothing more to write from here. Everything is as usual in Banaras. Here, no Pundit has come forward for the debate. Further developments, if any, will be informed to you. There is nothing more to write.

Swami Dayanand Saraswati

Letter No. 204

To Munshi Manohar Lal

(Māgha 30, Saṁvat 1936 i.e. February10,1880)

This letter, written in Hindi, was sent from Banaras to Patna. This letter was copied by Sadhu Mahesh Prasad Maulvi Fazil, Prof. Kashi Hindu Vishvadyalaya from its original copy attached with the Hindi translation of the Quran rendered by Munshi Manohar Lal Rais when Sadhu Mahesh visited Ajmer to verify the translation. This copy was passed on by him to Pt. Bhagavadatta along with his letter dated 7.8.1943. Here it may also be informed that Swami Ji had got the Hindi translation of the Quran done by Munshi Manohar Lal Rais, Gurhatta, Patna, who was a great scholar of Arabic.

May you be happy Pundit Manohar Lal Ji!

You may send send the complete Quran or only the checked and verified portion as soon as the necessary checking and verification has been done. I am having to to consult it time and again. I am sending the complete set of papers through Jagannath. Keep them safe.

Swami Dayanand Saraswati

Letter No. 205

To the Editor, Theosophist

(Māgha Kṛṣṇa 30, Saṁvat 1936 or February 10, 1880)

This letter was written by Swami Ji in reply to a letter written by Padri Gray of Ajmer, which was earlier published in the Theosophist Journal.

During the meeting at Ajmer, I have requested Padri Saheb to come to the Meeting venue for the debate, which he declined. Therefore, I don't think it proper to have a debate with him now. However, if some learned Bishop is ready for debate through your newspaper, I will certainly do it.

Swami Dayanand Saraswati

Letter No. 206

To Lala Mool Raj

(Māgha Śukla 6, Saṁvat 1936 i.e. February 16, 1880)

This letter, written in Hindi, was sent from Banaras to Lala Mool Raj, M.A, Additional Assistant Commissioner, Multan (now in present Pakistan). The English version of the original letter was published in the Gurukula Magazine, Gujranwala, Oct.-Dec. 1908, p. 248. The original letter fell to the menace of mice due to the negligence of Lala Rajaram.

Namaste! Your letter dated 11th February 1880 was received. It gave me immense pleasure to hear of your appointment as an Extra Assistant Commissioner. May God promote you still higher.

As regards matters over here, the Lt. Governor has as yet sent us no reply. The Magistrate Saheb verbally tells us to commence lecturing but hesitates passing an order in writing. We have come to know that Lt. Governor forwarded our application to the Magistrate for his remarks, and the Magistrate returned it (about one week ago) saying that he had stopped the lectures on account of the Muharram procession, lest riots break out. We expect to get a reply in a day or two. We have not thought it proper to commence lectures without a written order of the Local Government. This will settle the matter once for all.

We will commence our series of lectures with great earnestness. A printing press, named Vedic Press has been started. A notice to that effect has been sent separately today. Namaste to all.

Swami Dayanand Saraswati

Letter No. 207

To Mukand Singh

This is the summary of the letter, written in Hindi, sent from Banaras to Chhalesar. This summary is quoted in 'Pitṛ Yajña Mīmānsā' authored by Bhumitra Sharma printed at Bhaskar Press Meerut on Bhādrapad second, Badi 1, Saṁvat 1974.

The Satyarth Prakash, which has been printed by Raja Jai Krishan Das Ji, has content which goes against the Vedas, in some places. With regards to Śrāddha, the provision of meat and Śrāddha for the dead, they both go against the Vedas. As you must know, in the book Pañcha Mahāyajña Vidhi which was published in Śaka 1976 (or Vikrami Saṁvat 1931 or 1874 A.D.), at the Arya Printing Press Mumbai, I criticised the practice of Śrāddha for the dead. This book was published a year before the Satyarth Prakash was printed by Raja Ji. Therefore, please don't undertake such an act as it is against the Vedas.

Swami Dayanand Saraswati

Letter No. 208

To Col. H.S. Olcott

This is a summary of the letter, written in Hindi, sent from Banaras. It was published in 'The Theosophist' in April 1880 i.e. Chaitra 197 on page 190.

Despite being anxious that my autobiography, which you will be publishing in your journal, has not as yet been drafted, I (must tell you that I) have not been able to find the time necessary to do it. But, I will try to send the draft to you as soon as possible.

Swami Dayanand Saraswati

Letter No. 209

To Raja Shiva Prasad

(Chaitra Śdi 12, The Tuesday, Saṁvat 1937 i.e. April 22, 1880)

This letter, written in Hindi, was sent from Banaras. The original letter is preserved in the collection of Pt. Bhagvadatta.

Be happy Raja Shiva Prasad Ji!

I received your letter dated Chaitra Śukla 11 (or April 21, 1880), Wednesday, and came to know its purport. That day (16th December) our discussion remained incomplete due to a lack of time at our end. Neither was I able to complete my point nor were you able to listen to it thoroughly, because you had come to meet those Sahebs, and that was your main interest. Afterwards, there have been no further interactions to facilitate further talks on the matter. Now, I am likely to proceed to the western side within the next eight to ten days. During this period you can meet me as per your convenience. We can discuss it at some other time also. I would have met you myself, but my busy schedule doesn't permit it. You will appreciate that by having face-to-face discussions, the issue can be understood straightaway unlike through correspondence.

Your Question: What is your belief?

My Answer: Vedic

Your Question: What do you mean by Veda?

My Answer:. Saṁhitas

Your Question: Don't you consider Upaniṣads as Veda?

My Answer: Iśāvāsya Upaniṣad is included into Veda (being the 40th chapter of Yajurveda). The rest of the Upaniṣads are the part of the Brahmaṇa texts, so they cannot be called Veda, as they are written by seers and so authorship by God cannot be assigned to them.

Your Question: Don't you consider Brāhmaṇa Granthas as Veda?

My Answer: No, as Veda is the knowledge of creation made by God, so its authorship can be assigned to God only. Man-made knowledge cannot be called Veda. The Brāhmaṇa texts are elucidations on the Vedas by seers as their authors, whereas Saṁhitas deal directly with the knowledge of God i.e. His creation. Like, whatever emanates from Omniscient God (Īśvara), being the infallible truth can be acceptable, the same does not hold true of man-made knowledge, emanating from those who are not omniscient and so cannot be accepted. But Brāhamaṇa texts are also acceptable to the extent that they are in conformity with the Vedas, otherwise they cannot. Vedas are homo-mensura (svataḥ prāmāṇa) i.e. self-evident, whereas Brāhmaṇa need Vedas as evidence to prove their authenticity. From the aforementioned, it becomes evident that Brāhmaṇa texts contrary to Veda can be discarded, but the Veda, even if contrary to Brāhmaṇa texts, cannot be discarded, because Veda is to be accepted by all means.

Regarding the issue of considering Brāhmaṇas on a par with the Veda, one may refer to the chapters dealing with 'The Origin of Vedas', Eternity of Vedas' and 'Subject matter of Vedas' of 'Ṛgvedādibhāṣya Bhūmikā (p. 9-88)' written by the me, the author of these words, in order to find an answer. Therein, I have stated my opinion clearly on all such issues. Having gone through it, you will be able to arrive at a decision similar to mine.

Swami Dayanand Saraswati

Letter No. 210

To Raja Shiva Prasad

(Chaitra Vadi 7, Saṁvat 1937 i.e. May 1,1880)

This letter, written in Hindi, was sent from Banaras.

May you be happy Raja Shiv Prasad Ji!

I have received your letter and got to know its intentions. What I could conclude going through your letter is that you are unable to understand the intended sense of the books right from the Vedas to Pūrva Mimānsā. That is why you failed miserably to understand what I intended to say in my Vedabhāṣya Bhūmikā as well. Had you learnt it from me, you would have been able to understand it a little bit.

However, should you desire to have answers to your questions, you should approach Swami Vishudhananda Saraswati and Bal Shastri Ji. They may be of some help to you. Just think, without having a first-hand knowledge of these books, how can you know about the internal relationship between the Vedas and the Brāhmaṇas? The intents and the objectives of the Vedas should be regarded as being independent authorities and the Brāhmaṇas should be viewed as being dependent on the Vedas for their authority. Without proper insight into all these issues, you will remain ignorant of the truth.

Swami Dayanand Saraswati

Letter No. 211

To Munshi Bhaktawar Singh

(Vaiśākha Kṛṣṇa 30, Saṁvat 1937 i.e. May 9, 1880)

This letter, written in Hindi, was sent from Lucknow to Banaras. This letter was discovered by Mamraj Ji from an old collection of letters retained by Lala Ram Sharan Das of Meerut. The original copy is preserved in the collection of Pt. Bhagvadatta, BA. This letter mentions Swami Ji's departure from Lucknow to Kanpur. This event has been missed by his biographies.

May you be happy Munshi Bhaktawar Singh Ji!

I hope you might have received the letter sent to you yesterday. Today, the Arya Samaj will start functioning here (in Lucknow). I will be delivering lectures for two days. On Wednesday, I will stay here. On Thursday morning, I will be proceeding to the Kanpur Cantonement. Good-quality kharbooza (melons) are not available here in the market. Whatever is available is not of a sweet quality like that of Kashi (Banaras) due to the effect of the monsoons. I have told Ramadhar Bajpai to send you good quality kharbooza (melon), whenever they reach the markets here.

Please send the following books to Pundit Inder Narain:

Ṛgveda: 8th & 10th issues

Yajurveda: 8th, 10th and 12th issues

Satyarth Prakash: 1 copy

Sanskāra Vidhi: 1 copy

Varṇochāraṇa Śikṣā: 1 copy

Sanskrit Vākya Prabodha: 1 copy

Bhrānti Nivāraṇa: 1 copy

Aryoddeṣya Ratanmālā: 1 copy

However Bhimsena has not left the leaves of 'Strain̩a-taddhita' here. Please also let me know where one should start writing on a particular leaf from, and please show me what has already been penned down and to what extent, by marking the papers properly.

Please take note of all letters, as the same instructions will not be repeated.

Pundit Inder Narain deposited Rs. 5 with me, out of which one anna and 2 paise are for the postal charges and Rs. 4, 14 annas, 2 paise are for the cost of books. If the postal charges are more than one anna and 2 paise, then it can be recovered from him. Furthermore, whatever books you send to Ramdhar Bajpai, please tell him to pass on those books to Pundit Inder Narain quickly.

The Brahmachari, who used to cook meals in Kashi, has left Kashi and has arrived here to stay with me. Bhairava Kahar gives one rupee to Narsingh Thapa. Bhim Sen can go and meet him at the Rani of Nepali's palace and he will hand over one rupee and get due acknowledgement for having done so. He (Bhairava) should be introduced to the peon, so that whenever Bhairava gives money for him, it may be passed on to him.

Swami Dayanand Saraswati

Letter No. 212

To Munshi Bhaktawar Singh

(Vaiśākha Śukla 12, the Friday, Saṁvat 1937 i.e. May 21, 1880)

This letter, written in Hindi, was sent from Farrukhabad. The original letter is preserved in the collection of Pt. Bhagvadatta.

Be happy Munshi Bhaktawar Singh Ji!

After reaching safely at Farrukhabad having travelled from Kanpur on Baisakh Śudi 11 (May 20, 1880) I am staying in the garden of Ram Charna Kali Charan at Toka Ghat, Farrukhabad. You must be busy doing what was instructed to you to do in the last letter. I hope that the typing fonts etc. have arrived from Calcutta and that the printing work of the Vedabhāṣya has already been started. If not received, please immediately move to Calcutta to get the type fonts so that the printing work of the Vedabhāṣya may be started early. The printing work of the book 'Sandhi Viṣaya' should also be undertaken quickly. Please send a copy of the 'Vyavahāra Bhānu, if it has come out of the press. Please do all the work as instructed in my last letter. Also, reply to my last letter. Convey my namaste to all.

Swami Dayanand Saraswati

Letter No. 213

To Munshi Bhaktawar Singh

(Jyeṣṭh Śukla 6, Saṁvat 1937 i.e. June 14, 1880)

This letter, written in Hindi, was sent from Farrukhabad to Benaras. This letter was recovered from the collection of Lala Ram Sharan Das Rais of Meerut by Mamraj Ji. The original letter is preserved in the collection of Pt. Bhagvaddatta.

Be joyful Munshi Bhaktawar Singh Ji!

This is to acknowledge receipt of your letter dated June 10 (i.e. Jyeṣṭha Śukla 2, the Thursday, Saṁvat 1937). I have been briefed on events over there. When I left Banaras one and a half months ago, there was a small part of the Vyavahāra Bhānu that had not been printed. After one and a half months, has any progress been made? Also, only one frame of the book 'Sandhi Viṣaya' has been printed so far. So the Vyavahāra Bhānu is incomplete, the Sandhi Viṣaya has only been printed up to one frame. Tell me, were you able to complete any book so that it is now ready for reading? Please get the pending frame of the Vyavahāra Bhānu printed now and send it wherever it needs to be dispatched. Moreover, the work relating to the Vedabhāṣya should also continue unhindered.

I appreciate that an arrangement for a foundry has been made. I am well aware of the lethargic attitude of Abhay Lal and Chunni Lal. We may get orders related to the foundry from rich clients. Please get Bhimsen to bring three gold coins (Ashrafi) and some gold, or if the weavers create problems, to tell them that we will sell the product directly on the market. You can sell it through Babu Avinash Lal, Chowk Khambe Wala, who is a member of the Arya Samaj. Keep the proceeds from this sale safely. There is no need to spend it for some other purpose because it is earmarked for the weavers only.

I have seen the frame of the Vedabhāṣya, and you may also compare it. It is half a finger less than that of Mumbai. Will it be suitable for binding? The bottom margin is also comparatively less. It should be proportionately equal on all sides like that of the Mumbai printing. However, for want of it being the same size as the paper, we have no other choice but to go for it. The critique of Shiva Prasad is ready. It is entitled 'Bhramochedan' i.e. (The Elimination of Confusion). It should be sent for corrections. Change 'rachitā' on the title page into 'rachitaḥ'.

Has Daftari left his job? I feel now that (at last) the work will happen smoothly and you will take care of it. Yesterday, the Arya Samaj was set up in Farrukhabad. Books are to be sent now in the name of Jais Raj Goti Ram at Farrukhabad. These may be sent via Kalu Ram Sewa Ram and sent to the same shop addressed to the Kanpur Cantonment by train. From there, they may be transferred to Farrukhabad. Also, write him a letter telling him to transmit them to Farrukhabad. In the event a direct train is introduced for Farrukhabad, then the supply (of books) may be made directly to Jais Ram Goti Ram at Farrukhabad.

Please reply whether you have made a payment to Inder Mani or not. If not, please reimburse his dues. During my Lucknow stay, I wrote to you to send all the books required by Ramdhar Bajpai, but you failed to do so. This was maybe because of your busy schedule of work. This should not be repeated. He has complained about it. I am forwarding the same to you for your information. I shall inform you about my departure.

The book on Sandhi Viṣaya corrected by me is also being sent. The quality of the ink for its printing should be the same as that of the Vedabhāṣya. Recently, new issues have come which will be checked for correctness. Please add an errata page prepared by Bhimsen to the Vayahārabhānu, because there are numerous mistakes in it. Because the paper used in the printing of the Vedabhāṣya is of a shorter size, paste a notice on the title page that such large paper is not available for the printing of the Vedabhāṣya as it was available only in Mumbai. Therefore, it will be printed on what is currently available. I am happy and I hope you are also there. I also wish for the smooth functioning of the Arya Samaj.

Please advise Bhim Sen to prepare well for talks. He should pursue his study, teaching, and research in a careful manner. Convey my namaste to Pundit Sube Rao and Hari Pundit. Has Pundit Amar Nath recovered from his illness or not? Please report all news to me from your end on every 8th day. I will also write to you whenever I feel it necessary.

Swami Dayanand Saraswati

Letter No. 214

To Munshi Bhaktawar Singh

(Āṣāḍha Kṛṣṇa 2, Saṁvat 1937 i.e. June 24, 1880)

This letter, written in Hindi, was sent from Farrukhabad to Banaras. The original letter was preserved in the collection of Pt. Bhagavaddatta.

May you be happy Munshi Bhaktawar Singh ji!

I will send Raja Shiva Prasad's reply today by registered post. Please acknowledge receipt. Bhimsen should first check this book and make things clear to the compositor so that no mistakes can creep in. The note should be printed as it is. Get 2000 copies of it printed. You can dispatch it along with the Vedabhāṣya to the places you feel necessary. You may send it to all (Arya Samajs) as well as to Sanyasis. Also, one copy each may be sent to those subscribers of the Vedabhāṣya who are worthy of it. Do send it to all Colleges, Government Schools, and Government Libraries.

I have instructed Seth Nirbhay Ram to send the lead type, as per your requisition and the same will come from Calcutta. But, first, send Rs 100 as a deposit to Jaissi Ram Gutt. Your requirements will be met out of this deposit. You have informed me that Abhey Ram Chunni Lal does not manage the finances that are properly deposited with him. So, I have made an arrangement with a rich person at Kashi for managing the funds deposited with him. You may now deposit money with him. Keep a balance of Rs. one hundred with Abhey Ram Chunni Lal, so that our dealings may continue. Later, on Diwali, you may settle your account finally. We have received the parcel that was sent by you in an instact state, but I wonder why its postal charges are very high? Please award Rs. 3 to the weaver who made this scarf and shawl.

I am well aware that you work wholeheartedly. Don't be mistaken by the repetition in my writing. This is because you don't distinguish between your work and my work. You have asked for papers of the 'Sandhi Viṣaya' and the 'Vedabhāṣya', which could not be sent, as I was preoccupied with giving a reply to Shiva Prasad. Bhairava Kahar, who came along with me, has stolen Re one and 8 annas and Rs. 2 and 8 annas from my pen holder. Therefore, he has been fired after the payment of his monthly dues and 13 annas which went towards his return fare.

Please don't make the contents (of the book) known until this Bhramochedan book comes out of the Press. Upon its publication, one copy each may be given to the Ruler of Kashi, Raja Shiva Prasad, Vishuddhanand, Bal Sastri, and for the Library of Rai Shankar Prasad, and also to Pundit Sube Rao and Hari Pundit. You may distribute it among those whom you deem fit and suitable for it. The balance may be sold out. Please convey my namaste to all. I am happy here and hope for the same at your end.

Swami Dayanand Saraswati

Letter No. 215

To Rama Bai

(Āṣāḍha Śukla 6, Saṁvat 1937 i.e June 28, 1880)

This letter, written in Sanskrit, was written from Meerut to Pandita Ramabai in Calcutta.

Ramabai was born on 23 April 1858 in the Canara district of British India (now in Karnataka). Her Family belonged to the Mala Kattemane Dongare Family. Her father, Anant Shastri, was an intellectual Brahmin, who from his study of Hindu texts, believed that women should be educated. His second wife, Ramabai's mother, Lakshmibai, was a child bride at nine years of age. Against the prevailing Hindu traditions, he decided to educate her. The village Brahmins responded by ostracising him, so Shastri left the village to make a home in the forest. The family moved from place to place. Whenever he could, her father would lecture on the need for female education. He taught Ramabai to read and write Sanskrit, as well as how to interpret Vedic texts. By the age of twelve, Ramabai had memorised 18,000 verses from the Puranas. Besides Sanskrit, Ramabai learned the Marathi, Kanarese, Hindustani, and Bengali languages. When her parents died in the 1877 famine, Ramabai and her brother decided to continue their father's work. She and her brother travelled all over India. Ramabai's fame as a lecturer reached Calcutta, where the pundits invited her to speak. In 1878, Calcutta University conferred on her the title of Pandita, as well as the highest title of Saraswati in recognition of her interpretations of various Sanskrit works.

She came in contact with Swami Ji. Swami Ji wanted her

to join the Arya Samaj and work for the education and reformation of women while remaining a celibate. After the death of her brother in 1880, Ramabai married a Bengali lawyer, Bipin Behari Medhvi and they had a daughter whom they named Mano. Medhvi was a Sudra, so her marriage was inter-caste. But as ill-luck would have it, Medhvi died. After Medhvi's death, Ramabai moved to Pune where she founded Arya Mahila Samaj under the influence of Swami Dayanand Saraswati. The purpose of the society was to promote the cause of women's education and deliverance from the oppression of child marriage. When in 1882 a commission was appointed by the Government of India to look into education, Ramabai gave evidence before it. In 1883, Ramabai was awarded a scholarship to train as a teacher in England. During her stay in England, she was converted to Christianity and joined the Anglican Church and thus Swamiji's plans to set up a women's wing of the Arya Samaj to look into the cause of women empowerment was plagued.

May God bless Ramabai, one of the noblest, well-read, and studious of ladies. Here everything is going well, and I hope all is even more better at your end. It gave me immense pleasure to hear about your scholarship. I am writing this letter to tell you about my mission and I would like your response as soon as possible.

I want to know about your future plans. Do you plan to live a life of a celibate as often talked about? Is it a fact that you deliver lectures to the public? I have also heard that you want to choose a life partner of similar Guṇa (merit), Karma (action) and Svabhāva (nature). Is it true?

My opinion is that you can contribute more to the welfare and upliftment of women as a celibate like lady scholars like Gargi etc. than as a married woman because there are many restrictions on married women. In light of all these reasons, would you prefer to lead a normal married life like other ladies or to work for the education of girls and women? Why don't you travel outside Bengal? I think a widely travelled person can contribute more to the welfare of society than a person who remains confined to one place.

If you want to visit this place, you are welcome. Your travel expenses will be reimbursed. If so, let us know in advance about your arrival programme, so that the necessary arrangements for your stay may be made here. Moreover, if you want to take a lecture tour to various places, the people of Meerut would be happy to sponsor your lecture tours. My postal address is:

Swami Dayanand Saraswati

C/o Babu Chedi Lal Gumasta Kamsaryat,

Meerut Cantonment, Meerut

There is nothing more required for a learned lady.

Swami Dayanand Saraswati

Letter No. 216

To Pundit Gopal Rao Hari

(Āṣāḍha Kṛṣṇa 8, the Wednesday, Saṁvat 1937 i.e. June 30, 1880)

This letter, written in Hindi, was sent from Farrukhadabad to Benaras. The original letter was with Pt. Bhagvaddatta which was passed on to Mahesh Prasad. From Mahesh Prasad, it reached Mamraj on 20.1.1951.

May you be happy Pundit Gopal Rao Hari!

I hope you will duly accept the following duties assigned to you:

1. For the Mīmānsaka Upasabhā, the following five members have been appointed: You yourself, Babu Ji, Lala Jagan Nath Prasad, Lala Ramcharan, and Lala Nirbhey Ram and in their absence Lala Narain Dass Mukhi, Lala Har Narain, Purohit Munni Lal, Lala Kali Charan, and one of the sons of Lala Nirbhayaram, or any of the three who is available.

2. If possible, you should also deliver a lecture at the Arya Samaj, if you are there.

3. As the monthly issue will be arranged by you, please make the necessary corrections if needed.

Swami Dayanand Saraswati

Letter No. 217

To Shyam ji Krishna Varma

(Āṣāḍha Kṛṣṇa 6, the Tuesday, Saṁvat 1937 i.e. July 13, 1880)

This letter, written in Sanskrit, was sent from Ajmer to England. Its English translation was published in England in 'Ethinium' magazine by Prof. Monier Williams. In India also the same English translation was subjected to Hindi translations from time to time. The present English translation is based on the original Sanskrit letter preserved at the Paropakarini Sabha. The copy of the original letter was published by Diwan Bahadur Har Bilas Sarda in Dayanand Granthmala Centenary Edition.

A lot of blessings from Swami Dayanand Saraswati to my best disciple Shyam Ji Krishna Varma who is a noble Arya Scholar, dedicated to treading the Vedic path, ready to preach the duties ordained in the Vedas and to set aside what is anti-Vedic. He is a prolific speaker who uses languages decked with wise sayings and is always engaged in receiving and imparting knowledge and who is honoured by all good scholars.

We are fine and pray for your wellbeing over there.

Having been disappointed for a long time due to the absence of any letter on your part, this letter is being written to you in the hope that on receiving a quick reply from you soon, that I may become happy once again.

What type of people live over there? What kinds of flora, fauna, and environment do they have there? How are you? Is the purpose of your trip being served? How many people are learning Sanskrit from you? What subjects do they opt for? What is your monthly income and expenditure there? What are your study and teaching timings? When will you decide to come over here? What is the reason behind your name and fame not spreading as quickly across the nations as it did here? Is it because of the distance, that you have not been able to come here? Or have you not had the chance as you are too preoccupied with your studies? If it is so, I would like to advise you not to come back without taking up the task of delivering lectures on the Vedas upon the completion of your studies. This is because earning a good name and fame is more beneficial than earning money. What are the views of Prof. Monier Williams and Max Mueller about the Vedas? What about their will and dedication for the cause of Vedas? Is there any institution backed by the Theosophical society for the propagation of Vedas in London? Have you ever met the Queen and visited the House of Commons? Convey my namaste to Prof. Monier Williams and inquire about his health on my behalf. Let me know about his reaction and give all the information worth mentioning whether enquired by me or not. There is nothing more to say to such an accomplished scholar.

Swami Dayanand Saraswati

Letter No. 218

To Ramabai

(Āṣāḍha Śukla, 15, Saṁvat 1937 i.e. July 21, 1880)

This letter, written in Sanskrit, was sent to Calcutta.

May God bless Ramabai, who is faultless, well-versed in the Śāstras, decked with knowledge, who has set an example of scholarship among the uneducated women of India, who expresses her views through articles which are appreciated by experts in the field, and who is very straightforward and loving.

Here everything is fine, and I hope for better things at your end. I was happy to receive your affectionate letter. Hope you wouldn't mind if I give you some more trouble. It's with regret that the letter sent in anticipation of happy news at your end, was followed by your reply evoking both grief and joy. I don't know why. Your straightforwardness in the letter is the cause of happiness, but the news of the sad demise of your brother is painful. I hope you will be able to bear this unbearable loss. What is your place of birth, age, and education? Do you know any foreign language in addition to Sanskrit? Where do you come from? Where do your family members live? Do you have any other brother and sister other than the one who was ill? Was the latter your elder or younger brother? Do you have any of your surviving family members to accompany you, or are you now completely alone? It was a coincidence like the story of crow and fruit that my letter and sorrow descended together. But I am convinced that scholars like you can come out of this grief. If you need travel expenses, let me know without hesitation how much money you need. Don't think that you are a stranger. If you have made arrangements, then there is no need to write about it, you will be reimbursed for the expenses as soon as you reach here.

You have mentioned two options with regards to your arrival here. According to the first option, you are supposed to reach here after a month. I think that this also suits me. I am planning to stay here for 25 days. If you happen to come here within this period, we shall be able to meet. Afterwards, you will be intimated of my itinerary. I think what I have said is enough for a scholar like you.

Swami Dayanand Saraswati

Letter No. 219

To Pundit Bhim Sen

(Āṣāḍha Kṛṣṇa 2, 1936, i.e. July 23, 1880, Friday)

This letter was written in Hindi. In this letter, Swami Ji talks about the will document prepared for the foundation of the Paropakarini Sabha in Ajmer. The original letter is preserved in the collection of Pt. Bhagvadatta.

May you be happy Pundit Bhim Sen ji!

Now, after an interval of eight days, you have stopped writing letters regularly. Please write regularly informing me about how many books have been printed in a week, what tasks have been accomplished, what is being done now, and what more is planned for the next week. Before you take up writing a letter do get inputs from Munshi ji about the number of books printed during the last eight days. As Munshi ji tells us about the income from the sale proceeds every month, occasionally get inputs on this score too and tell Munshi Ji to speak freely and without any reservations.

You should resign from your government job. You are welcome to join us for life or for as long as you can. We may also ask your advice even after you are relieved of your work. All signatories to the will document are from the Arya Samaj. They will not do any harm to him. Munshi (Bakhtawar Sing) Ji is also a man of integrity and will not do anything against Dharma. It has been laid down in the 'will document' that the members of Sabha are obliged to act according to the provisions of the will. I have reserved the right to amend the 'will', if necessary, and to appoint a new member or oust any existing one. Such provisions have been made for the proper functioning of the Sabha so that it may achieve its goals. These members are friends of Munshi Ji. They are all scholars and dharmic. They don't entertain any ill-will against anybody, so there is no possibility of them working against Munshi ji. Moreover, dharmic people are always dharma-loving and oppose adharma. Both myself and they are all very well aware of the credentials of Munshi Ji. Read this letter to Munshi Ji in private and he can keep this letter with him. This letter is addressed to you so that you may also become a witness to it. Moreover, the same has been written by me in my own handwriting, so that it may remain as an authentic secret for the future if need be.

Swami Dayanand Saraswati

Letter No. 220

To Col. H.S. Olcott and H.P. Blavatsky

(Śrāvaṇa Vadi 6, Saṁvat 1937 i.e. July 14, 1880)

This letter, written in Hindi, was sent from Meerut on 27 July after being translated into English.

May you be happy Colonel Olcott Saheb and Madame H.P.Blavatsky! Namaste!

I am well now. Hopefully, you are also keeping well. I learnt that you visited Ceylon (Sri Lanka). I hope you returned safely. What happened there? Presently I am in Meerut for about a month.

We are pleased to go through your letter that was written in Hindi, addressed to me in Kashi, and which mentions that the Vedas as the most sacred, the eternal composition of God and is for the altruistic welfare of all. It is true that 'aṅgikritam sukritinaḥ pripālayanti' i.e. all dharma abiding scholars always keep up Dharma.

Now, let me clarify that the Vedic Śākhā (Branch) in the Theosophical Society belongs independently to both the Arya Samaj and the Theosophical Society. Neither is the Arya Samaj a branch of the Theosophical Society nor is the latter a branch of the Arya Samaj. However, the Vedic Śākhā is the connecting link between both the Arya Samaj and the Theosophical Society. This may be publicised by both of us in our respective organisations. We should not keep this fact a secret, because both the members of the Arya Samaj and the Theosophical Society should know this, so that all doubts about it may be avoided.

Furthermore, whatever I have said to Sinnett Saheb (the editor of the Pioneer, Allahabad) is correct. I don't believe in miracles whether it is through trickery or through the yoga system. This is because no-one can ever appreciate the importance of yoga for its own sake and have an interest in it without practising yoga. If it is not practiced, then everybody will just long for miracles and want to be mere miracle men. And so the very purpose of the promotion of yoga will be marred. Neither have I demonstrated, nor do I wish to demonstrate any miracle to Sinnett Saheb. I am not bothered whether he is satisfied or annoyed, because if I indulge in such things, then all the communities of the learned and the laity will expect me to make such demonstrations for their recreation. I don't want to subject myself to such spectacles as Madame H.P. Blavatsky.

Instead of taking some benefit from the scholarship of Madam H. Blavatsky, people want to see some tricks or miracles. So, I don't want to indulge in such things. However, I can teach the method of yoga, if so desired by a seeker so that he may himself experience all the divine power emanating from the practice of yoga. There is no greatness in it (the demonstration of miracles). I am happy to know that you have rejected all modern man-made faiths like Christianity and have accepted the most sacred, eternal, and natural Vedic faith. I am impressed by your statement that you are not going to desert the Vedic path, even if I may desert it. This is not a small thing. This is the outcome of God's grace who has impelled us on the Vedic path.

We cannot thank Him enough for this grace. How I wish, God could shower his grace upon each and every human being so that they may also tread the true Vedic path, which would enable (him/her) to get rid of all false beliefs. Thus, they would also be blessed with happiness like us. I am also pleased to inform you that a will has been prepared to appoint 18 executors, including you and Madam Blavatsky and 16 other reputed persons from Arya Samajs in India. After the registration of the will (the will was registered on August 16, 1880), all of you will be informed about the rules and regulations to ensure that there is no confusion afterwards (after my death), and all assets are utilised for the benefit of all humankind. These executors will be deemed to represent me (for the purpose stipulated therein). Therefore, please keep that letter securely at your end, as it will be of use to you in the future. What more needs to be written to affectionate learned people (like yourselves).

Swami Dayanand Saraswati

Letter No. 221

To Babu Mulraj

(Śrāvaṇa Kṛṣṇa 6, the Tuesday, Saṁvat 1937 i.e. July 27, 1880)

This letter was written in English.

My dear Babu Mulraj Ji, M.A.

For a long time, I have heard nothing from you. Still, I hope you are quite well and wish that you may keep informing me occasionally, if not regularly, about your postal address. I have been in Meerut for the last fortnight and I intend to stay here for another 20 days or more.

I want to lodge a petition with the government on a subject of public interest, which has also been ratified by the hundreds of people who have attended my lectures. The government should pass a resolution entitling the children of widows the right to property, both movable and immovable, of their parents, and that anyone trying to injure (harm) the widow in any way should be made liable to punishment by the government.

As a result, the lives of thousands of children will be saved, abortions will be minimised or stopped completely. Niyog (the legitimate right to have a child from the deceased husband's brother or any other relative, in case the widow doesn't have a child from her husband) or the remarriage of widows will be allowed. But this issue cannot be handled by an ordinary person, so I entrust the responsibility to you to look into this matter and to frame regulations giving all the requisite details. I hope you will agree with me and do the needful. I have given you only some hints. You have to do the homework and frame rules complete in all respects, having sections, subsections, clauses, etc. that cover all the issues. This draft regulation may be sent to me as soon as it is ready for submission to the government under my signature, but the sooner it is done, the better it will be.

There is bad news also which requires your attention and advice. I think you are familiar with Munshi Inder Mani of Muradabad. He is now President of the Arya Samaj and a person of unrivalled excellence. He is well known, so it is not necessary to give you more details about him. The Mohammadans are his greatest enemies. In the past, they vainly tried to defame him. However, this time they succeeded in framing him. This is not only a personal attack on Munshi Indraman but on all Aryas.

The facts of the case are that a newspaper called Jam-i-Jamshed of Muradabad, published an article last May on the 16th, stating that Munshi Indraman, an enemy of Islam had recently published some books against Mohammaddanism (Islam?), which would incite riots and rebellion in the Mohammadan community, and that he would one day, lose his life as a consequence. We are at loss, as to how the Magistrate and Collector of the city allowed (the newspaper) this liberty. Now, the government are being requested to ban controversial books and the printing press.

The (above) said newspaper was shown to the government (I mean H.E. the Lt. Governor). He got this matter investigated through district authorities and imposed a fine of Rs. 5000 on Munshi Indraman on 24th and confiscated all of the books, without any proper inquiry instituted for this purpose. It is a matter of great concern, not only for Munshi Indraman but for the whole country and for all of us. I, therefore, seek your advice on this matter as to how to proceed (further). In the meantime, arrangements will be made to file an appeal in the case. A prompt reply with full directions as to how to proceed with regards to this critical matter is requested.

I have yesterday, received a letter from a gentleman from Germany (Prof. G. Wise). He is ready to train our people in any subject. This is a good opportunity. I would like you to allow your brother to try his luck in this regard. Any other Arya gentlemen worthy of this may also be recommended. Full particulars as to expenses, voyage, etc. will be communicated to you later, as soon as the time permits.

All is well here and hope the same at your end.

Hoping to hear from you soon.

Swami Dayanand Saraswati

Letter No. 222

To Babu Mulraj

(Śrāvaṇa Sudī 4, the Tuesday, Saṁvat 1937 i.e. August 20, 1880)

This letter, written originally in Hindi and translated into English, was sent from Meerut.

May you be joyful Babu Mulraj Ji!

The letter drafted in Urdu regarding Munshi Indraman is to be translated into English. The letters received from Germany, have been sent to you for your perusal through Lala Anandi Lal. Please let me know what reply should be sent to them. In my view, some people should be sent to Germany to learn some arts and skills. But if we can get such people (who can teach) in India, there will be no need to send our people to Germany.

We have raised Rs. 3000 for the Munshi Inderman case. We have sent all the necessary papers of this case to you, to decide it on merit. Please prepare the appeal after considering all the advantages and disadvantages of the case, because we are to send it to many reputed giants. For filing an appeal Rs. 1500 is to be raised from Panjab and Rs.1500 from other states. It would be better that you kindly arrange Rs. 1500 from Panjab.

I am sorry to say that the letter which was dictated to deal with emergent circumstances, could not convey to you the actual intended sense.

You have pointed out that the rule talks about re-marriage and not Niyoga. I have prepared another draft legal proposal (legislation) to deal with the pitiable condition of widows. The same will be dispatched to you for necessary amendments. 1). It will deal with Niyoga. 2). According to this legislation, the widow's children from Niyoga will have a right over the (assets) of the deceased husband of the widow. 3). They (the children of a widow begot through Niyoga) should not be construed as illegitimate or outcasts. 4) People of the widows' community or relatives should not torture or create problems for them in any way. 5) The law should not punish them (widows). Upon enactment of such a law, the tendency of getting abortions will be stopped, and the lives of hundreds of children will be saved. If legitimacy is granted to the child born through Niyoga, the tradition of inheritance of ancestral property or Jagir will not be discontinued for want of a legitimate child born to legally wedded wife and husband, and the family line will also not be discontinued as is the practice now-a-days. This is because the child born through Niyoga will have the same rights as those born to a legally wedded wife and husband. Moreover, there will be no discrimination on that score. It makes no difference whether such rules are presented before the public in this shape or a bit differently. The draft legislation will be on the above lines. Until the receipt of the next letter on this matter, this issue may be understood in the above framework.

Swami Dayanand Saraswati

Letter No. 223

To Prof. G. Wise

(October 9, 1880)

This letter, written in Hindi, was sent from Meerut to Prof. Wise L., Wörtstraße, Baden, Germany.

It is the considered view of a Committee (formed for the purpose of looking into this matter) and of learned people, that there is no need to send young Arya Samajists to Europe to learn the arts and other skills.

Swami Dayanand Saraswati

Letter No. 224

To Shyam ji Krishna Varma

(Āśvina Kṛṣṇa 6, the Saturday, Saṁvat 1937, i.e. September 25, 1880)

This letter, written in Sanskrit, was sent from Ajmer. The original letter is preserved by Prof. Dhirendra Verma. Its copy received by Pt. Bhagwadatta was full of mistakes, so was edited by him. This English translation is based on the same.

May Krishan Varma succeed in his endeavour due to the efforts made by various scholars. He honours Vedic principles due to his acquaintance with them. He is endowed with various merits due to his rational efforts and defeats all wrong notions prevalent in various places and countries.

We are extremely happy to receive a letter bearing good news at your end.

It's a pleasure to know that you are exposing anti-Vedic ideology in your lectures.

We have received hoards of letters from Germans who excel in several arts and skills. It is necessary to understand their points of view.

Since these foreigners have extended their support to train the people of Bharat in various arts and skills for their benefit, you should treat them generously.

It is advised that before your arrival, you should also visit the prosperous land of Europe and deliver lectures on the Vedas to people who are interested.

Also, tell them that I am not able to respond to

their letters because of my unfamiliarity with their language. You have not informed me about Monier Williams. Have you conveyed my namaste to Monier Williams? I want to leave this place for Dehradun.

You must also deliver a lecture in the House of Commons and make the members familiar with the rules of Śāstras and other Vedic texts, so that they may realise the misery of the pitiable. The British are persecuting Indians because of their mean mentality.

The Muslims believe that they are the only superior race. In view of this wrong notion, they want to eliminate people who follow the Vedas. For example, Munshi Indraman, a resident of Moradabad, is a follower of the Vedic path and famous for his Vedic practice and manners. He is busy in counteracting their faith. And because of his stance against Islam, the magistrate has banned his two books and imposed a fine of Rs. 500. He has filed an appeal with the judge. The judge has withheld the decision of the magistrate condemning him to pay Rs. 400.

Government servants are often negligent of their duty and are mostly busy grinding their own axes. There are very few who look to the interests of others.

It is highly painful to tell you about the British. Until the time that Manu's Penal Code is implemented, they will not be able to do real justice while pronouncing decisions in court cases.

They often express their confused position in matters related to Dharmic acts. They are shortsighted, full of jealousy, highly greedy, and add fuel to the fire.

Present your view in the House of Commons in such a way, that Vedic principles and related corroborative evidence do not contradict each other.

I am not able to reply quickly to the letters of Dr. Massey, president of Theosophical Society, due to my unfamiliarity with his language. Presently I am not in a position to afford an interpreter. I have informed Colonel Olcott to appoint an interpreter if he desires a quick reply from my end. If you also happen to meet the president of the society there, who has expressed his wish to hear from me soon, tell him about these facts.

The books required by you were permitted to be sent on that very day. You were to receive them from Kashi. Have you received them or not? There is no need to pen down anything further. We have established a 'Paropakarini Sabha' here. You are also a member. Its Memorandum of Association is being sent for your perusal and record. Keep it as your personal document. It will be useful later. Keep me informed about the news over there.

Swami Dayanand Saraswati

Letter No. 225

To Atma Ram

(Kārtika Sudi 13,1937 or November 14, 1880)

This letter, written in Hindi, was sent from Dehradun. The original letter is preserved in the collection of Pt. Bhagwadatta.

Respected Atma Ram Ji,

Namaste.

Your letter dated November 4, 1880, was received on the evening of 10th November 1880. Upon its perusal, I became happy. I will now give a pointwise reply to your letter:

Question 1: It is written in Satyarth Prakash Chapter 12, page 396, line 16, that at the time of dissolution pudgals (the entity that reincarnates as an individual or person, i.e., the bundle of tendencies that keeps an individual reincarnating until they attain enlightenment) get separated, while it is not maintained (in the Jain Faith).

Ans. I have sent a letter responding to the letter of Thakurdas through Arya Samaj Gujranwala, which might have reached you. In this letter, I have stated that there is no difference in so far as Jains and Buddhists are concerned. We come across many references where Mahavira and other Jain Tirthankaras have been mentioned as Buddha and Buddhists and at several other places they have been referred to as Jina, Jain, Jinavar, and Jinendra, etc. (cf. Vivekasāra, p. 65, line 13). We also find a reference to Buddha, Buddhists, and many Siddhas (ibid. p.113, line 7). Reference to the story of four Buddhas (ibid. p. 136, line 8). Reference to Story of Each Buddha (ibid. p. 138, line 21). Reference to the story of Buddha himself (ibid. p. 152, line 14).

Four Buddhas attained Mokṣa (salvation) simultaneously. A similar type of narrative is traceable to other scriptures as well, which neither you nor any other Jain scholar will dispute.

You have already accepted the veracity of many ślokas in this regard produced by us in reply to the first letter of Thakurdas. A copy of that reply is available in Meerut and will perhaps be available to you. In the Introduction of Kalpa Bhāṣya, Raja Shiv Prasad has mentioned his father and other ancestors as followers of Jainism. The same has been produced as evidence. In the book 'Timira Nāśak', Vol. 3, p.8, line 21 to p. 9, line 32, it has been clearly stated that Jains and Buddhists are the names of one and the same thing.

At several places, Mahavira and other Tirthankaras have been depicted as Buddhists, and you call them as 'Jain' or 'Jina', etc. So far as the branches of Buddhism, like Chārvāka, Ābhāṇaka, etc. are concerned, they are just like branches of your sect Śvetāmbara, Digambara, Dhūṇḍia, etc. Some of them believe in Śunyavāda, others in Kṣaṇikavād, yet others believe the world to be eternal. There are some who take the world as being perishable and others see the world as undergoing a natural cycle of creation and dissolution. There a set of scholars who consider that the Ātmā (soul) is made up of five elements and is perishable (cf.

Ratnāvali, p. 32, line 13 to p. 43, line 10).

Similarly, Chārvākas, who are divided into many branches, call your pudgal an atom, a combination of which leads to creation, and whose decombination leads to dissolution. This is not essentially different from the philosophy of the Jains and Buddhists. Just as in the Paurāṇikas, the branches of Ramānujis and Vaiṣṇavas while different in name, are essentially one. Pāśupatas and Śaivaits are also essentially one though different in name. The branches of the Ten Mahāvidyāas of the Vāma-mārgis are essentially one. In Christianity, Roman Catholics and Protestants although they differ ideologically, are essentially one in so far as the Bible is concerned. Similarly, in Islam, Shia and Sunnis may differ ideologically but are essentially one in so far as the Quran is concerned. Similarly, Jains and Buddhists though different in name are essentially one.

Had you gone through the Tantra Siddhants (Principles of Tantra) of each of the branches of the Buddhists and Jain sects, you would not have questioned the chapters of the Satyarth Prakash dealing with the creation and dissolution of the universe.

Question 2: In the Satyarth Prakash (p.397, line 24) it has been stated that human beings are mindful of acts of crimes or other acts committed by them (animals do so instinctively, unaware of the ethics behind them). Therefore, giving punishment to human beings for the crime committed by them is not a crime. This is not supported by Jain ideology.

Ans. Please refer to the Jain scripture 'Vivekasāra' (p.22, line 10-15), wherein, it is clearly mentioned that Viṣṇu Kumar following someone's order kicked out a priest named Namuchi, who was an opponent of Jina, to the Seventh hell. There are many more statements similar to it.

Question 3: In the Satyarth Prakash (p. 399, line 3) it mentions viewing the animate and inanimate world sitting on a lotus hill.

Ans. Please refer to the portion of the conversation between Mahavira and Gautam registered in the (Jain) scripture Rattansāara (p. 23, line 13-24), to verify the above fact.

Question 4: It has been alleged in the Satyarth Prakash (p.401, line 23) that according to Jains if someone doesn't belong to the Jain faith, he doesn't deserve any service, even the offer of water, however superior or senior he is.

Ans. Please refer to the Jain scripture 'Vivekasāra' (p.221, line 3-8), which prohibits the following six things:

1. Praise of other faiths
2. To have dialogues with followers of other faiths
3. To offer a seat to followers of other faiths
4. To offer eatables and drinks to followers of other faiths
5. To offer fragrant flowers to followers of other faiths
6. To worship murtis of other faiths

Question 5: It has been alleged in the Satyarth Prakash (p.401, line 27) that upon the visit of a Sadhu (Saint), followers of the Jain faith forcibly pluck hairs off their chins, moustaches, and heads.

Ans. Please refer to the (Jain) scripture Kalpa Bhāṣya (p.108, line 4-9). This text and every other Jain text clearly sanctions the hair-plucking rite at the time of the initiation ceremony. Hair plucking is accomplished among Dhundies either by the person concerned or his disciple or his Guru.

Question 6: The ślokas quoted in the Satyarth Prakash (p. 402, line 20 onwards) in the name of the Jain faith doesn't belong to Jainism.

Ans. Its reply has already been given vide my letter dated Kārtika Śudī 4, Saturday, Saṁvat 1937. Please refer to it.

Question7: According to the Satyarth Prakash (p. 403, line 11), the Jain faith recognises only Artha and Kama as the objective of human life.

Ans. This view is expressed by the Charvaka sect which is a sub-division of the Jain faith. The Charvakas have coined their own ideology :

'Live with comfort until death'

'No living being is devoid of death'

'The body once consecrated to fire is not reborn'.

Similarly, according to Niti and Kāma Śāstra, Artha and Kama, are the only objectives of life.

The above, in brief, is the reply to your queries. As a complete clarification can not be possible through correspondence whenever we may happen to meet each other, I may clarify your doubts by citing appropriate evidence from the scriptures. If you have any other doubts about the 12th Chapter of Satyarth Prakash, you may seek clarifications by writing to me (through the Arya Samaj at Meerut), and a proper reply will be sent to you. Now, I will be here for a few more days. If you come to Ambala, you can inform me about your itinerary by telegram by November 17, 1880, before 8 a.m in Dehradun, and after that in Agra. I don't think a wise person like you needs more clarification.

Swami Dayanand Saraswati

Letter No. 226

To Pundit Bhim Sen

(Kārtika Sudī 14, the Tuesday, 1937 i.e. November 15, 1880)

This letter, written in Hindi, was sent from Dehradun. The original letter has been preserved in the collection of Pt. Bhagvadatta.

May you be happy Pundit Bhim Sen Ji.

To whom and where did you give the two bags containing my clothes, a pair of shawls, kitchen wares, etc? Also let me know the details of the expenditure money withdrawn by you from the office, and how much money has been handed over to whom by you.

Write and send all the precise details to my Kashi address, whether you personally know of the irregularities committed by Munshi Bhaktawar Singh, through servants and other employees (of the printing press) that you have come across, or whether you have noticed some foundry or wooden items being made or got made by him. Do reply to me soon. He speaks of his innocence and accuses you of everything. There is a mismatch in his accounts and everything is not properly maintained. He is not able to give a satisfactory reply. Moreover, he starts quarrelling whenever pushed to the wall. Nevertheless, Master Shadi Ram Ji and Pundit Jwala Dutt are competent people, so they are not offended by him. Instead, they try to get him to work. He wants to drag you too into controversy and pass the burden on you. His lie has been detected by Masterji. He repeatedly says that he doesn't know anything, Bhim Sen may be aware of it. For instance, he set up a forma in English, and you reminded him about taking permission from Swami Ji. He retorted however that if he takes it to some other place, it would cost him four to five hundred rupees. He also denies any knowledge of the withdrawal of money from the office.

I am sure that you may not be having the date-wise detail of income and expenditure. If it is there, it would be very helpful. You may also try to get this detail from the office. Write a letter to the Kashi address with a copy to me giving details of all items that are in your custody, so that he may not escape by blaming you, and tell the truth.

Please send the following account as soon as you can:

-Whatever knowledge you have about the money deposited, handed over, or used by Munshi Bakhtawar Singh.

-The cash amount available with Munshi Ji and the amount available with the office which was reported by me when I left the place.

Also, inform the concerned people at Kashi so as to enable them to file a case against Munshi Ji in court. Then Munshi Ji will also not be able to level false allegations against you. Whatever clinching evidence you have about wooden items or foundry items used by Munshi Ji, or any other written proof you have against Munshi Ji may be sent to me as well as to Kashi.

Now, it is hoped that work over there will go on

smoothly under the supervision of Master Shadi Ram and Pundit Jawala Dutt, and Munshi Ji will stand exposed completely. It is a matter of chance that you fell sick at the same time and had to leave abruptly. Master Saheb and Pundit Jawala Dutt could not reach there to be in your presence. All this gave Bhaktawar Singh an opportunity to commit wrongs in the printing press. It would not have happened had you been there. Just see, Munshi Ji has cleverly taken half of the material of the printing press in his possession. He is not ready to clear his account. When Master Ji or Pundit Jawala Dutt ask him to accompany them to the office to do the office accounts, he tries to evade the matter and starts abusing them. This all point to the misappropriation of funds on his part.

I will be reaching Agra on Margshir Vadi 2, 1937 (Thursday) or November 18, 1880. It is, therefore, vital on your part to give appropriate information about everything to me in Agra. Also, write as soon as possible a letter giving details of everything you know. Let me know about your health and whether your physical condition allows you to be here. If you come, then I may not engage any other Pundit. Please write in detail and inform me soon.

Swami Dayanand Saraswati

Letter No. 227

To H.P. Blavatsky

(Mārgaśirṣa Vadi 6, 1937 i.e. November 23, 1880)

This letter was written to Madam H.P Blavatsky. This letter indicates that Theosophists were trying to convert Arya Samajists into their fold by projecting Swami Dayanand as a member of the Theosophical Society without taking Swamiji into their confidence. Swamiji raised strong objections about it. This letter shows how the relations between Theosophists and Swamiji were severed.

Be happy Madam H.P. Blavatsky!

Your letter dated October 8, 1880, has reached me at Dehradun through Babu Chedi Lal Rais, Meerut. I give below a point wise reply to it.

After an exchange of letters, we met at Saharanpur, Meerut, Kashi, and again at Meerut. While my stand continues to be the same, in accordance with the understanding reached between us in those meetings, there appears an apparent change in your stand, because, whatever stand you have taken earlier in writings and conveyed during mutual interactions, is no longer maintained in this letter. This fact you may decide upon by examining your own conscience. Earlier it was decided that Sanskrit would be studied to obtain Vedic learning, and to make the Theosophical Society a branch of the Arya Samaj, etc. The stand taken in earlier correspondence is published and is known to everybody. Moreover, copies of the letters sent by me are also available in our record. For example, just recall the discussions on that night at

Meerut about the rules of the Arya Samaj and of the Society, when I said in the presence of everybody that there is nothing special in the Society's rules vis-a-vis the rules of the Arya Samaj. The same thing I also wrote to you in my letter from Bombay. In accordance with what had been discussed, I still uphold and reiterate that it is not desirable to merge the Arya Samaj with the Society for religious purposes, etc. Furthermore, had not you and Colonel H.S. Olcott written the same thing in your book 'Lectures and Dialogues' that "Whatever concerning the True Dharma (Satya Dharma), True Knowledge (Satya Vidya), Right Reform (Sudhar), and Parma Yoga, etc. are prevalent in the people of Āryāvartta and directed in the Vedic scriptures. They do not' exist anywhere else." Now, consider this: should the Theosophical Society merge with the faith of the people of Aryāvartta or should the people of Aryāvartta become Theosophists.

Nonetheless, please try to recall whether I or anyone in the Arya Samaj has ever tried to convert any Theosophist. On the contrary, you are trying to convert Arya Samajists and bring them into the fold of the Theosophical Society and you are even taking a membership fee of Rs. 10 from many Arya Samajists. Have you not asked Babu Chedi Lal at Ambala to become a Theosophist by approaching him earlier at Meerut? Did you not also send him a letter from Shimla? For that reason, I have certainly cautioned everybody at Meerut Arya Samaj that if Madame Blavatsky or Colonel H.S. Olcott or any other Theosophist on their behalf, asks anyone to become a member of Theosophical society, they should be given the reply that if the objectives and rules of the Arya Samaj and that of the Society are the same, then there is no reason for an Arya Samajist to become a member of the Theosophical Society. If however they are opposed, then there is no need for any Arya Samajist to join a Society opposed to the Arya Samaj. Moreover, the rules of the Arya Samaj are intact until something questionable about them is pointed out.

So, now you should decide whether the Pope of Rome, who is not a confused person, speaks your language and mine. As I have already said, non-native societies cannot befriend and be of as great a mutual benefit to indigenous ones as indigenous societies can be for each other. In the context of a rule in Pāṇinian Grammar असिद्धं बहिरङ्गमन्तरङ्गे (asiddhaṁ bahiraṅgamantaraṅge) which means that outsiders cannot exist effectively with insiders, it has already been explained to you, and I am explaining it to you again and will forever more explain it to you that; only people coming from a similar cultural, linguistic, or regional background can benefit each other and can institute faster progress. This mutual benefit and progress is much more than those coming from different backgrounds. For example, due to the difference in language, I and the Europeans have not been able to derive much mutual benefit through the sharing of ideas. Language, religion, region, and culture are in fact vital connecting factors. Our connections and intimacy depend greatly upon these factors. I elaborated on this, on the following day, by stating that precautions and medication are but the requirements of a patient and not that of a healthy person.

We (the Arya Samajists) treat the Theosophists like brothers. They are a part of the Arya Samaj, and we will continue to believe so. That is why, we have never forced them to merge with us, nor charged them a membership fee of Rs. 10, nor do we intend to do so even now. Instead we love them and work for their welfare. However, non-Arya Samajists and non-Theosophists are free to exercise their own will after attending our lectures and to join the Vedic fold. We must not prohibit them at all. With regards to your statement that with the exception of myself, Arya Samajists from Mumbai, Lahore, and other places have joined your society without being pressured to do so, I maintain that this is not true at all. In Mumbai you had requested Munshi Samarathdan and others to join the Society. Moreover in Prayag (Allahabad), Pundit Sunder Lal and other members of the Arya Samaj were approached too. I witnessed it myself and I heard it from the horse's mouth. My name has been included in the members' list of your society without consulting me. There is no doubt in my mind that the same exercise might have been repeated elsewhere.

Additionally, it is against the rules of the Arya Samaj to respect all religions equally, to allow people from other religions to join our society but not to raise any questions about other religions. We certainly do allow people coming from other religions to join us as brothers, even though they may then be stopped from being members of the Theosophical Society. In this regard, let me ask you a question. What is your religion? Should you say that your religion is opposed to all other religions, then a person from another religion can never join your society. Should you say that your religion is not opposed to any other religion, then what is the need of a person from another religion to join your society, because they all are the same. For example, Muslims call people from other religions Kaffirs and never allow any form of closeness with them. Obviously, such people won't join your society, as should they have brotherly relations with persons from other religions, they will lose their religion, and if they retain theirs, you will lose yours. One mind cannot be applied to more than one thing at one time. Please ponder over it and reply back. The remaining decisions to be made, are subject to face-to-face discussion.

It is impossible for Theosophists to say that 'for two and a half years Swami Ji has been one of our honoured members' when I myself would like to know when I had filed an application for membership of your society and when I had expressed my willingness to be a member of it. I had written in my letter dispatched from Mumbai that - "I neither accept nor will accept any other rules of any other Society or Samaj, except that of Vedic Sanatan Dharma of Āryāvartta." Have you forgotten this? As this is my firm conviction, I cannot oppose it even at the cost of my life. However, it is a mistake on your part to include my name in the list of members of the Society of your own accord without consulting me. This is not the truth.

Don't you remember that I lodged my objection with Colonel Olcott in your presence regarding the inclusion of my name in your Council. I also clearly told you not to do anything on my behalf which has not been agreed by me and if you happen to do any such thing of your own accord, I will never accept it. Colonel Olcott assured me that you would not to do such a thing. I also wrote a letter from Mumbai requesting you to remove my name from all the places that you have included it on your own accord. Despite all of this, whatever you have written in your letter cannot be proved true by anybody. It is a matter of great surprise that the people who had come as students, to become disciples, now want themselves to replace the teachers. Doing such contradictory things ill behoves everybody.

You do not believe in God, as the Creator and Sustainer. This was proved in the month of Bhādrapada in the current Saṁvat 1937. Prior to this, you never said to me, nor have I heard it from anyone else, that you don't consider God as the Creator and Sustainer, except during an interaction with Promod Dass Mittar and with Dr. Lazurus Saheb in Kashi. Don't you remember the statement, Promod Das Mittar made, when we were sitting in the evening on a mound outside the Kothi (residence) of Dr. Tibo Saheb in Kashi? He told me about you, that you (Madam) are an atheist and a non-believer. I, then, replied to him that he may not be able to understand your mind. I enquired from Damodar Das whether Madam believes in God or not. Then Damodar replied, after consulting you, that you believe in God. Is this also untrue? It is not my statement, rather it is your statement that appears different and surprising. I considered you like a sister and a friend and will continue to do so until and unless there is some compelling reason or circumstance not to do so. It is because all Arya persons of

Āryāvartta, including me, have always been generally treating and will continue to treat the Europeans, Americans, and other inhabitants of the globe like brothers and friends. but only if their understanding is based on truth and dharma, and not on untruth and adharma. Similarly, English people in India, whether they are Government officers or commoners, may treat Aryan people and me as they deem fit and suitable. As far as I am concerned, I have always treated everyone, regardless of who they are, in a friendly manner without any discrimination and will continue to do so. There appears to be no solid reason behind their conviction that they cannot treat other Aryasamajists in a like manner, as they did with Swami Ji. In fact, they have put forward this opinion because they are ignorant of history, and are unschooled in the characteristics of good conduct, true progress, true knowledge, the real objectives of life as ordained in Shastras, the system of (Dharmic) justice, the good qualities of the Aryans, and the true significance of the Vedas and Vedic Shastras. All their doubts will be set aside in the due course of time, as soon as they become aware of the reality.

Still, I am indebted to God who has been graceful enough to save us from mutual rivalry, division, anti-social activities, confusion, and atrocities, like those perpetrated by Jains and Muslims and instead freedom of speech, expression, and belief have been accorded to us. Had Her Majesty, the Queen of England, the ruler of India, the House of Commons and the Government officers in Āryāvartta (India) not been religious, learned and decent persons, it would not have been possible for me and others to deliver lectures happily and to compose books explaining the true significance of the Vedas and other Vedic texts. Not only this, our lives would have been under constant threat. Therefore, we extend our sincere thanks to all gentlemen.

I hope you remember the observations that you made in a letter dispatched from Kashi, in which you said that you are not going to abandon the Vedas even if we abandon them. This statement of yours is praiseworthy and we express our heartfelt thanks for it. If all Europeans would extend their support for this supreme cause, it would indeed be a welcome step. If they don't want to support this noble cause, Aryans and the Arya Samajists are not going to be affected adversely, because this is not a new thing for us. From the creation of the world and the advent of the light of the Vedas (up to today), we have continued to believe in them. It is a different matter that now-a-days, some people are following an opposite path, due to ignorance and the lack of proper teaching. Now, people are free to join or not to join the Arya Samaj in the interest of their individual or universal progress. If they opt-out of joining the Arya Samaj, it will be their loss and not ours. It is our aim, cherished wish, and endeavour to consider the progress of an individual within the collective progress of the whole universe. To say otherwise would make it is easy for anyone to say that there is a clash of opinions between us. You maintain that if someone considers God to be the Creator and Sustainer of the universe, the question should arise as to why this person should be supported. However this very thought defeats the very objective of your society, according to which, everybody should be treated in a brotherly fashion. Just think it over, whose approach is causing loss and harm? Our main objective is to help the whole world without causing loss or harm to anybody. Here, it can be stated categorically that if the Theosophists oppose the Arya Samajists, it will not harm our cause, but will harm their own cause of brotherhood. We shall continue to the greatest extent possible to put in our best efforts to have friendly relations with people of high moral and ethical values and inculcate in a brotherly manner, moral and ethical values upon those who are devoid of these. Now, you can decide what is in your interest.

Please convey my namaste to Colonel Olcott Saheb and others.

Swami Dayanand Saraswati

Letter No. 228

To Pundit Jwala Dutt

(Pauṣa Kṛṣṇa 5, 1937, or December 22, 1880)

This letter, written in Hindi, was sent from Agra. The original letter is preserved in the Paropakarini Sabha.

May you be happy Pundit Jwala Dutt ji.

Your letter is received and its contents apprised. It is a matter of great concern that you have been repeatedly told not to add new things in Vyakarana (book on Sanskrit grammar) and that it is to be printed as decided in Dehradun. Please print the Nāmika (the book dealing with Sanskrit nominal stems) as it is. There are no need for new additions. The Kārakīya (the book dealing with the Sanskrit case system) will follow the Nāmika book in the press. I was not aware that you are not mature enough to take up the job of proofreading. I am sending four to five specimen copies, highlighting the mistakes in your proofreading of the Vedabhāṣya. Similar mistakes have crept in. Take care that the same things are not repeated in the future. Proofreading should be done carefully and attentively so that no mistakes occur.

Swami Dayanand Saraswati

Letter No. 229

To Pundit Jwala Dutt

(Māgha Kṛṣṇa 2, 1937, Monday, i.e. January 17, 1881)

This letter, written in Hindi, was sent from Agra. The original letter is preserved in the collection of Harbilass Sarda It was first published in the 'Works of Swami Dayanand' by Shri Harbilas Sarda, Ajmer 1952 p. 127.

May you be happy Pundit Jwala Dutt ji!

I would like to inform you that the papers relating to the Eighth Chapter of the Yajurveda sent by you have been received. However these are of no use because there have been a lot of cuttings in them. You may seek an easy excuse by saying that you had no time to devote to it. The Nāmika (the book dealing with Sanskrit nominal stems) may be published as it is in the best format. Take care that it does not have mistakes like those seen in Sandhi Viṣaya (the book dealing with Sanskrit Euphonic combinations). When I went through the proofs of Sandhi Viṣaya, I found that the type of silly mistakes committed by you, would not have even been committed by a person with much less knowledge than you. Now, I am advising you to be careful. Instead of taking offence, follow my advice to improve your skills. There are fewer mistakes, much less even in the case of Sanskrit, in the 40 pages of Sandhi Viṣaya corrected by Bhim Sen. On the other hand there 51 mistakes in the 40 pages corrected by you. Even the correct usages have been uncorrected by you. Also, 24 pages that were corrected, contained 59 mistakes and the majority of them pertain to Sanskrit rather than Hindi. When I will go through the proofs of the Sandhi Viṣaya corrected by you as well as Bhim Sen, I cannot say with certainty, how many more mistakes will be detected. Forget about it now, but be mindful of not repeating these mistakes in the future. In the future, I will try to scrutinise all, my dictated versions and your corrected versions. From now on, I will check the Vedabhāṣya for mistakes, if any.

It is a matter of great surprise that such mistakes never occurred when the printing was done at Mumbai at Lazarus's but now takes place when it is done in our own printing press. Regarding such mistakes, there is a need to add a corrigendum to avoid the publishers getting a bad name as well as the printing press.

Swami Dayanand Saraswati

Letter No. 230

To Atma Ram

(Māgha Kṛṣṇa 6, 1937 i.e. January 21, 1881)

This letter, written in Hindi, was dispatched from Agra. It was first published in Dayanand Digvijayark 1st Vol. p. 52-54. It was also published by Pt. Lekhram in the Urdu Biography of Swami Dayanand Saraswati, p. 695-698. (See Hindi Edition, p. 716-719).

Anand Vijay Atma Ram ji,

Namaste!

Your letter dated Māgha 8 has reached me and I have got to read its contents. I am extremely happy to know that you didn't find it objectionable when I recognised Buddhism and Jainism as one and the same faith. It is becoming of gentlemen to accept the truth and discard untruth. However regarding your assertion that four sects consisting of 'Yogāchāra' etc. belong to the Jain-Buddhists faith, giving the Buddhist sect, one Śāstra different from the Jains, I have already replied that a particular sect may have divisions and sub-divisions based upon minor differences of faith and traditions, but those divisions and subdivisions are but the substreams of the mainstream and cannot be considered different from it. For instance, the Chāravākas are no different from other non-believers (atheists). If you should ask for their history and biography, it has already been given in the third chapter of the book called 'Timiranāśaka'. You can refer to it.

The Buddhists, whom you consider belong to a separate sect from yours (Jain), cannot be considered as being separate in so far as their faith is concerned. For example, some Shvetambar Jains criticise other Digambar Jains and call them outsiders. This has been made clear in many books. The book 'Samyaktva Nirṇaya' also raises this issue. Come what may, you cannot establish a separate identity for yourselves from the Buddhists and vice versa. No scholar would even recognise them as a separate sect looking at their principles. While the possibility of conceptual differences cannot be ruled out.

I was surprised to know that, according to you, the Chārvakas existed during the time of Mahavir Tiranthkar and not after. Are you unable to prove the existence of the Chārvaka faith prior to the 23 Tiranthkars? The 23 Tiranthkars being those that preceded Mahavir Tiranthkar. Some may say that Ṛṣabh Dev also emanated from the Charvāka faith. Do you have any counter argument to this statement? The Charvakas do not comprise, even one single class out of the total of 15 mentioned in your faith. None among them was called 'Siddha' (perfect) or 'Mukta' (emancipated one). Can they be differentiated from your principles and scriptures?

Besides, you have already accepted that the Buddhist faith is not different from your Jain faith because you have considered the Karkanda, etc. as Buddhists. I have also given documentary proofs to prove that Buddhists and Jains are but two sides of one and the same coin. So, raising a question for the second time on this issue is meaningless. When a law suit is proved, with the evidence proferred by the accused himself, the magistrate need not take into consideration any further witness, nor evidence of any other persons. How can you question the veracity of observation made by Raja Shiv Prasad, whose family for many generations have followed the Jain faith, or Europeans who take a keen interest in writing history? They have also come to the conclusion that Buddhists and Jains are not different faiths. According to them, Jainism is the result of borrowings from both the Aryans and Buddhists.

So far as your reply to the second question is concerned. It is stated by you that the non-believer Namuchi was an enemy of Jainism. He used to torture and expel Jain sadhus. So he was executed and sent to the seventh hell. You were unable to make this statement in the context of the Satyarath Prakash. If you say that Namuchi was killed, because he was the enemy of Jainism, do you mean that he did not commit any crime deliberately? It is a matter of great concern that you have got the wrong end of the stick.

While replying to the third question, you have quoted a śloka of the Prākṛta language without writing its meaning, leaving its meaning at my disposal. This omission implies that I will not be able to pluck out its real significance. Of course, I am not well versed with the languages of all countries, except Sanskrit and the languages of some countries. However I have developed a better understanding of various branches and sub-branches of different faiths, and principles of various schools of thoughts based on my studies and knowledge of them gained through interactions with concerned scholars. People like you and your Acharyas, whose thoughts are not based upon reasoning and evidence, adopt such an Apbhranśa (corrupt) language, that it is very difficult to understand and thus communicate with each other. For instance, in your language, you call 'dharma' 'dhamma'. In your language, you often use unconventional code words which are very difficult to comprehend. For example, madya (drink) is denoted by the word tirtha (pilgrimage), mānsa (meat) by the word puṣpa (flower), so that no one else, except you, can comprehend them properly. Kings, who are judicious, lay down such a straight path that even a blind man can reach his destination, are contrary to their opponents, who spoil the path in such a way that none can walk smoothly on it despite much effort and a lot of trouble having been taken. It makes no difference, whether you disapprove of the authenticity of the Jain book titled 'Ratnasāra', as several other Śrāvakas and followers of Jainism actually believe in its authenticity.

Please reflect on this: despite being a learned scholar, you still spell 'mūrkh' as 'mūrṣa' and so needlessly throw many tantrums while trying to justify these mistakes. How reprehensible it is that you don't have a command over local languages, not to speak of Sanskrit. There would have been no harm in accepting the possibility of errors in your letter, instead of giving wrong arguments to justify them, as to err is to be human.

Your reply to question 4 is quite astonishing. The desire to gain knowledge is expressed before a person who is senior to you in knowledge. You will appreciate the fact that I have also learnt from scholars and Acharyas, who were wiser and more learned than me. Shouldn't learned people from other faiths be treated as disciples rather than Gurus after assessing their ability? Even while giving donations, you never take the issue of salvation into consideration but have some other purpose behind such acts. You want to appreciate your own faith and its sadhus, but take a reverse stand when it comes to the matter of other faiths and sadhus. This is unbecoming of learned and good people. In fact, it is the moral duty of inquisitive minds, spiritual persons, and great personalities to recognise good people as good, and bad people as bad, irrespective of religion or region. This is what is expected from all of us including you. The actual intent of my letter will be revealed to you when we meet face to face. Having gone through my work the 'Satyarth Prakash', none can conclude that Jains deserve to be long suffering, that they don't deserve alms or donations etc. and that they are dishonest. Instead, the Satyarth Prakash purports to say that good, honest and helpless people should always be supported and bad people should always be reformed.

But these six do nots have cast such a slur on you that it can only be washed away with God's grace. This will depend on your genuine, unprejudiced and unbiased efforts. When there is a clear statement (emanating from your side) not to appreciate other religious faiths, and not to feed meals and water to needy people coming from other religions, how can you undo such statements? Such statements are quoted in hundreds of your scriptures, so please don't think that I am making these things up. If you review these statements of yours seriously, you will see a need to get rid of them and you will do so. The remainder is up to you.

Your reply to question No. 5 no longer answers my objections. The evidence of 'pulling hairs' has been furnished by me from your scriptures. This evidence cannot be denied by any argument or plea.

With reference to question no. 6, it has already been proved that the Jains and Buddhists belong to the Jain faith which has Charavaka as one of its branches. It cannot be disapproved otherwise.

Moreover, if your Jain scriptures misquote something about us, which is not recorded in our scriptures, this is moral defamation. Therefore, we request you to furnish documentary evidence in support of your misquotations quickly by return of post. Please, be careful to indicate the name of the relevant Bhāṣhya (commentary), along with the correct address(es) of the publishers. The page and line numbers of the relevant portions may also be cited, in the same manner as I did in my reply to you, otherwise it will bring shame on you for misquoting the Vedic texts. Please don't take it lightly and ensure not to prolong it further. An early reply from your end will be appreciated.

Some objections on the Jain scripture titled Vivekasāra.

Objection No. 1: Vivekasāra (page 10, line 1) mentions that Shri Krishna went to the third hell.

Objection No. 2: Vivekasāra (page 40, lines 8-10) mentions that Harihar Brahmā, Mahādeva, Rāma, and

Krishna, etc. were amorous, full of anger, ignorant and womanisers. They were like boats made of stones, the kind that sink along with their passengers.

Objection No. 3: Vivekasāra (page 224, line 9 to page 225, line 15) mentions that Brahmā, Viṣṇu, and Mahādeva are all not gods worthy to be worshipped.

Objection No. 4: Vivekasāra (page 55, line 12) mentions that no parmārtha (emancipation) can be achieved by visiting places of pilgrimages like Ganga and Kashi, etc.

Objection No. 5: Vivekasāra (page 138, line 12) mentions that a Sadhu (saint) of the Jain faith, even if corrupt is superior to sadhus (saints) of other religions.

Objection No. 6: Vivekasāra (page 1, line 1) mentions that Jainism consists of branches of Buddhism, etc. It proves that Buddhism is a branch of Jainism.

Swami Dayanand Saraswati

Letter No. 231

To Mahadev Govind Ranade

(January 24, 1881)

This letter, written in Hindi, was sent from Agra to Mumbai through Rao Bahadur Gopal Rao Deshmukh.

Mahadev Govind Ranade!

You are a great saviour of the nation. As you are keeping a close watch on the whole of the nation, please shower your blessings on Kutch Bhuj as well. Rao Saheb (Khengraji) (of Kutch Bhuj) is presently a minor, who needs education. I am hopeful that you will do the needful.

Had I been there at this juncture, I would have met all of you, but I was not aware of your visit. I am busy with lectures and there are many other matters also to attend to. So it is not possible to come over there. On my visit to Rajputana, I will try to make it if time permits. I will inform you in due course. It is better to visit new places, so that other people over there may also be benefitted.

Swami Dayanand Saraswati

Letter No. 232

To Col. H.S. Olcott and H.P. Blavatsky

(Chaitra Kṛṣṇa 4, Saturday, Saṁvat 1937 i.e. March 19, 1881)

This letter, originally written in Hindi, was sent from Bharatpur. It was published in the Paropakari (Ajmer) on Kartika Sudi 1, Saṁvat 1946 (pp. 33-34). The original letter is preserved in the Paropakarini Sabha.

May you be happy Shri Colonel H.S. Olcott Saheb and Madam H.P. Blavatsky!

1. I would like to inform you that Madam Blavatsky's letter dated January 17, 1881, has been received and their current status apprised. My reply to it is appended below. I will never change my stand.

2. You did not reveal your mind to Moolji Thakursee during chats with him. Maybe you kept it a secret. I know at that time you believed in God, but in Meerut, we observed a change in your stance. We don't want to harbour any ill-will with anybody except those who indulge in acts of immorality, unethical behaviour, and injustice.

3. The Arya Samaj is based entirely on the Vedic faith, and there is no deviation in its objectives. Your concept of 'Brotherhood' cannot occur until religious factions, and rivalries are completely over. I think you are lacking information about the rules of the Arya Samaj. Moreover, I told you earlier that, as long as the rules of any Sabha (institution) coincide with the rules of the Arya Samaj, they will be regarded as being in harmony, the opposite will mean that they they will not. Two contradictory things cannot be true. It is

evident that only one of them will be true i.e. untruth always stands in opposition to truth, and truth always stands in opposition to untruth.

4. You have been repeatedly writing that the rules of the Pope are also similar to the ones of the Arya Samaj. The rules of the Pope and those of the Arya Samaj are poles apart. The rules of the Arya Samaj are just like the nectar of knowledge, whereas the rules of the Pope are opposed to knowledge and full of selfish motives behind them. If the same accusation is levelled against you what will be your answer?

5. In 1879, I clearly told Colonel Olcott in Saharanpur that I didn't have any competent scholars of English at my disposal, and, therefore, I was having difficulty in replying to your English letters. So I authorise you now to reply to letters written in English. If you want me to reply, then the letter should be sent to me with an Hindi translation. I am a preacher who preaches in only one language. I find it difficult to converse in any other language. When Colonel Olcott functioned as my representative in the General Council, it was not necessary to add my name. He could have done as he deemed fit and suitable (in his name only).

6. I befriend a person until the time he indulges in lustful actions. When I see injustice I sever my links with the perpetrator, whoever he may be, Harish Chander or anyone else.

7. I remember all the main points. When the Theosophical society was registered, its purpose was to be a subsidiary of the Arya Samaj. As things have now changed, this registration document cannot be taken as evidence. When the registration papers of your society reached me, while I may have acknowledged its

receipt, I never consented to be a member of your society.

8. In the way that you don't accept bad elements as members, neither does the Arya Samaj. Please have a look at the rules of the Arya Samaj. 'One should always deal with others affectionately and ethically in the same manner as one is being dealt with.' You can verify this rule.

9. I don't wish to start any new faith but instead shed a light on the Sanatan Vedic faith. A non-follower may be the loser and not me. As you love me with sincerity and truthfulness, so do I you and all good people.

10. It is a good thing that we are mutually contributing to the progress of the world. I teach and preach the Vedas, as per my capability and resources. I don't want any post or position except that of a preacher and teacher. You can refer to me by different designations, 'member' or anything else, but I don't want any honour or praise. What I wish to undertake is a major mission. So I hope that with the grace of God and with the cooperation of all good and learned people, I will succeed in my mission.

Now, the reply to the query of Colonel Olcott Saheb, is that I (presently) don't have any spare time. Whenever I get to visit Mumbai, I will spare some time for you. Otherwise, I will only have some free time upon the completion of the Vedabhāṣya. Our meeting will be useless, if the very purpose of the meeting is not fulfilled. Please inform Damodar that Sewak Lal Krishan Dass has failed to reply to our registered letter. Ask about the reason and let me know accordingly. Convey my namaste to all concerned. Today, I am proceeding from Bharatpur to Jaipur.

Swami Dayanand Saraswati

www.ingramcontent.com/pod-product-compliance
Lightning Source LLC
LaVergne TN
LVHW051108080426
835510LV00018B/1954
* 9 7 8 8 1 8 7 7 1 0 9 5 0 *